国际会计英语核心词汇双语词典

财务管理

双语名词与解析

杜　英　徐金姝　编著

上海财经大学出版社

图书在版编目(CIP)数据

财务管理双语名词与解析:汉文、英文/杜英,徐金姝编著. —上海:上海财经大学出版社,2023.1

(国际会计英语核心词汇双语词典)

ISBN 978-7-5642-3937-4/F·3937

Ⅰ.①财… Ⅱ.①杜…②徐… Ⅲ.①财务管理-名词-词汇-汉、英 Ⅳ.①F275

中国版本图书馆 CIP 数据核字(2021)第 278592 号

□ 责任编辑 吴晓群

□ 封面设计 张克瑶

财务管理双语名词与解析

杜 英 徐金姝 编著

上海财经大学出版社出版发行

(上海市中山北一路 369 号 邮编 200083)

网 址:http://www.sufep.com

电子邮箱:webmaster@sufep.com

全国新华书店经销

上海叶大印务发展有限公司印刷装订

2023 年 1 月第 1 版 2023 年 1 月第 1 次印刷

890mm×1240mm 1/32 12.75 印张(插页:2) 308 千字

定价:68.00 元

Foreword / 前言

本书适合自学英文“财务管理”课程的学生参考，特别适合要参加 ACCA FM 和 AFM 全球考试的人员。第一单元到第七单元是 ACCA FM 的内容，第八单元到第十二单元是 AFM 的内容。

在多年的全英文教材《财务管理》的教学使用过程中，笔者发现很多学生对专业词汇没能充分理解。其原因有两点：一是专业词汇本来就难理解，二是专业英语的理解与表达问题。因此笔者以 ACCA 教学大纲为框架，梳理了财务管理的主要专业词汇，用双语解析的方式来帮助大家更全面、更深入地理解“财务管理”课程的内容。

此外，本书还补充了学习提示、知识点拓展与巩固等板块的内容。学习提示旨在给学生一些学习目标、知识点学习和理解的技巧。知识点巩固与拓展意在通过一些习题和例子来检验和巩固学生对各专业词汇的理解，并拓宽学生对某一知识点理解的广度和深度。

本书的编写虽然力求准确，但鉴于编者英语水平和专业水平的局限，可能会有一些错误和瑕疵，欢迎各位读者批评指正！

编　者

2023 年 1 月

Contents / 目录

Module One

Financial Management Objectives and Environment/财务管理的目标和环境

本单元的学习目标是了解财务管理的框架、环境和目标。

学生应加强:(1)对概念和专业术语的记忆和理解;(2)对财务比率及其公式的掌握、计算和分析;(3)对财务管理框架(财务管理目标、环境以及基本的财务管理活动)的掌握。

A

Agency Theory

There exists an agency relationship between management and shareholders. Managers act as agents of shareholders. So managers should act in the best interests of shareholders. But sometimes, managers may pursue their personal objectives at the expense of shareholders. We call this agency problem. In order to solve agency problem, regulators may enact stricter corporate governance and stock-exchange listing rules. The business may improve corporate governance practices and introduce managerial incentive schemes. All these measures incur agency cost. In addition, agency costs also include losses suffered by business from opportunistic behaviours of management.

代理理论

企业管理层和股东之间存在一种代理关系。管理层是股东的代理人,管理层应该以股东最大利益为出发点。但是,有时管理层会为了追求自身的利益而牺牲股东的利益。这就是代理问题。为了解决代理问题,监管者会制定更加严格的公司治理和证券交易所股票上市规则,企业可以改进公司治理和引进管理层薪酬激励计划。这些措施都会使企业产生代理成本。另外,代理成本也包括因管理层的机会主义行为而给企业带来的损失。

【知识点巩固与拓展(一)】

代理理论是财务管理中用于解释股东、债权人以及企业管理者之间关系的一个重要理论。企业管理者受外部投资者(股东和债权人)所托,代理他们来管理企业,帮助外部投资者得到一定的投资回报。虽然管理层有自己的私利,当跟外部投资者利益有冲突时,为了自己的利益,可能牺牲股东的利益,或者为了自己和股东的利益而牺牲债权人的利益,但是由于企业的治理机制和法律法规的限制,以及管理层为了自己的职业生涯考虑,在其行动的时候还是有所顾忌的。所以,代理问题虽然存在,但不要过分夸大代理问题。

【知识点巩固与拓展(二)】

一、代理问题产生的原因是什么?

一是公司所有权和控制权的分离;二是不确定性的存在;三是外部投资者和管理层之间信息的不对称,即对于公司的具体运营情况,管理层掌握的信息更多。

二、股权越分散还是越集中,股东和管理层之间的代理问题越严重?

股权越分散,股东的影响力越弱,管理层对公司的控制越强,机会主义行为就会越多,代理问题就越严重。

三、解决代理问题的方法有哪些?

一是加强对公司的监管(regulating),比如关于公司治理和上市公司有关的法律法规的颁布和实施;二是通过设计合适的管理层薪酬计划(managerial reward schemes)来把管理层与股东的利益绑定(align interests of management with shareholders)。

Arbitrage

Arbitrage refers to the practice of buying a goods in a market where the price is lower and then selling it in another market where the price is higher. The arbitrageur will make a profit by taking advantage of the price difference in the two markets.

For example, in market A, Mr. Li borrowed $1 000 000 at an annual interest rate of 5%, and he then lent $1 000 000 to Ms. Wang in Market B at annual interest of 5.5%. Li made a profit of $5 000[1 000 000×(5.5%−5%)]from the arbitrage.

套利

套利是指从价格低的市场买进，然后在价格高的市场卖出去的行为。套利者利用两个市场的价差盈利。

例如：李先生在市场 A 以 5%的年利率借入 1 000 000 美元，然后在市场 B 以 5.5%的年利率借给王女士。通过这一套利行为，李先生盈利 5 000 美元。

Assets Turnover

It can be calculated as sales revenue divided by operating assets. It measures the efficiency of assets utilisation. The more efficient of the asset usage, the bigger the assets turnover.

For example, extracts from the annual financial statements of Company A in Year 2020 are as follows: sales revenue \$4 000 000, non-current assets \$40 000 000, current assets \$12 000 000, current liabilities \$10 000 000.

Assets turnover＝400/(4 000＋1 200－1 000)＝9.5%. Company A earn \$9.5 per \$100 operating assets (capital employed).

资产周转率

资产周转率用销售收入除以经营资产来计算。它计量资产(资本)的利用效率。一家企业的资产(资本)利用效率越高，其资产周转率就越高。

例如：根据 A 公司 2020 年年报，其销售收入为 400 万美元，非流动资产 4 000 万美元，流动资产 1 200 万美元，流动负债 1 000 万美元，其资产周转率＝400/(4 000＋1 200－1 000)＝9.5%，即每 100 美元的经营资产或所用资本一年带来 9.5 美元的收入。

【知识点巩固与拓展】

在ACCA的课本里,资产周转率用销售收入除以经营资产(operating assets)获得,这里的经营资产是用非流动资产加流动资产减流动负债获得。经营资产等于所用资本总额(total capital employed)。而有些书中的资产周转率是用销售收入除以总资产获得。分母有时用期末数,有时用期初和期末的平均数。所以虽然都是资产周转率,但用的公式不同,计算结果就不同,所代表的意义也有差异。

ABS (Assets-backed Securities)

ABS are securities that are backed by a pool of specific assets. The pool of specific assets are usually illiquid assets which are hard to be sold individually. For example, mortgage-backed bonds issued by banks.

资产支持证券

资产支持证券是由特定一组资产所支持的证券。这组资产一般流动性较差,单独出售比较困难。例如银行以借出去的房产抵押贷款为担保而发行的债券。

B

Bill of Exchange

A bill of exchange is a short-term debt instrument that is issued by the drawer promising to pay the face value to the holder at maturity.

汇票

汇票是一种短期债务工具。出票人承诺在到期日向持票人支付票面价值。

Banker's Acceptance(BA)

BA is a bill of exchange accepted by a bank. The bank makes a promise to settle the bill and make payment to the bill holder at maturity. The bill holder can sell the bill at a discount before maturity to raise immediate cash. It is of high liquidity and of low risks to the investors.

银行承兑汇票

银行承兑汇票是指由银行承兑的汇票。银行承诺在到期日兑现汇票并向汇票持有人支付汇票款项。持票人可以在到期日前把汇票折价销售出去以快速筹得资金。对投资者来说，它是一种高流动性、低风险的投资产品。

【学习提示】

银行承兑汇票是一种折价交易的货币市场工具。

C

Capital Employed

Capital employed refers to long-term funds raised for investments in non-current assets and working capital.

Total capital employed＝debt capital＋equity capital＝operating assets＝non-current assets＋(current assets－current liabilities)

所筹资本

所筹资本指企业为了投资非流动资产和营运资本而筹集的长期资金。

所筹总资本＝债务资本＋权益资本＝经营资产
＝非流动资产＋(流动资产－流动负债)

Capital Markets

Capital markets are markets for long-term funds, where a listed company can raise money by issuing shares or bonds and investors can buy and sell securities. The Stock Exchange of a country is the main capital market. A country may also has second-tier, third-tier or even fourth-tier markets. Capital markets include primary markets and secondary markets.

资本市场

资本市场是筹集长期资金的市场。在资本市场，上市公司可以通过发行股票和债券筹集资金，投资者可以买卖证券。一个国家的证券交易所是主板市场，还会有二板、三板甚至四板市场。资本市场包含一级市场和二级市场。

【学习提示】

金融市场包括资本市场和货币市场。资本市场为企业提供长期资金，销售的证券有债券和股票等金融工具。货币市场为企业提供短期资金，银行承兑汇票(BA)、大额存单(CD)、国库券(treasury bills)以及商业票据(CP)等都是货币市场上流通的金融工具。

Commercial Paper(CP)

CP is a short-term unsecured corporate debt, usually issued by large organizations with good credit ratings to fund short-term expenditures. Commercial paper is usually sold at a discount from face value.

商业票据

商业票据是一种短期无担保的公司债务，通常是一些信用级别较好的大型组织机构为支持短期支出而发行的。商业票据一般以低于面值折价销售。

【学习提示】

商业票据是一种折价交易的货币市场工具。

Corporate Governance

Corporate governance refers to the system by which organizations are directed and controlled. It involves risk management and internal control, accountability to shareholders and other stakeholders and conducting business in an ethical and effective way.

公司治理

公司治理指指导和控制组织机构的体系。它涉及风险管理与内部控制、对股东和其他的利益相关者的责任以及以道德、有效的方式经营企业。

【学习提示】

公司治理是解决代理问题的方法之一，它通过立法来规范管理层的行为。

Cum-div.(Cum-dividend)

Cum-dividend means the buyer of shares is entitled to receive the next dividend payment.

含息

含息股票的购买者有权收到即将派发的股利。

Cum-div. Price

It refers to the quoted share price that include the forthcoming dividend payment.

Cum-div. price=ex-div. price + next dividend per share

含息股价

含息股价指报价里包含即将派发的股利的股票价格。

含息股价＝除息价＋即将派发的每股股利

【学习提示】

注意含息价和除息价之间的区别和换算。

Certificates of Deposit(CD)

CD is a certificate of a time deposit at a bank at specified interest rate. It is a short-term marketable security issued by a bank to a depositor, who is usually another bank or a large business organization, acknowledges that a certain amount of money has been deposited with it for a certain period of time at a certain amount of interest.

大额存单

大额存单是一种固定利率的定期存款凭证。它是一种短期有价证券，一般是银行签发给另一家银行或大型企业等储户，证明储户已将一定数量的货币以一定的利息存储一定期限的凭证。

【学习提示】

大额存单是货币市场上一种计息的金融工具。

D

Dividend Yield

It measures the return a shareholder can obtain from investing in a share in the form of dividends. It calculated as either the company's total annual dividend payments divided by its market capitalization, or the dividend per share, divided by current share price.

股利收益率

股利收益率计量股票投资者以股利形式得到的投资回报率。用派发的总股利除以股票总的市值或者用每股股利除以现时每股价格即可得出。

【学习提示】

股利收益率＝每股股利/现时每股价格。一般用这个公式是指，一个新的股票投资者现在以现时股价买进一股，持有一期，可以得到的股利回报率。如果是一个老的股东想算算一期下来以股利形式得到的投资回报率，则用每股股利除以期初股价。例如，公司现时股价为 10 元，年初股价为 6 元，本期每股股利为 1 元，则对新的股东，股利收益率为 1/10＝10％，而对一个老的股东，其股利收益率为 1/6＝16.7％。

Dividend Cover

It measures how many times of earning attributable to ordinary shareholders can cover dividends paid.

$$\text{Dividend cover}=\frac{\text{earnings attributable to ordinary shareholders}}{\text{dividends paid}}$$

$$\text{Dividend cover}=EPS/\text{dividend per share}$$

股利保障倍数

股利保障倍数计量归属于普通股股东的收益是当期派发的股利的多少倍。公式一是归属于普通股股东的收益除以当期派出的股利总额，公式二是每股收益除以每股股利。

【学习提示】

公式二(股利保障倍数＝每股收益/每股股利)用得较多。

【知识点巩固与拓展】

Dividend yield is 20%, market price per share is $10. EPS is $4.4. Calculate dividend cover.

股利收益率为20%，股票当前市价为每股10元，每股收益为4.4元。计算股利保障倍数。

Dividend yield＝dividend per share/current share price

20%＝dividend per share/10

Dividend per share＝$2

$$\text{Dividend cover}=EPS/\text{dividend per share}=\$4.4/\$2=2.2$$

【知识点巩固与拓展】

股利保障倍数反映企业对派发股利的保障程度，从这个意义上来说，这个比率越高越好。但如果我们取其倒数，即每股股利除以每股收益，就是股利支付率。股利保障倍数越高，股利支付率越低，则未必是一件好事。

Deregulation

Deregulation is the opposite of regulation, that is, the removal or weakening of any form of regulation.

去管制

即管制的相反做法，指废除或削弱任何形式的管制。

Debt Capital

Debt capital refers to long-term funds raised through borrowing and issuing preference shares.

The book value of debt capital = non-current liabilities (book value) + preference share capital

The market value of debt capital = *MV* of non-current liabilities + *MV* of preference shares

债务资本

债务资本指通过借债或发行优先股而筹集到的长期资金。

债务资本的账面价值＝非流动负债的账面价值＋优先股的股本

债务资本的市场价值＝非流动负债的市场价值＋优先股的市场价值

【学习提示】

这是ACCA书上对债务资本的定义。但优先股不同于传统债务资本的融资工具(比如债券),企业对优先股的股息没有必须支付的义务。

Disintermediation

It describes an increase in direct link of funds suppliers and funds users without financial intermediaries.

去中介

去中介是指资金提供方和资金使用方绕过金融中介直接联系的情况日益增多的现象。

Discount Instruments

Discount instruments refer to money market instruments that do not pay interest, are traded at a discount to the face value and are redeemed at par at maturity.

折价交易的工具

折价交易的工具指货币市场流通的一类金融工具,不付息,一般以票面价值的折扣价交易,在到期日由发行单位以面值赎回。

E

Earnings Attributable to Ordinary Shareholders

It is equal to PBIT less interest cost, income tax and preference dividends.

归属于普通股股东的收益

它等于息税前利润减去利息费用、所得税以及优先股股利。

EPS

Earnings per share is calculated by dividing earnings attributable to ordinary shareholders by the weighted average number of ordinary shares outstanding.

每股收益

用归属于普通股股东的收益除以同期发行在外普通股股数的加权平均数，即可获得每股收益。

【知识点巩固与拓展】

某公司 2020 年息税前利润为 5 000 000 美元，利息费用为 100 000 美元，所得税税率为 30%，优先股股利为 400 000 美元。发行在外普通股股数 1 000 000。计算每股收益。

PBIT $5 000 000, Interest cost $100 000, corporation tax rate 30%, preference dividends paid $400 000. Number of ordinary shares outstanding is 1 000 000. Calculate *EPS*.

Earnings attributable to ordinary shareholders

=($5 000 000−$100 000)×(1−30%)−$400 000

=$3 030 000

EPS=$3 030 000÷1 000 000=$3.03

Equity Capital

Equity capital refers to long-term funds raised through issuing ordinary shares and through retained cash. The book value of equity capital = ordinary share capital + reserves. Reserves include capital reserve and revenue reserve. Reserves + share capital = owner's equity.

权益资本

权益资本是通过发行普通股而筹集的长期资金加上企业自己的留存资金。权益资本账面价值＝普通股股本＋所有的公积。公积包含资本公积和盈余公积。公积＋股本＝所有者权益。

Ex-div.（Ex-dividend）

Ex-dividend means that the purchaser of shares is not entitled to receive next dividend payment.

除息

除息股票的购买者无权收到即将派发的股利。

Ex-div. Price

The share price that does not include next dividend paid.

Ex-div. price = cum-div. price − next dividend per share

除息股价

不包含将要派发的股利的股价。

除息股价＝含息价－将要派发的每股股利

【学习提示】

公式里用到的股价，一律是除息价（Ex-div. price）。

Externalities

Externalities refer to positive or negative effects on a party who is neither a buyer nor a seller of the product or the service causing the effects. For example, the car makers and car users pollute the environment and endanger the health of the public.

外部性

外部性指一种产品或服务给既不是买方也不是卖方的第三方所带来的正面或负面的影响。比如汽车制造商和汽车使用者污染了环境而危害了公众的健康。

Eurocurrency

Eurocurrency is the currency which is held by individuals and institutions outside the country of issuing that currency. For example, dollars outside USA are called Euro-dollars.

离岸货币

离岸货币是由发行该货币的国家以外的个人和机构持有的货币。比如流通在美国以外的美元被称为离岸美元。

Eurobond

Eurobond refers to a bond that is denominated in a foreign currency which is often differs from the currency of the issuing country and is usually sold to investors in several countries simultaneously.

欧洲债券

欧洲债券指以不同于发行国货币的外币计价而且通常在几个国家同时销售的债券。

EMH

The efficient market hypothesis is the hypothesis that the share prices in the stock market reflect all the available information. Efficiency means information processing efficiency, that is the ability of a stock market to price shares fairly and quickly. There are three forms of stock market efficiency: weak form, semi-strong form and strong form efficiency.

有效市场假说

有效市场假说，假设股票市场上的股票价格反映所有可得信息。有效意指信息处理的有效性，即指股票市场快速、公允地为股票定价的能力。股票市场的有效性分为三种：弱型有效、半强型有效和强型有效。

【知识点巩固与拓展】

弱型有效市场的股价充分反映了过去的信息，包括过去股价的波动信息。半强型有效市场的股价充分反映了所有公开可得的信息，包括公布的财报信息和股价的历史波动信息。而强型有效市场的股价反映了所有的信息，包括未公开的内部信息。

市场有效性假说的理论前提:(1)假设投资者是理性的;(2)各个投资者的理性偏差是独立的;(3)理性的专业投资者有套利行为。行为理论和一些经验证据都对市场有效假说提出了挑战。

F

Financial Management

Financial management is a management activity involving financial planning, financial control and financial management decision-making, aimed at achieving the objectives of the organisation. Long-term financial management involves capital budgeting (capital project investment decision making) and meeting funds requirements for these projects. Short-term financial management involves working capital management, that is, the management of current assets and current liabilities. Both long-term and short-term financial management involve risk management.

财务管理

财务管理是为完成组织目标所进行的一种管理活动,主要进行财务规划、财务控制和财务决策。长期财务管理主要涉及资本预算(资本预算项目的投资决策)以及解决这些项目的资金需求。短期财务管理主要涉及营运资本管理,即流动资产和流动负债的管理。不管长期还是短期的财务管理,都涉及风险管理。

Financial Management Decisions

Financial managers make investment decisions, financing decisions and dividends decisions. And risk management must also be considered. These decisions are interrelated. Investment in assets needs funds, which is raised after financing decisions. Dividend decisions affect retention of profit, which is an internal financing source for future reinvestment. If the business makes successful investments, there is more funds available for future dividend payments and capital projects investment. Risk management should be involved in the whole financial management process and all financial management activities.

财务管理决策

财务经理需要做投资决策、融资决策和分红决策。此外，还必须考虑风险管理。这些决策是相互关联的。资产的投资需要资金，资金在融资决策后筹集。分红决策影响留存收益，而留存收益是企业用于未来再投资的内源性资金的来源。如果企业投资成功，那就会产生更多的资金来支付将来的股利和用于资本项目的投资。风险管理应贯穿于财务管理的全过程以及所有财务管理活动中。

Financial Market

Financial market is a market where funds suppliers can find diversified investment opportunities and funds users can raise funds from various sources, usually with the help of financial intermediaries. Financial market includes capital market and money market.

金融市场

在金融市场，通常在金融中介的帮助下，资金投资方可以找到多样化的投资机会，而资金使用方可以通过多渠道筹集资金。金融市场包含资本市场和货币市场。

Fiscal Policy

Fiscal policy is the macro-economic policy employed by the government to influence the aggregate demand and business cost through managing the government expenditure or through the tool of taxation。

财政政策

财政政策是政府宏观经济政策的一种，通过管理政府支出和税收工具从而影响总需求和企业经营成本。

Financial Intermediary

A financial intermediary is a go-between of surplus units and deficit units in funds market. It links surplus units with deficit units by obtaining funds from surplus units and investing them to deficit units. Financial intermediaries can aggregate smaller funds and invest in larger amounts, can reduce risk for individual funds suppliers by pooling, can also provide maturity transformation. Commercial banks, finance houses and investment funds are all examples of financial intermediaries.

金融中介

金融中介是资金市场上资金盈余机构和资金短缺机构的中介。它通过吸收资金盈余机构的资金并将其投资给资金短缺机构，从而把资金盈余机构和资金短缺机构联系在一起。金融中介可以把很多小笔资金集中在一起，然后做大笔资金的投资；金融中介可以集中很多个人或机构的资金并且做广泛的投资，这就降低了单个投资者所需承担的风险；另外，金融中介也解决了投资方和资金使用方期限不匹配的问题。商业银行、金融公司、投资基金都是金融中介的例子。

Fixed Exchange Rate

It refers to exchange rates kept by a government at a fixed level against a major currency or against a basket of other currencies or kept it within a specified value range.

固定汇率

在固定汇率机制下，一国政府试图使本国的货币相对某种主要货币或者相对一揽子其他货币的汇率保持在一个固定的水平或范围之内。

Floating Exchange Rate

It refers to exchange rates which are determined by demand and supply conditions in the foreign exchange market and are allowed to fluctuate freely.

浮动汇率

在浮动汇率机制下，汇率完全由外汇市场上的供求关系决定，可以自由上下浮动。

G

Green Policy

It is a policy that aims to protect environment and to deal with the problems of pollution.

环保政策

环保政策是旨在保护环境和处理污染问题的政策。

H

Hedging

Hedging is the practice of offsetting the risk incurred by an investment through entering into a counterbalancing contract.

For example, A UK company bought goods from an American supplier, and will pay out USD $1 000 000 in three months time. So the business exposed to dollar exchange risk. In order to reduce the risk, the UK company may enter into a hedging contract to buy in $1 000 000 in three months time at a specific price.

套期保值(对冲风险)

签署一个对冲的合同以抵消某项投资所面临的风险。这样一种金融行为就称为套期保值或对冲风险。比如一家英国公司从一家美国供货商那里购买货物，预计在三个月后要支付 100 万美元，这样，这家英国公司在这三个月里就面临英镑兑美元的汇率风险。为了规避此风险，该英国公司就可能签署一个以一定价格在三个月以后买进 100 万美元的对冲合同。

I

Institutional Investors

Institutional investors are institutions which have large amounts of funds to invest, such as insurance companies, investment trusts and venture capital organisations.

机构投资者

机构投资者指有大量资金用于投资的机构，比如保险公司、信托投资机构以及风险投资机构。

【学习提示】

相比个人投资者，机构投资者往往对企业有更大的影响力。

Interest-bearing Instruments

Interest-bearing instruments are one kind of money market instruments that investors receive interest and principal at maturity, such as money market deposits, certificates of deposit and repurchase agreement.

计息工具

计息工具是一种货币市场工具，投资者在到期日可以收到利息和本金，比如货币市场存款、大额存单以及回购合约等。

Interest Cover (Interest Coverage Ratio)

It measures how many times of PBIT of a business can cover interest expense of the same accounting period. Interest cover = *PBIT*/ interest expense. It measures the safety of interest payment and reflects financial risk of a business. The lower the interest cover, the higher is the financial risk.

利息保障倍数

它计量的是息税前利润为同期利息费用的倍数。利息保障倍数 $=\frac{\text{息税前利润}}{\text{利息费用}}$。它衡量利息支付的安全性，并反映企业的财务风险。利息保障倍数越低，表示该企业的财务风险越高。

【学习提示】

从利息支付保障的角度来说，这个比率越高越好。它是衡量财务风险(financial risk)的一个指标，这个比率越低，说明企业财务杠杆越高，财务风险越大。这个比率的倒数就是一个财务杠杆的衡量指标。

【知识点巩固与拓展】

税后利润 6 300 000 美元，企业所得税税率 30%，利息费用 1 000 000 美元。计算利息保障倍数。

Profit after tax \$6 300 000, corporation tax rate 30%, interest expense \$1 000 000. Calculate interest cover.

$PBIT = \$6\ 300\ 000/0.7 + \$1\ 000\ 000 = \$10\ 000\ 000$

Interest expense $= \$1\ 000\ 000$

Interest cover $= \$10\ 000\ 000/\$1\ 000\ 000 = 10$

Interbank Market

It is a market where banks lend funds to each other.

银行间拆借市场

它是指银行间互相拆借资金的市场。

M

Managed (Dirty) Floating Rate

It refers to exchange rates which are allowed to fluctuate but from time to time the government will intervene in the foreign exchange market through buying and selling their domestic currency.

有管理的浮动汇率

在有管理的浮动汇率机制下，允许汇率自由浮动，但是为了维护国家的利益,政府会通过不时地买进或卖出本国货币来干预外汇市场。

Market Failure

It occurs when the market mechanism fails to allocate economic resources efficiently. The market mechanism is that the interaction of supply and demand results in a market clearing price and quantity supplied and demanded. Market failures, such as imperfect competition, social costs, imperfect information and social inequity, can be corrected by the regulation of markets.

市场机制失效

当市场机制不能够使经济资源有效配置时,就出现了市场机制失效现象。市场机制指供求关系决定了市场结算价格和市场上的实际供应量与需求量。不完全竞争、社会成本、信息不完全以及社会不公正等市场机制失效的表现形式可以通过政府对市场的管制来纠正。

MBS(Mortgage-backed Securities)

MBS are securities issued that are backed by mortgage loans from banks.

抵押贷款支持证券

指由银行贷出的抵押贷款所支持而发行的证券。

【学习提示】

抵押贷款支持证券属于资产支持证券。

Monetary Policy

Monetary policy is a kind of macro-economic policies employed by the government to influence the aggregate demand and business cost through control of the monetary systems by operating on such variables as money supply, interest rate, availability of credit and exchange rate.

货币政策

货币政策是政府宏观经济政策的一种，通过调整货币供应量、利率、信贷量以及汇率等经济变量来控制货币体系，进而影响总需求和企业经营成本。

Monopoly

It refers to a market situation where there is only one supplier of a good or service, it is characterized by a lack of economic competition to produce the good or service and a lack of viable substitute goods

垄断

垄断指一种市场状态，在垄断市场，对于某种商品或服务，整个市场只有一个供货商，缺乏竞争和有效的替代品。

Money Market

Money market is a market for short-term funds. Money market instruments include interest-bearing instruments (such as money market deposits, Certificate of Deposit and Repurchase agreement), discount instruments (such as Treasury bill, Banker's Acceptance, and Commercial Paper) and derivatives (such as forwards, futures, swaps and options).

货币市场

货币市场指短期资金市场。货币市场的工具有计息工具(货币市场存款、大额存单、回购合约)、折价交易工具(国库券、银行承兑汇票、商业票据)以及衍生工具(远期合约、期货、互换、期权)。

N

Negotiable Securities

Negotiable securities are securities that can be resold.

可流通证券,可转让证券

指可以被转手卖掉的证券。

Non-negotiable Securities

Non-negotiable securities are securities that cannot be resold.

非流通证券,不可转让证券

指不可以被转手卖掉的证券。

O

Operating Assets

Operating assets are economic resources needed for everyday operations of a business, including non-current assets and working capital.

Working capital = current assets − current liabilities

经营资产

企业每天运营所需的经济资源，包括非流动资产和营运资本。

营运资本＝流动资产－流动负债

P

Profit Margin

It refers to the profit percentage of sales. It can be calculated as profit divided by sales revenue. Gross margin = gross profit/sales; Operating profit margin = operating profit/sales; Net profit margin = net profit/sales. Profit margin reflects profitability of a business.

利润率

指销售收入的获利百分比，用利润除以销售收入来计算。毛利率＝毛利润/销售收入，营业利润率＝营业利润/销售收入，净利润率=净利润/销售收入。利润率反映了企业的盈利能力。

【知识点巩固与拓展】

销售收入 600 万美元，销货成本 300 万美元，其他经营费用 100 万美元，利息费用 30 万美元，企业所得税 34 万美元。计算毛利率、营业利润率和净利率。

Sales revenue \$6m, cost of sales \$3m, other operating expenses \$1m, interest expense \$0.3m, corporation tax \$0.34 m. Calculate gross margin, operating profit margin and net profit margin.

Gross profit = \$6m − \$3m = \$3m

Operating profit = \$3m − \$1m = \$2m

Net profit = \$2m − \$0.3m − \$0.34m = \$1.36m

Gross margin = \$3m/\$6m = 50%

Operating profit margin = \$2m/\$6m = 33%

Net profit margin = \$1.36m/\$6m = 23%

【学习提示】

注意：不同的利润率代表的意义不同。毛利率反映一家企业在整个供应链当中的实力，如果一家公司对于上游的供货商和下游的客户都不可或缺，那它的毛利率就会比同行企业高。营业利润是毛利润减去销售费用、管理费用等经营费用以后的利润。如果毛利率比同行高，而营业利润比同行低，就说明企业经营费用控制得不好。如果营业利润率比同行高，而净利率比同行低，则是因为利息费用等没控制好。

还要注意，根据不同准则编制的利润表，关于营业利润的定义可能有区别。这里用的是ACCA“财务管理”课程对此的定义。

Profit Maximisation(英)/Maximization(美)

Profit-oriented organizations seek to maximise the bottom line of the Income Statement, that is to maximise the reported accounting profit figure. Profit is a short-term performance measure, and can be manipulated by different accounting policies.

利润最大化

营利性的机构力求把利润表的最后结果最大化，即最大化所公布的会计利润。会计利润是一个短期指标，可以通过改变会计政策人为地操纵。

【学习提示】

注意利润最大化和股东财富最大化的一致性和非一致性。

从长期来说，利润最大化必然带来股东财富最大化，二者是一致的，但由于利润是财务报表中披露的会计利润，它是可以在短期内通过人为方法而被操纵的，因此，短期内，利润最大化未必带来股东财富最大化。

P/E Ratio

It reflects the market's expectation of a share's future prospects. P is for market price per share. E is for EPS. It is calculated as market price of a share divided by EPS.

市盈率

市盈率(P/E)反映市场总体对某一股票前景的期望。P 是指每股价格,E 是指每股收益。市盈率$=\frac{\text{股票价格}}{\text{每股收益}}$。

【知识点巩固与拓展】

一家公司的增长前景、风险状况以及会计政策的稳健性都会影响股票投资者对其股票前景的判断,进而影响市盈率。

A 公司当前股票价格为每股 100 美元,每股收益 2 美元,计算市盈率。

Current share price of Company A is ＄100 per share, $EPS=$ ＄2. Calculate P/E ratio.

$P/E=\$100/\$2=50$

Privatization

Privatization is a practice of introducing private sector enterprises into industries which were previously state-owned or state-operated. Transferring the ownership of assets from the state to private shareholders, contracting out public projects to private firms and allowing private firms to compete against state-owned businesses are all forms of privatization.

私有化

私有化指允许私营企业进入原本只有国家所有或国家经营的行业。把国有资产的所有权转给私营股东,把公共项目承包给私营企业以及允许私营企业与国营企业自由竞争都是私有化的形式。

Primary Market

Primary market is a market that enables organizations to raise new finance, by issuing new shares or bonds.

一级市场

在一级市场,机构可以通过发行新的股票或债券来筹措新的资金。

【学习提示】

注意区分一级市场和二级市场。企业发行新的证券在一级市场,而投资者想买卖已发行的证券是通过二级市场交易。

R

Repos

Repurchase agreements (Repos) are agreements under which one party agrees to sell a financial instrument to another party for an agreed price on an agreed date, and at the same time agrees to buy it back at a later date for an agreed higher price.

回购合约

在回购合约中,一方承诺以一定的价格在协议日出售金融工具给另一方,并同时承诺在将来某日以更高的价格回购。

【学习提示】

有金融工具而需要短期资金的公司可以与银行等金融机构签订回购合约，从而获得资金；相反，如果有短期资金需要投资，则可签逆回购合约。

ROCE

Return on capital employed (ROCE) is also called return on investment (ROI). It is calculated as PBIT divided by total capital employed. It measures how much the business can earn with one unit of currency invested by investors. It indicates the earning power of a business. In order to increase ROCE, a business must increase profit margin and/or asset turnover.

资本回报率

资本回报率，也叫投资报酬率，用息税前利润除以所筹总资本来计算。它计量企业用投资者投入的一个货币单位资金可以赚多少钱，反映了企业的盈利能力。一家企业要提高资本回报率，就需提高利润率和(或)资产周转率。

【知识点巩固与拓展】

因为 Operating assets = total capital employed，所以 $ROCE=\frac{PBIT}{\text{operating assets}}$。

而通常所讲的资产报酬率（ROA）$=\frac{PBIT}{\text{total assets}}$。

【知识点巩固与拓展】

利润率指标：

$$\frac{\text{息税前利润}}{\text{销售收入}}=25\%$$

资产周转率指标：

$$\frac{\text{销售收入}}{\text{经营资产}}=1.4$$

计算资本回报率。

$$\frac{PBIT}{\text{Sales revenue}}=25\%$$

$$\frac{\text{Sales revenue}}{\text{Operating assets}}=1.4$$

Calculate *ROCE*.

ROCE(资本回报率)$=25\%\times1.4=35\%$

ROE

Return on equity (ROE) is calculated as earnings attributable to ordinary shareholders divided by equity capital. It shows the earning power of the ordinary shareholders' book investment. In order to increase ROE, a business need to optimize ROCE and financial gearing.

权益资本回报率

权益资本回报率，用归属于普通股股东的收益除以权益资本而获得。它反映了普通股股东的账面投资的盈利能力。为了提高权益资本回报率，企业应该优化资本回报率和财务杠杆。

【学习提示】

这里的分母是权益资本(equity capital),而不是资产负债表里的所有者权益(owner's equity)。权益资本的账面价值=所有者权益－优先股股本。而有些书中,ROE 的分母是所有者权益,因为所有者权益=资产－负债,所以称为净资产收益率。大家要注意区分上述概念。

【知识点巩固与拓展】

税后利润 600 万美元,优先股股息 50 万美元,普通股股本 1 000 万美元,留存收益和其他公积共 5 000 万美元。计算 *ROE*。

Profit after tax ＄6m, preference dividends ＄0.5m, Ordinary share capital ＄10m, Retained earnings and other reserves total ＄50m. Calculate ROE.

Earnings attributable to ordinary shareholders

=Profit after tax－preference dividends

=＄6m－＄0.5m=＄5.5m

Equity capital =ordinary share capital ＋ reserves

=＄10m＋＄50m=＄60m

ROE =earnings attributable to ordinary shareholders/equity capital=＄5.5m/＄60m=9.17%

Reverse Yield Gap

Normally, debts involve lower risk than equity investment, so investors expect a lower yield on debts than on equity shares. But sometimes, the opposite applies and the yields on shares are lower than on low-risk debts, and a reverse yield gap exists in this situation. The main reason is that the shareholders may be willing to accept a lower return in short-term for anticipating a long-term higher capital gains in the future.

收益率倒挂现象

在正常情况下，对投资者而言，债务投资比权益类投资风险低，因此投资者期望的债务工具的收益率比买股票的收益率低。但是，有时情况正相反，股票的收益率低于债务工具的收益率，这就出现了收益率倒挂现象。主要原因是股东愿意接受短期的低收益而期望得到未来长期的更高的资本利得。

S

Secondary Market

Secondary market is a market for the trading of existing shares or bonds after they are issued in primary markets.

二级市场

股票和债券在一级市场发行以后，投资者之间在二级市场进行交易。

Securities

Securities are tradeable financial instruments which can take the form of equity(such as shares), debt(such as bonds) or derivatives.

证券

证券是指可交易的金融工具，可以是权益类（比如股票）、债务类(比如债券)或者是金融衍生工具。

Security

Security refers to a financial arrangement using assets as collateral for debts.

担保

担保是指在举债时用资产作为担保品的金融安排。

Securitization

Securitization is a way of raising funds by issuing marketable asset-backed securities (ABS).

证券化

证券化是通过发行由资产支持的有价证券而融资的方式。

Semi-strong Form Efficiency

A form of capital market efficiency. In this kind of market, share prices reflects publicly available information as well as historical information, including information about past share price movements. The share price adjusts quickly after the announcement of a piece of new information. Investors cannot obtain above normal profit only through analysing publicly available information. Only inside information can make investors earn above normal profit.

半强型有效市场

这是有效资本市场的一种类型。在半强型有效市场,股价反映所有公开可得的信息,也包括历史信息,比如过去股价的波动信息。一条新信息公布后,股价会很快进行调整。单纯靠分析公开可得的信息,投资者无法获得超常利润,除非可以得到内部信息。

Shareholder Wealth Maximisation

The usual assumption of the financial objective of a private company is to obtain the maximum wealth for their ordinary shareholders. The wealth of the ordinary shareholders comes from dividends received plus market value of shares.

股东财富最大化

通常假设私营企业的财务目标是为普通股股东获得最大的财富。股东财富主要由企业派发的股利和所持股份的市值两部分组成。

【知识点巩固与拓展】

李先生在 2021 年 1 月 1 日购进 Starplus 公司 1 000 股股票。目前股价为每股 5 美元,2021 年 4 月 1 日李先生收到 1 500 美元股利,那么作为 Starplus 的股东,李先生获得的财富为 1 500 美元的股利加上 5 000 美元的现时股票价值,总共是 6 500 美元。

Mr. Li bought 1 000 ordinary shares of Starplus plc. in 1 January, 2021. The current share price \$5 per share, and Mr. Li received \$1 500 dividends on 10 April, 2021. So the total wealth of Li as a shareholder of Starplus plc. = \$1 500 + 1 000 × \$5 = \$6 500.

Shareholder Return

Shareholders' return on investment takes two forms, one is dividends received and the other is capital gains from share price appreciation.

股东投资回报

股东的投资回报有两种：一种是收到的分红（股利），另一种是股票升值所带来的资本利得。

【知识点巩固与拓展】

李先生在2020年1月1日以每股4美元的价格购进1 000股Starplus公司的股票。到2020年12月31日，股价升到每股5美元。在2020年4月10日，李先生共收到1 500美元的股利。求2020年李先生作为股东的回报率。

Mr. Li bought 1 000 ordinary shares of Starplus plc in 1 January, 2020 at \$4. On 31 December, 2020, the share price rised to \$5 per share, and Mr. Li received \$1 500 dividends on 10 April, 2020. Calculate the total shareholder return (in %) in Year 2020.

Dividends per share = \$1 500/1 000 = \$1.5

每股股利1.5美元

Share price movement (capital gains) = \$5 − \$4 = \$1

每股股票升值（资本利得）1美元

Total shareholder return (in dollars) = \$1.5 + \$1 = \$2.5

每股股票总的回报（以美元计）为2.5美元

Total shareholder return (in %) = 2.5/4 = 62.5(%)

股东年投资回报率为 62.5(%)

Stakeholders

Stakeholders refers to individuals or groups who are affected by or affect the activities of the firm. They can be classified as internal, connected and external stakeholders.

利益相关方

利益相关方是指影响企业经营活动或被企业经营活动所影响的个人或团体。利益相关方可以划分为内部利益相关方、业务往来利益相关方以及外部利益相关方。

【知识点巩固与拓展】

内部利益相关方有企业管理层和雇员。业务往来利益相关方有客户、供货商、股东以及债权人等。外部利益相关方有政府及其他与企业没有直接契约关系的个人和团体。

Strong Form Efficiency

A form of capital market efficiency. In this kind of market, share prices reflects all information, including inside information. The share price adjusts even before the announcement of a piece of new information. The investors cannot obtain above normal profit under any circumstances, because the share price is already a fair price.

强型有效

这是有效资本市场的一种类型。在强型有效市场，股价反映了所有信息，包括内部信息。股价在一条新信息公布之前就开始调整。由于股价已是一个公允价格，在任何条件下投资者都无法获得超额利润。

T

Treasury Bills

Treasury bills are short-term debt instruments issued by the government. It is usually highly liquid, and has negligible default risk. It is one of discount financial instruments traded in the money market. Its yield to maturity is often taken as an approximation to risk-free interest rate.

国库券/短期国债

这是政府发行的短期债务工具。它通常流动性很强，违约风险几乎可以忽略不计。它是货币市场上折价交易的一种金融工具。短期国债的到期收益率通常被拿来作为无风险利率的近似值。

V

Value for Money(VFM)

VFM refers to getting the best possible outputs from the least inputs, which means maximizing the benefits at the lowest cost. It requires three Es (economy, efficiency and effectiveness).

钱尽其用

钱尽其用指用最小的投入取得尽可能多的产出，指用最小的成本取得最大的收益。它要求做到"三个 E"(经济、效率和效果)。

【学习提示】

不管是营利机构还是非营利机构，都要追求 VFM。

【知识点巩固与拓展】

经济(economy)主要指投入。它要求以尽可能低的投入，提供既定数量和质量的产品或服务。

效果(effectivenss)主要指产出或目标的达成。相同的投入，产出越多或目标达成得越好，越有效果。

而效率(efficiency)是指投入产出比。

Y

Yield Curve

Yield curve is the graphic depiction of the relationship between the yield on bonds of the same credit quality but different maturities. On the yield curve, the maturities are represented on the x-axis, and the yield is represented on the y-axis. That is, if the yield curve slopes upward, it indicates that interest rates for long-term debt securities are higher than short-term debt securities; this is called a normal yield curve. A negative yield curve indicates that interest rates for short-term debt securities are higher, and a flat yield curve indicates that they are roughly the same. Yield curves are most commonly plotted with government bonds with different maturities; this is used to predict future trends in interest rates. If the yield curve slopes upward, it reflects the market participants expect the interest rate will rise. If the yield curve slopes downward, the market participants may expect the interest rate will go down.

收益率曲线

指描述债券的收益率和债券到期期限之间关系的曲线。X 轴代表债券的到期期限，Y 轴代表债券的收益率。如果收益率曲线向上倾斜，则表示长期债券的利率高于短期债券的利率，这是正常收益率曲线。负收益率曲线表示短期债券的利率高于长期债券的利率。而平的收益率曲线表示长期利率与短期利率相等。普遍的做法是用到期期限不同的国债来画收益率曲线，并以此预测未来利率的走向。如果收益率曲线向上倾斜，则反映市场参与者期望利率走高；如果收益率曲线向下倾斜，则反映市场参与者期望利率走低。

【学习提示】

收益率曲线是预测未来利率走向的一个工具。

Module Two

Investment Appraisal (Capital Budgeting Decisions)/投资评估(资本预算决策)

本单元的学习目标：

(1)熟悉投资决策(资本预算决策)的过程以及需要全面考量的因素。

(2)掌握各种投资评估方法(ARR, Payback, NPV, IRR, Sensitivity Analysis, Probability Analysis, Discounted Payback, Profitability Index, EAC)的原理、决策原则以及优缺点，特别注意在具有风险和不定性的情况下决策的辅助方法以及资本配置(有资本约束)时的决策方法。

(3)重点掌握净现值方法。

A

Adjusted Payback

Adjusted payback(Discounted Payback) is the time taken for the cumulative present value of relevant cash flows from a project to recover the initial investment cost.

调整回收期

调整回收期又叫折现回收期,指项目相关现金流的累计现值可以收回项目初始投资成本所需要的时间长度。

【知识点巩固与拓展(一)】

一般回收期法没有考虑现金流发生的不同期间(timing of cash flows)以及货币的时间价值(time value of money),而调整回收期(折现回收期)克服了这一缺陷,它使用的是折现后的现金流。调整回收期(折现回收期)比一般回收期长,考虑了更长时间的现金流。但不管是一般回收期还是调整回收期,都没有考虑项目周期所发生的所有现金流(all the cash flows during project life),均忽略了回收期以后的现金流(cash flows after payback)。

【知识点巩固与拓展(二)】

Starplus 公司计划购置一台成本为 150 万美元的机器。机器的使用年限为 5 年,残值估计为 0。第一年到第五年的现金流分别如下:500 000

美元、520 000 美元、530 000 美元、600 000 美元、610 000 美元。折现率为 10%。计算调整回收期(折现回收期)。

Year	*CFs*($)	*DCFs*($)at 10%	Cumulative *DCFs*
0	(1 500 000)	(1 500 000)	−1 500 000
1	500 000	454 500	−1 045 500
2	520 000	429 520	−615 980
3	530 000	398 030	−217 950
4	600 000	409 800	191 850
5	610 000	378 810	570 660

Starplus Ltd. is planning to buy a machine which costs $1 500 000. Its useful life is 5 years. Its residual value is estimated to be nil. The estimated cash flows generated by this machine from Year 1 to Year 5 are as follows: $500 000; $520 000; $530 000; $600 000; $610 000. The discount rate is 10%. Calculate adjusted (discounted) payback.

Adjusted payback=3+217 950/409 800=3.53(years)

Annuity

Annuity refers to any terminating stream of constant amount of cash flows over a specified period of time. For example, an investment can earn a constant return of $1 100 for ten years starting from next year. The return of $1 100 per year for ten years constitute an annuity.

年金

年金指等额、定期的系列现金流。比如,一项投资期限 10 年,从下一年起,每年可以得到 1 100 美元的回报。这笔 10 年期每年 1 100 美元的回报就是一笔年金。

ARR

The accounting rate of return, also called ROCE, it is calculated as profits divided by investment.

会计报酬率

会计报酬率又称资本投资回报率,用会计利润除以投资金额计算得出。

【学习提示】

在计算会计报酬率时,通常分子用年均利润,分母用平均投资额。

平均投资额=(期初投资额+期末残值)÷2

ROCE=average annual profit/average investment

Average investment=(initial investment + scrap value)/2

式中,有时分子用第一年的利润,分母用期初投资额。

【知识点巩固与拓展(一)】

ROCE (ARR)因其计算和理解都比较简单,所以成为投资项目评估的一种广泛使用的方法。它使用的是会计利润,这项数据比较容易获得,但会计利润容易受到人为操纵。这是一个比率,便于不同投资规模的项目进行比较,但仅仅据此来决策,容易被误导。

【知识点巩固与拓展(二)】

Starplus 公司计划购置一台成本为 150 万美元的机器。机器的使用年限为 5 年,残值估计为 0。第一年到第五年的利润分别如下:200 000 美元、220 000 美元、230 000 美元、300 000 美元、310 000 美元。计算 ARR (ROCE).

Starplus Ltd. is planning to buy a machine which costs \$1 500 000. Its useful life is 5 years. Its residual value is estimated to be nil. The estimated profit generated by this machine from Year 1 to Year 5 are as follows: \$200 000; \$220 000; \$230 000; \$300 000; \$310 000. Calculate ARR (ROCE).

Average annual profit =(\$200 000+\$220 000+\$230 000+\$300 000+\$310 000)/5=\$252 000

Average investment=(\$1 500 000+0)/2=\$750 000

ARR=252 000/750 000=33.6%

Asset Replacement Decisions

Asset replacement decisions are decisions on when and how frequently an asset should be replaced.

资产重置决策

资产重置决策关于何时以及间隔多久一项资产应该被重新购置的决策。

C

Capital Allowance

Capital allowance refers to tax allowable depreciation, which is the depreciation expense that can be allowed to be deducted from taxable profit in calculating corporation tax.

资本折让(资本免税额)

资本折让指计税允许扣除的折旧费用,即在计算企业所得税时被允许从应纳税所得中扣除的折旧费用。

Capital Budgeting

Capital budgeting, or investment decision-making, is the planning process used to determine whether an organization's long term investments projects are worth pursuing. It involves stages such as identifying and screening projects, analysing and selecting proposed projects, monitoring the progress of the project.

资本预算

资本预算,或者投资决策,是用来决定企业是否值得去投资于某些长期项目的计划过程。它涉及找寻和筛选项目、分析和选择拟议项目,以及监督项目的进展等阶段。

Capital Rationing

A business has several investment projects but the capital for investment is limited to a certain amount, so it needs to compare the projects and allocate the limited funds to the projects effectively. Such situation is called capital rationing. Soft capital rationing is brought about by internal factors; Hard capital rationing is brought about by external factors.

资本配置

一家企业有几个投资项目,但可用来投资的资金有限,因此企业需要比较各投资项目,然后把有限的资金进行有效的分配。这种情形就是资本配置。软资本配置是由企业内部因素导致的。硬资本配置是由企业外部因素导致的。

【学习提示】

在企业面临资本约束的情况下,首先应该寻求摆脱或减弱资本约束,其次寻求用有限的资本取得最大的净现值。对于单期的资本分配,如果项目是可拆分的,则用获利指数(profitability index)来对项目进行排序,就可获得最大的净现值。

Compounding

Compound interest arises when interest is added to the principal, so that, from that moment on, the interest that has been added also earns interest. This addition of interest to the principal is called compounding. For example, an investor lend \$1 000 to other people at an annual compound interest rate of 10%. For one year, he can earn interest $\$1\ 000 \times (1+10\%) - \$1\ 000 = \$100$. For two years, he can get interest $\$1\ 000 \times (1+10\%)(1+$

10%) − \$1 000 = \$210. And for n years, he can get interest \$1 000×(1+10%)^n − \$1 000.

复利计息

复利是指把利息加入本金,从这时起,加入本金的利息也获得利息。把利息加入本金的做法叫复利计息。例如,某位投资者以每年10%的复利借出1 000美元给别人,借一年,他可得到利息1 000×(1+10%)−1 000=100(美元);借两年,他可得到利息1 000×(1+10%)(1+10%)−1 000=210(美元);借n年,他可得到利息1 000×(1+10%)^n−1 000。

【知识点巩固与拓展】

假设某位投资者以每年10%的单利借出1 000美元给别人。则他每年得到的利息是相同的,都为1 000×10%=100(美元)。

Certainty Equivalent Approach

The expected cash flows of the project are converted to riskless equivalent amounts by being multiplied by adjusting factors and are discounted at a risk free rate. The greater the risk of an expected cash flow, the smaller the certainty-equivalent value (for receipts) or the larger the certainty equivalent value (for payments).

确定等值法

把项目的预计现金流乘以调整因子转换成无风险的等值,然后用无风险利率来折现。预计现金流的风险或不确定性越大,对于现金流入，确定等值就越小；预计现金流的风险或不确定性越大，对于现金流出，确定等值就越大。

【知识点巩固与拓展】

Starplus 公司计划购置一台成本为 150 万美元的机器。机器的使用年限为 5 年，残值估计为 0。第一年到第五年的现金流分别如下：500 000 美元、520 000 美元、530 000 美元、600 000 美元、610 000 美元。第一年到第五年的调整因子分别为 0. 9、0. 8、0. 7、0. 6、0. 5。无风险利率为 4%。在确定等值法下计算净现值。

Starplus Ltd. is planning to buy a machine which costs \$1 500 000. Its useful life is 5 years. Its residual value is estimated to be nil. The estimated cash flows generated by this machine from Year 1 to Year 5 are as follows：\$500 000；\$520 000；\$530 000；\$600 000；\$610 000. The adjusting factor for Year1 to Year 5 are as follows：0. 9，0. 8，0. 7，0. 6，0. 5. The risk-free rate of interest is 4%. Calculate *NPV* under certainty equivalent approach.

Certainty equivalent value for Year 1 to Year 5：

Year 1 \$500 000×0. 9=\$450 000

Year 2 \$520 000×0. 8=\$416 000

Year 3 \$530 000×0. 7=\$371 000

Year 4 \$600 000×0. 6=\$360 000

Year 5 \$610 000×0. 5=\$305 000

Discount rate is 4%.

NPV=\$450 000×0. 962+\$416 000×0. 925+\$371 000×

0.889＋＄360 000×0.855＋＄305 000×0.822－＄1 500 000＝＄206 029

Conventional Cash Flows

Conventional cash flows refers to cash flows that the initial cash outflow is followed by a series of cash inflows and there is no cash outflows at future project life. For example, the cash flows of a project are as follows: Year 0 －＄16m; Year 1 to Year 8 ＄4m each year. There is only one cash outflow which occurs initially.

传统现金流

传统现金流指期初有现金流出，此后，在项目周期内的未来期间，都是现金流入而没有现金流出。例如，某项目的现金流：第0年支出1 600万美元，第一年到第八年每年流入400万美元。只有一期现金流出，那就是期初的投资支出。

Critical Factors

Critical factors are factors that are critical to the success of the investment project.

关键因素

这是指对投资项目成功非常关键的因素。

D

DCF

Discounted cash flow (DCF) is an investment appraisal technique which takes into account all the relevant cash flows during project life and the time value of money. There are two DCF methods，one is NPV，the other is IRR.

折现现金流法

折现现金流法是一种投资项目评估方法，它考虑项目周期所发生的所有相关现金流以及货币的时间价值。折现现金流法有两种：一是净现值法，二是内部收益率法。

Discounting

Discounting is the process of determining the present value of a payment or a stream of payments that is to be received in the future.

折现（贴现）

折现指计算将来收到的一笔或多笔现金的现值的过程。

Discounted Payback

Adjusted payback，the time taken for the cumulative present value of cash flows of a project to recover the initial investment.

折现回收期（又称调整回收期）

折现回收期是指将一个投资项目的未来收益折算为现值，使其累计现值等于初始投资所需要的时间长度。

Discount Factor

The factor that is multiplied by a future cash flow to get the present value. It can be calculated as $(1+\text{discount rate})^{-n}$ (n is the number of periods that the cash flow occurs). For example, if cash flow in period 2 is \$1 000, the discount rate is 10%. The discount factor is $(1+10\%)^{-2}=0.826$. The present value is \$1 000 $\times 0.826=$ \$826.

折现系数(贴现因子)

未来的某期现金流乘以折现系数就得到其现值。计算公式如下：

折现系数$=(1+$折现率$)^{-n}$(n 是现金流所发生的期数)

例如，在第二期发生的现金流为 1 000 美元，折现率为 10%，则折现系数为$(1+10\%)^{-2}=0.826$。现值为 $1\ 000\times 0.826=826$(美元)。

【学习提示】

折现系数可以查现值系数表(present value table)得到。

Discount Rate

Discount rate is the interest rate used in discounting to get the present value of a future cash flow. The discount rate chosen is usually the required rate of return by investors after considering the risk level of the underlying investment project. Often the cost of capital of the company is used as the discount rate for NPV analysis in investment appraisal.

折现率(贴现率)

折现率指为计算未来现金流的现值而用来折现的利率。所选用的折现率通常是考虑所投项目风险水平以后所要求的回报率。投资评估时,在净现值分析中经常用公司的资本成本作为折现率。

E

Equivalent Annual Annuity (EAA)

EAA refers to the annual annuity which gives the same NPV as the actual uneven cash flows of an investment project. If the annuity is negative, we call Equivalent Annual Cost (EAC). If the annuity is positive, we call Equivalent Annual Benefit (EAB). $EAA = NPV$ of project/annuity discount factor. EAC(B) is a method which is most useful for evaluating projects which are assumed to have unequal but repeating life spans, eg. asset replacement decisions.

等额年金

使投资项目的每期实际不等额现金流的净现值相等的年金值就是等额年金。如果这个年金值是负的,就叫等额年金成本。如果这个年金值是正的,就叫等额年金收益。等额年金=项目的净现值/年金折现系数。等额年金成本(收益)主要用来评估那些年限不等但项目投资可以重复的项目,比如固定资产重置决策。

【学习提示】

本来项目各期发生的现金流是不均匀的，而EAA就是当净现值相同时，现金流均匀分布，每期应发生的现金流量。

Equivalent Annual Cost (EAC)

EAC refers to negative equivalent annual annuity. For example, an equipment is replaced every two years, its purchase cost is \$200 000. The operating costs of the equipment in Year 1 and Year 2 are \$22 000 and \$30 000 respectively. Its residual value at the end of Year 2 is \$60 000. The discount rate is 10%.

NPV of one replacement cycle $= -\$22\ 000/(1+10\%) - \$30\ 000/(1+10\%)^2 - \$200\ 000 = -\$244\ 778$

Cumulative discount factor (annuity factor) = 1.736

$$EAC = \frac{\$244\ 778}{1.736} = \$141\ 001$$

等额年金成本

即负的等额年金。例如，一台设备每两年重置一次，其购置成本为200 000美元，在第一年和第二年的经营成本分别为22 000美元和30 000美元。在第二年年末的残值为60 000美元。折现率为10%。

一个重置期的 $NPV = -22\ 000/(1+10\%) - 30\ 000/(1+10\%)^2 - 200\ 000 = -244\ 778$(美元)

年金折现系数=1.736

等额年金成本(EAC)=244 778/1.736=141 001(美元)

Equivalent Annual Benefit (EAB)

EAB refers to positive equivalent annual annuity. A capital project has a three-year life. Its cash flows during the three years are as follows: Year 1—$200 000; Year 2—$300 000; Year 3—$350 000. The initial investment is $250 000. The discount rate is 12%.

$NPV = \$200\ 000/(1+12\%) + \$300\ 000/(1+12\%)^2 + \$350\ 000/(1+12\%)^3 - \$250\ 000 = \$416\ 900$

Cumulative discount factor (annuity factor) = 2.402

$EAB = \$416\ 900/2.402 = \$173\ 564$

等额年金收益

即正的等额年金。例如，一个资本预算项目的期限为 3 年，3 年期间的现金流如下：第一年 200 000 美元，第二年 300 000 美元，第三年 350 000 美元。初始投资 250 000 美元。折现率为 12%。计算其等额年金收益。

净现值 $= 200\ 000/(1+12\%) + 300\ 000/(1+12\%)^2 + 350\ 000/(1+12\%)^3 - 250\ 000 = 416\ 900$(美元)

等额年金收益(EAB) $= 416\ 900/2.402 = 173\ 564$(美元)

H

Hard Capital Rationing

It refers to a situation where limited amount of capital needs to be allocated to different potential projects, where the capital constraint is brought about by external factors, such as restrictions on bank lending and/or the depressed share price.

硬资本配置

硬资本配置指企业需要把有限的资本在不同的潜在投资项目之间进行配置,而这种资本约束主要是由外部因素导致的,比如对银行借贷的限制以及遭重挫的股价等。

【学习提示】

有时候,由于金融市场这一环境因素,企业通过正常渠道很难再从外部筹集更多的资金,这种硬性的资本约束是企业自身很难改变的。

Internal Rate of Return (IRR)

IRR is the discount rate used in investment appraisal that makes the net present value of all cash flows from a particular project equal to zero.

内部收益率

在投资评估中,使一个项目的现金流的净现值等于 0 的折现率即为内部收益率。

【学习提示】

净现值等于 0 这一点是财务上的盈亏平衡点

(financial break-even point)。$NPV>0$，项目可接受；反之，$NPV<0$，项目不可接受。内部收益率就是使财务盈亏平衡的折现率。

【知识点巩固与拓展】

Starplus 公司计划购置一台成本为 150 万美元的机器。机器的使用年限为 5 年，残值估计为 0。第一年到第五年的现金流分别如下：500 000 美元、520 000 美元、530 000 美元、600 000 美元、610 000 美元。计算 IRR。

Starplus Ltd. is planning to buy a machine which costs $1 500 000. Its useful life is 5 years. Its residual value is estimated to be nil. The estimated cash flows generated by this machine from Year 1 to Year 5 are as follows: $500 000; $520 000; $530 000; $600 000; $610 000. Calculate IRR.

可用 Excel 里的 IRR 公式计算得到 23.42%。

也可以用以下方法估算 IRR：

折现率 10%时，$NPV=570\ 660$(美元)

折现率为 25%时，$NPV=-40\ 156$(美元)

$IRR=10\%+(25\%-10\%)\times[570\ 660/(57\ 660+40\ 156)]=24.01\%$

L

Leasing

Leasing is a commonly used source of finance, where the lessee who needs a specific asset but does not want to borrow to buy it, enters into a contract with the lessor who owns such an asset, to hire the asset and to pay specified rentals over a certain period of time.

租赁

租赁是一种普遍使用的筹资方法。承租人需要某项资产但又不想借钱去买,于是跟拥有资产的出租方签订一份租赁合同,并在租赁期内支付一定的租金。

Lessor

Lessor is one party in a leasing contract who owns a specific asset and leases it to the lessee in return for specified rentals over a certain period of time.

出租方

出租方是租赁合同的一方,把拥有的某项资产出租给承租方并在指定期间内收取一定租金。

Lessee

Lessee is one party in a leasing contract who hires a specific asset from the lessor and pays specified rentals over a certain period of time.

承租方

承租方是租赁合同的一方,从出租方那里租来某项资产,并在指定的期间支付一定租金给出租方。

M

Mutually Exclusive Projects

Mutually exclusive projects refer to two or more capital investment projects from which only one can be chosen.

互斥项目

指两个或多个资本投资项目，但企业只能从中选取一个。

Money Cash Flow

Money cash flow is also called nominal cash flows. It is the actual expected cash flow at future price level, that is inflated cash flow after considering inflation.

货币现金流

货币现金流又称名义现金流，是以未来物价水平预估的实际现金流，即考虑了通货膨胀以后的现金流。

Money Discount Rate

Money discount rate is also called nominal discount rate. It is a rate relating to current market rate of return after considering both real rate of interest and inflation rate. It changes with different inflation rates.

货币折现率

又称名义折现率，即在考虑实际利率和通货膨胀率后，与当前市场回报率相关的折现率。它随着通货膨胀率的变化而变化。

【学习提示(一)】

计算净现值,若考虑通货膨胀,则应注意匹配原则,即货币现金流(名义现金流)用货币折现率(名义折现率)折现,实际现金流用实际折现率折现。名义折现率和实际折现率之间的折算公式为:

1+名义折现率=(1+实际折现率)×(1+通货膨胀率)

【学习提示(二)】

假设以当前物价水平估计的一年以后的现金流为20 000美元。这是实际现金流。假设通货膨胀率为2%,则货币现金流(名义现金流)为20 000×(1+2%)=20 400(美元)。

如果实际利率为6%,则货币折现率(名义折现率)为(1+6%)×(1+2%)-1=8.12%。

N

Net Present Value(NPV)

NPV is the value obtained by discounting all relevant cash inflows and outflows of a capital investment project by a chosen discount rate. It represents the value created by a project.

净现值

净现值是指用选定的折现率把一个资本投资项目的所有相关

现金流入和流出折现所得到的值。它代表一个项目所创造的价值。

【学习提示】

(1)在实际计算 NPV 时,项目周期中产生的现金流都是估算出来的,而折现率的选择也带有主观性。所以,企业在用 NPV 做投资决策时,要谨慎。假设估算无误,净现值大于 0,则意味着一个项目为企业创造了价值,应该接受。

(2)NPV 只考虑了财务方面的影响,没有考虑非财务方面的影响。而一个大的资本项目的决策,非财务因素,比如战略影响、社会和法律影响等也应考虑进去。

(3)在净现值的计算中,首先确定相关现金流。一般把相关现金流分成四部分:一是与固定资产有关的现金流(包括投资成本以及项目结束时的残余价值),二是与营运资本有关的现金流(包括增量投资以及项目结束时的资金回笼),三是经营现金流(=增量销售收入-增量成本),四是企业所得税(=经营现金流的所得税支出+计税折旧费的税收抵扣)。

Non-conventional Cash Flows

Non-conventional cash flows refers to cash flows where there are cash outflows not only initially but at other future periods. For example, a project's cash flows during project life are as follows: Year 0 −\$10m; Year 1 to Year 5 \$1.5 m each year; Year 6 −\$2m; Year 7 to Year 10 \$1.6m each year. There is another cash outflow during Year 6 in addition to the initial cash outflow of \$10m.

非传统现金流

除了初始有现金流出以外,在以后期间也有现金流出的现金流。例如,某项目的现金流如下:第 0 年,支出 1 000 万元,第一年到第五年每年流入 150 万元,第六年再支出 200 万元,第七年到第十年每年流入 160 万元。除了初始的 1 000 万元支出,在第六年有第二笔投资支出 200 万元。

Nominal Cash Flow

Nominal cash flow is also called money cash flow. It is the actual expected cash flow at future price level, that is inflated cash flows after considering inflation.

名义现金流

名义现金流又称货币现金流,是以未来物价水平预估的实际现金流,即考虑了通货膨胀以后的现金流。

Nominal Discount Rate

Nominal discount rate is also called money discount rate. It is a discount rate relating to current market rates of return after considering both real rate of interest and inflation rate. It changes with different inflation rates.

名义折现率

名义折现率又称货币折现率,是指在考虑实际利率和通货膨胀率后,与当前市场回报率相关的折现率。它随着通货膨胀率的变化而变化。

【学习提示】

money cash flow 与 nominal cash flow，money discount rate 与 nominal discount rate 意思相同。

【知识点巩固与拓展】

投资项目 A 的预估现金流：第一年 6 000 万美元，第二年 7 200 万美元，第三年 7 500 万美元。实际折现率为 9%，通货膨胀率为 3%，计算名义现金流和名义折现率。

(1)名义现金流：

第一年　$6\ 000\times(1+3\%)=6\ 180$ 万(美元)

第二年　$7\ 200\times(1+3\%)^2=7\ 638$ 万(美元)

第三年　$7\ 500\times(1+3\%)^3=8\ 195$ 万(美元)

(2)名义折现率：

$(1+9\%)(1+3\%)-1=12\%$

The expected cash flows of Project A during three-year project life are as follows: Year 1 $60 million; Year 2 $72 million; Year 3 $75 million. The real discount rate is 9%, and the general inflation rate is 3%. Calculate the nominal cash flows and the nominal discount rate.

The nominal cash flows:

Year 1　$\$60m\times(1+3\%)=\$61.80m$

Year 2　$\$72m\times(1+3\%)^2=\$76.38m$

Year 3　$\$75\times(1+3\%)^3=\$81.95m$

The nominal discount rate:

$(1+9\%)(1+3\%)-1=12\%$

O

Opportunity Cost

Opportunity cost refers to the maximum benefits foregone by making a choice. For example, a project needs a machine, which has a net realisable value of 2 million dollars and no other uses. In evaluating this project, the opportunity cost of this machine is its net realisable value of 2 million dollars as this is the benefits foregone by using the machine in the project instead of being disposed.

机会成本

机会成本就是因做出某个选择而牺牲的最大利益。例如:一台闲置机器,其报废价值为 200 万元,除了用于某项目,没有其他用处。那这台机器投资于某项目的机会成本为 200 万元的报废价值。

P

Payback Period

Payback period refers to the time taken for the cash inflows from an investment project to recover the cash outflows.

投资回收期

投资回收期指投资项目的现金流入把投资项目的现金流出都

收回所用的时间。

Postponability Index

Postponability index is an index that can be used to decide on which projects should be postponed first, and which projects should be postponed last. It can be calculated as Loss in NPV from the postponement/outlay deferred from Year 0. The project which has the lowest postponability index should be delayed first.

投资推迟指数

投资推迟指数是指用来决定哪个项目应首先推迟、哪个项目应最后推迟的指数。它是用推迟带来的净现值损失除以在第 0 年的支出来获得的。投资推迟指数最小的项目,应该首先推迟投资。

【知识点巩固与拓展】

假设项目 A 的净现值为 7 280 万美元,推迟一年投资的净现值为 6 945 万美元,项目初始投资 3 000 万美元。

则项目 A 的推迟投资指数为:

(7 280－6 945)/3 000＝0.1117

假设项目 B 的净现值为 4 588 万美元,推迟一年投资的净现值为 4 301 万美元,初始投资额为 1 990 万美元。

则项目 B 的推迟指数为:

(4 588－4 301)/1 990＝0.1442

因为 A 项目的推迟指数小于 B 项目,所以先投资 B 项目,A 项目其次。

The relevant information of Project A and B is as follows:

Project A *NPV*= $72.80 million

NPV if delay one year= $69.45million

Initial investment= $30million

Project B *NPV*= $45.88 million

NPV if delay one year= $43.01million

Initial investment= $19.90million.

Calculate postponability index of Project A and B respectively.

Perpetuity

Perpetuity refers to a constant stream of identical cash flows with no end. For example, a return on an investment of $1 000 per year from now on. There is no specified ending date.

永续年金

永续年金指一系列没有到期日的等额现金流。比如一项投资的回报,从现在起,每年可以获得 1 000 美元。没有指定的结束日期。

【学习提示】

永续年金的现值=每期现金流/折现率

比如:一项投资,从现在开始,每年年底可以获得 1 000 美元,没有指定期限。合适的折现率为 10%,则这项永续年金的现值是 1 000/10%=10 000(美元)。

Present value

The present value the current worth of a future sum of money or stream of cash flows given a specified rate of return as discount rate. For example, if discount rate is 6%, the present value of \$5 000 in Year 5 is \$5 000×0.747=\$3 735. And cash flows of \$1 000 each year from Year 1 to Year 5, the present value=\$1 000×4.212=\$4 212.

现值

现值是指用特定的回报率即折现率计算的未来一笔或多笔现金流现在的价值。例如，如果折现率为6%，则第五年的5 000美元的现值为5 000×0.747=3 735(美元)；从第一年到第五年每年1 000美元的现金流，其现值为1 000×4.212=4 212(美元)。

【学习提示】

现值可以用折现(discounting)得到。

Probability Analysis

There are three steps in a probability analysis. First, a probability distribution of expected cash flows is estimated, recognizing there are several possible outcomes. Second, calculate an expected value of the NPV. Third, measure risk, for example in the following ways by calculating the worst possible outcome and its probability or by calculating the probability that the project will fail to achieve a positive NPV or by calculating the standard deviation of the NPV.

概率分析

概率分析分三步。第一步，预计现金流可能的结果，以及估计每种可能的结果的概率；第二步，计算净现值的期望值；第三步，计量风险,比如计算一下可能发生的最坏结果及其概率,或计算一下净现值小于零的概率,或计算一下 NPV 的标准差。

【学习提示】

概率分析是投资评估中计量风险的一种有效方法。

Profitability Index

It is the ratio of the present value of the project's future cash flows divided by capital investment. It is also called the benefit-cost ratio. It is often used to rank divisible projects in single period capital rationing.

获利指数

获利指数又称效益-成本比率,用投资项目未来产生的现金流的现值除以投资金额可获得。它经常用于在单期资本分配的情况下对可拆分的投资项目进行排序。

【知识点巩固与拓展】

有 A、B 两个项目,A 项目的初始投资额为 2 000 万美元,B 项目的初始投资额为 1 500 万美元。A 项目预计未来现金流的现值为 3 849 万美元,B 项目预计未来现金流的现值为 2 176 万美元。要求:假设 A 与 B 两个项目可拆分,求获利指数,并建议最佳投资顺序。

则 A 项目的获利指数为 3 849/2 000=1.924 5,B 项目的获利指数为 2 176/1 500=1.450 7。在 A、B 两个项目可拆分的前提下,又本期资金有限,则 A 项目应优先投资,其次是 B 项目。如此,则可利用有限的资金取得最大的净现值。

Initial investment of project A \$20million.

Initial investment of project B \$15million.

Present value of future cash flows of Project A \$38.49 million.

Present value of future cash flows of Project B \$21.76 million.

Calculate Profitability Index of Project A and B respectively and determine the priority of investment. Assume both projects are divisible. *PI* of Project A=38.49/20=1.924 5, *PI* of Project B=21.76/15=1.450 7. Project A should be invested first. And then Project B.

【学习提示】

(1)用获利指数来做投资规划,只有在项目可分开投资且资本约束只有当期时,才能获得最大的净现值。在项目不可拆分或者资本约束是多期的情况下,这种方法就不适用了。

(2)有时,获利指数也用项目的净现值除以初始投资计算得出。计算公式如下:

$$获利指数=\frac{项目预计未来现金流的现值-初始投资}{初始投资}$$

Project Screening

Project screening is one of the stages in capital budgeting process. At this stage, each proposed projects must be carefully screened according to some criteria, such as payback period, strategic value, availability of resources, legal and regulatory requirements and risk exposure. The short-listed projects then go to the next stage for detailed further evaluation.

项目筛选

项目筛选是资本预算过程的一个阶段。在这一阶段,每一个提议的项目都会根据诸如投资回收期、战略价值、资源可得性、法律法规的要求以及风险情况等标准进行仔细筛选。筛选好的项目就进入资本预算的下个阶段,做进一步详细评估。

R

Real Cash Flow

Real cash flow is the cash flows in current price level without taking future inflation into account.

实际现金流

实际现金流是指以现在的物价水平衡量的、没有考虑未来通货膨胀的现金流。

【知识点巩固与拓展】

项目A的3年项目周期的名义现金流如下:第一年6 000万美元,第二年7 200万美元,第三年7 500万美元。名义折现率为12%,通货膨胀率为3%。计算实际现金流和实际折现率。

实际现金流如下:

第一年　6 000/(1+3%)=5 825(万美元)

第二年　$7\ 200/(1+3\%)^2=6\ 787$(万美元)

第三年　$7\ 500/(1+3\%)^3=6\ 864$(万美元)

实际折现率 $(1+12\%)/(1+3\%)-1=8.7\%$

Nominal cash flows of Project A during three-year project life are as follows: Year 1 \$60 million; Year 2 \$72 million; Year 3 \$75 million . The nominal discount rate is 12%, and the general inflation rate is 3%. Calculate the real cash flow and the real discount rate.

The real cash flows are as follows:

Year 1　$\$6\ 000/(1+3\%)=\$58.25$m

Year 2　$\$7\ 200/(1+3\%)^2=\$67.87$m

Year 3　$\$7\ 500/(1+3\%)^3=\$68.64$m

The real discount rate is $(1+12\%)/(1+3\%)-1=8.7\%$.

Real Discount Rate

Real discount rate is the discount rate which only reflects the time value of money without considering future inflation rate.

实际折现率

实际折现率指只反映货币时间价值而没有考虑未来通货膨胀率的折现率。

Reinvestment Assumption

Reinvestment assumption is an assumption underlying DCF analysis about the rate of return that any future net cash inflows generated during the project life can be reinvested. For NPV, it is assumed that the cash inflows can be reinvested at the cost of capital (that is, the discount rate). But for the IRR method, it assumes these cash inflows can be reinvested to earn a rate of return equal to the IRR of the project.

再投资假设

再投资假设是DCF分析中关于报酬率的假设,即项目周期内产生的任何未来现金净流入都可以何种报酬率再投资。净现值法,假设未来项目的现金净流入以等于资金成本(即折现率)的报酬率再投资,而内部收益法假设这些现金流入以等于内部收益率的报酬率再投资。

【学习提示】

IRR的再投资假设,即假设未来现金流入以等于内部收益率的报酬率再投资,这点往往被诟病,认为其跟现实投资报酬率相差较大。

Relevant Cash Flows

Relevant cash flows are cash flows that arise as a consequence of the investment decision under consideration. Relevant cash flows must be future and incremental.

相关现金流

相关现金流是指由投资决策而产生的现金流。相关现金流必须是将来发生的,并且必须是一个增量。

【学习提示】

在净现值分析中,相关现金流不包括利息支出。

因为，这是融资决策的现金流，而净现值不考虑融资的影响，只考虑投资项目本身。

相关现金流是投资项目所改变的现金流，这里有三个关键词：

一是必须是现金流。会计折旧以及资产的账面价值都不构成现金流，所以均无关。

二是必须是决策点以后发生的。在投资决策前发生的前期市场调研支出是过去发生的，是沉没成本，所以是无关的。

三是必须是增量，即因投资项目而增加或减少的现金流。比如投资一台新机器，每年节约生产成本共 1 000 万美元。这 1 000 万美元就是一个增量，所以属于相关现金流入。

【知识点巩固与拓展】

红星公司打算投资一套成本为 3 000 万美元的生产设备，前期市场调研已发生 80 万美元支出。设备的有效使用年限为 10 年，10 年后的报废价值为 20 万美元。如果引进这套设备，每年可多生产和销售 10 000 个单位的产品，现在年销量和产量均为 100 000 个单位。产品售价假设不变，仍为每单位 500 美元。新设备可节省单位变动生产成本 20 美元，每年增加固定成本 90 万美元。找出这个投资项目的相关现金流。

相关现金流有：

(1)期初第 0 年，设备成本为−3 000 万美元。

(2)第 10 年，设备报废价值为 20 万美元。

(3)第 1 年～第 10 年，增加的销售收入为 10 000×500＝500(万美元)。

(4)第 1 年～第 10 年，节约的变动成本为 110 000×20＝220(万美元)。

(5)第 1 年～第 10 年,增加的固定成本为－90 万美元。

注:前期已发生的市场调研费用 80 万美元是过去发生的沉没成本,与决策无关,不用考虑。

Redstar Ltd. is planning to purchase an equipment costing $30 million. Market research fee of $0.8 million was incurred already. The useful life of the equipment is 10 years. At the end of its useful life, its scrap value is estimated to be $0.2 million. And this equipment will help increase sales volume by 10 000 units. Currently its production and sales volume are both 100 000 units. Selling price is assumed to be constant, that is $500 per unit. The variable production cost will be saved by $20 per unit. And fixed cost will be increased by $0.9 million per year.

Find out relevant cash flows of this investment project.

Relevant cash flows are as follows:

1. Equipment cost －$30m Year 0

2. Scrap value of the equipment $0.2m Year 10

3. Annual sales increase 10 000×$500＝$5m Year 1－Year 10

4. Annual variable cost saved 110 000×$20＝$2.2m Year 1－Year 10

5. Annual fixed cost increase －$0.9m Year 1－Year 10

Risk

It relates to the variability of returns. The greater the variability is, the greater the risk is. There are several possible outcomes which probabilities can be assigned on basis of past relevant experience. Risk can be quantified by assigning probabilities.

风险

它与回报的波动相关。回报波动越大，风险也越大。有几种可能的结果，每一种可能的结果都可以根据相关经验估计所发生的概率。风险通过估算概率而被量化。

Risk-adjusted Discount Rate

It is a discount rate used in NPV calculation which reflects the specific risk level of the investment project under consideration.

风险调整折现率

在计算净现值时，风险调整折现率反映了所投资项目风险水平的折现率。

【学习提示】

项目风险越高，投资者期望得到的收益就越高，所以折现率就应该越高；同样的项目现金流，计算出的净现值就越低。这样可以让决策者对待高风险项目的投资决策更加谨慎。

S

Sale and Leaseback

Sale and leaseback is one of the sources of finance. When a business owns an asset, usually tangible non-current assets, and want to raise funds, it can sell the asset to a financial institution to get the funds needed, and at the same time lease it back and pay specified rentals to the financial institution during the lease term according to the sale and leaseback agreement.

销售回租

销售回租是筹集资金的一种方式。当一家企业拥有资产(通常是有形的固定资产)但需要筹集资金时,它可以找一家金融机构,把资产卖给它,以获得相应的资金,同时再把该项资产从这家金融机构手里租回来,并根据销售回租协议,在租赁期内支付指定的租金。

Sensitivity

Sensitivity means the responsiveness of the project's NPV to changes in the variables used to calculate NPV. Sensitivity = *NPV* of the project/present value of a project variable. The lower the percentage, the more critical of the variable to the success of the project.

敏感性

它是指项目的净现值对影响净现值计算的变量变动的反应程度。敏感性=项目的净现值÷所考查变量能影响的现值。计算出的百分比越小,说明这个变量对投资项目的成功越关键。

【学习提示】

这是 ACCA 书上对敏感性的计算公式。如果参加 ACCA 考试,就用这个公式。

这实际是计算了一个安全边际(管理会计的概念)即实际情况离盈亏平衡点的距离。安全边际越小,越不安全,所考察变量微小的变动就会对净现值产生较大影响,所以 NPV 对所考察变量越敏感。

【知识点巩固与拓展】

在其他书上,敏感性=因变量变化的百分比÷自变量变化的百分比。计算结果越大,表明因变量,比如净现值,对所考察变量的变化越敏感。

Sensitivity Analysis

Sensitivity analysis refers to a method that assesses how sensitive the project's NPV is to changes in the variables used to calculate NPV. It measures the percentage change in a variable before NPV equals zero. It analyses the uncertainty surrounding a capital investment project.

敏感性分析

敏感性分析是用以分析投资项目的净现值对某变量变化的敏感度的一种方法。它计量了某个变量变化多少百分比就会使净现值等于零。它分析了某个投资项目所面临的不确定性。

Simulation

Simulation is a method of incorporating risks and uncertainty into consideration when making investment decisions. It simulates what happens in the real world where variables change interdependently and any possibility occurs ad hoc. Firstly, think about the variables that affect the investment return and set up the decision model. Secondly, think about the possible outcomes of each independent variable and estimate the probability of each possible outcome, assign random number to each possibility to represent probability. For example, if the probability of a possible outcome A is 0.2, we can use number 0 to 19. If the probability of another possible outcome B is 0.8, we can use number 20 to 99. Thirdly, we choose a number from the 100 numbers . If 17, it means A. If 68, it means B. Repeat this process for each independent variables many times. Finally, we can get the possible values and the statistical distribution of the investment returns .

模拟法

在做投资决策时,模拟法是考虑风险和不确定性的一种方法。现实世界中,各种变量会相互影响并且随机发生,它试图模拟这一切。首先,想想有哪些变量会影响投资回报,建立决策模型。其次,想想模型中的自变量的几种可能值,估计每种可能值的概率,并从 0～99 这 100 个数字中给每种可能值派一组数字来代表其概率。例如,一种可能值 A,其概率为 0.2,可以用 0～19 这 20 个数字来表示;另一种可能值 B,其概率为 0.8,就用剩下的 80 个数字来表示,即 20～99。再接下来,从 0 到 99 这 100 个数字中任选一个数字,如 17,就对应着 A,如 68,就对应着 B。每一个自变量都重复这个过程许多次。最后,得到投资回报的各种可能值及其统计分布。

Single Period Capital Rationing

It refers to a capital rationing situation at which the business has capital constraints only for a single period.

单期资本配置

单期资本配置是指只有单个期间有资本约束的资本配置情形。

Soft Capital Rationing

It refers to a situation where limited amount of capital needs to be allocated to different potential projects, where the capital constraint is brought about by internal factors, such as the financing policy of the company.

软资本配置

企业需要把有限的资本配置到不同的潜在投资项目中,而其资本约束主要是由内部因素导致的,比如公司的融资政策。这样一种情形就称为软资本配置。

T

Tax-allowable Depreciation

It is also called capital allowance. It is the depreciation expense that can be allowed to be deducted from taxable profit in calculating corporation tax.

计税允许扣除的折旧费用

它又称资本折让,是指在计算企业所得税时被允许从应纳税所得中扣除的折旧费用。

【学习提示】

计税允许扣除的折旧费用,对投资项目评估的影响,就是相关的节税效应。比如:投资一台机器,每年计税允许计提的折旧为 300 万美元,所得税税率为 20%。则每年节税额(项目的现金流入)=300×20%=60 万(美元)。

U

Uncertainty

It relates to the length of time into the future. The longer time into the future, the more uncertainty. There are several possible outcomes that are difficult to assign probabilities.

不确定性

不确定性与未来距离现在的时间长短有关。时间越长,不确定性越大。有几种可能的结果,但每一种可能的结果的发生概率都很难估计。

【学习提示】

敏感性分析以及投资回收期等方法都是考虑投资项目的不确定性而采用的投资项目分析方法。

Module Three

Raising Finance/融资

本单元的学习目标：

(1)熟悉各种融资工具的特点；

(2)掌握融资决策，特别是资本结构决策应考虑的因素；

(3)熟悉中小企业融资困难的原因及其解决办法；

(4)掌握企业分红决策需要考量的因素。

B

Bonds

Bonds refer to various long-term debt instruments a company or a government may issue. The bondholder lends money to the issuer by buying the bonds, and in return the issuer pays interest and/or repay the principal to the bondholder later.

债券

债券是指企业或政府发行的各种长期债务凭证。债券持有人通过购买债券先把资金借给发行方。作为回报，发行方随后会支付利息并(或者)将本金返还给债券持有人。

【知识点巩固与拓展】

传统债券作为一种债务融资工具的特点：

(1)必须按时支付利息，支付利息是债务人的法律义务。

(2)必须按时返还本金或赎回，这也是债务人的法律义务。

(3)债务合约里面会有一些对债权人的保护性条款，以限制债务人的某些行为。

(4)用债券融资会增加企业的杠杆。

(5)相对股票融资成本，债券融资成本较低。债券对投资者来说比股票的风险低，所以投资者要求的回报就低。

(6)债券的利息可以作为费用在计算所得税之前扣除，因此可以减轻发行企业的所得税负担。

(7)债券发行不会影响现有股东对企业的控制权，即没有稀释股权。

Characteristics of conventional bonds:

1. Interest must be paid. Interest payment is a legal obligation of the debtor.

2. The bonds must be redeemed or repaid. This is also a legal obligation of the issuing company.

3. There are loan covenants in loan agreements which will re-

strict the actions of issuing company.

4. Raising funds by issuing bonds will increase gearing of the issuing company.

5. Cost of bonds is lower than that of shares. Bondholders bear lower risk than shareholders, so they will require lower return.

6. Interest payments of bonds are tax deductible, so the tax burden of issuing company will be reduced.

7. New issue of bonds will not affect the business control by existing shareholders, that is, there is no dilution of control.

Borrowing Capacity

Borrowing capacity refers to the ability of a company to borrow money from the outsiders. It depends on the assets available as security, gearing level, credit rating and its cash position etc.

借贷能力

借贷能力指一家公司向外部借钱的能力。这主要取决于可以用作担保的资产、杠杆水平、信用等级以及资金状况等。

Business Angels

Business angels refer to wealthy individuals and groups of individuals who would like to invest in small businesses usually in a less formal way than venture capital providers. Both business angels and venture capitalists are prepared to take high risks in exchange for high returns.

天使投资人

天使投资人是指愿意向小企业投资的富有的个人和团体。他们对投资的评估通常不如风险资本提供者正式。天使投资人和风险资本家都愿意通过承担高风险来获得相应的高回报。

C

Capital Structure

It refers to the relative proportion of the debt capital and equity capital in the total capital employed of a company. It can be measured by debt/equity ratio or debt/（debt ＋ equity）ratio. It affects financial risk of a business. Capital structure decision is an important financial management decision of a company, many factors such as gearing level, stability of sales, cost of capital and risk should be considered.

资本结构

它是指在企业所用的总资本中债务资本和权益资本的相对比例。它通常可用负债权益比或者负债比负债与权益之和来计量。资本结构影响企业的财务风险。资本结构决策是公司的一项重大财务管理决策，需要考量很多因素，比如杠杆水平、销售的稳定性、资本成本以及风险等。

【学习提示】

资本结构决策属企业的融资决策，涉及债务融资与权益融资的选择以及长期债务与短期债务的选择等。

【知识点巩固与拓展】

资本结构决策会影响企业的财务杠杆，即财务风险水平。如果企业本身的经营杠杆比较高，就可以适当地降低财务杠杆。如果企业本身的经营杠杆比较低，企业就可以考虑适当地增加财务杠杆。另外，如果企业本来的杠杆水平很高，则在用新的债务融资时要谨慎。

一家企业的销售如果比较稳定，则其承担风险的能力较强，所以，可以适当地增加财务杠杆。

企业选择债务融资还是权益融资，还要考虑投资者关于风险和收益的权衡，以及这种权衡对资金成本的影响。

企业要选择债务融资，还要考虑自己的借贷能力，以及借贷市场对企业的态度。

资本结构决策还要考虑债务融资和权益融资各自的优缺点。

Capital structure decisions will change gearing and thus risk level of the company. If a company has a higher operational gearing, it should lower its financial gearing. If a company has a lower operational gearing, it can afford a higher financial gearing. Also, if the current gearing is high, a company should be cautious in choosing further debt finance.

The stability of sales will give the company more potential to deal with risks. So it can use more debt finance.

Investors' return-risk trade-off will affect cost of capital of the investee, which should be taken into account in capital structure decisions.

Whether a business can raise new debt finance, it will depend on its own borrowing capacity and attitude of the lenders.

Both debt finance and equity finance have their own advantages and disadvantages.

Clientele Effect

If a business pursues a consistent dividend policy, it will attract a clientele who prefers its particular dividend payout ratio. And if the company changes its dividend payout ratio, it will attract another clientele who prefers the new payout ratio. This new clientele will be as good as the former one in terms of the valuation of the firm. So the change of dividend policy will not affect business value.

客户效应

一家分红政策稳定的公司，将吸引偏好其特定股利支付比率的投资客户群体。如果企业改变了股利支付比率，它就会吸引偏好新股利支付比率的另一客户群。新的客户群对企业的估值的影响跟老的客户群一样。因此，分红政策的改变不影响企业的价值。

【学习提示】

莫迪利安尼-米勒(Modigliani-Miller)用客户效应理论来支持其股利政策无关论。

MM(无税)理论认为，除了企业本身的盈利能力和经营风险，其他因素不会影响企业的价值和企业的资本成本。所以股利政策也不会影响企业的价值。

Convertible Bonds/Convertible Loan Notes

Convertible bonds refer to bonds that give the bondholder the options which are either to convert to ordinary shares at pre-determined conversion rate and time or just hold as a straight bond and receive the redemption value at the maturity date. If upon maturity date, the conversion value is greater than redemption value, a rational bondholder will convert the bonds to ordinary shares. And if the redemption value is greater than conversion value, a rational bondholder will choose to just get the redemption value.

可转换债券

可转换债券持有人可以选择要么在指定的时间以指定的转换率转换成普通股，要么只是作为普通债券持有，在到期日收到赎回价值。如果到期时，转换价值超出赎回价值，理性的债券持有人就会把债券转换成普通股。如果赎回价值大于转换价值，理性的债券持有人就会只选择得到债券的赎回价值。

【知识点巩固与拓展】

可转换债券的特点：

（1）可转换成普通股。在规定时间，如果转换价值大于赎回价值，投资者就拥有把可转换债券转换成普通股的选择权；反之，投资者也可以选择获得债券的赎回价值。

(2)票面利率比普通债券低。因为给予投资者选择权,所以风险比投资普通债券低,投资者要求的利率相对较低。

(3)递延权益。如果投资者将来把可转换债券转换成普通股,则发行企业的权益增加,债务减少。

(4)可能无须赎回。如果转换成普通股,企业就不需要筹集一大笔资金来赎回债券。

(5)潜在的稀释作用。一旦转换成普通股,现有股东的股权以及发行企业的每股收益就均被稀释。

(6)对杠杆的影响。一旦转换成普通股,则权益增加,负债减少,财务杠杆降低。

Characteristics of convertible bonds:

1. Conversion rights. Upon maturity, if the conversion value is greater than the redemption value, the bondholders will choose to convert the bond to ordinary shares. If the redemption value is greater than the conversion value, the bondholders will choose to just get the redemption value.

2. Lower coupon rate of interest. Compared with conventional bonds, convertible bondholders face lower risk as they have conversion rights, so they require lower coupon rate of interest.

3. Delayed equity. If converted to ordinary shares, equity is increased and debts are decreased.

4. No need to be redeemed. If converted, there is no need for the issuing company to raise a large sum of money to redeem the bonds.

5. Potential dilution. If converted, both control of the business by the existing shareholders and EPS (earnings per share) are diluted.

6. Decrease gearing . If converted, equity will be increased, financial gearing will be decreased.

Conversion Value

It refers to the value of convertible bonds if converted to shares immediately. Conversion value = conversion ratio × market price of ordinary shares converted. For example, the 7% convertible bonds can be converted to 25 shares per $100 nominal value, the current share price is $3. Conversion value = 25 × $3 = $75.

转换价值

转换价值就是把可转换债券马上转换成股票，所转换股票的价值。转换价值=转换率×普通股股价。例如：利率 7%的可转换债券，每面值 100 美元可以转换成 25 股，现在股票的市价是 3 美元，则转换价值为 25×3=75(美元)。

【学习提示】

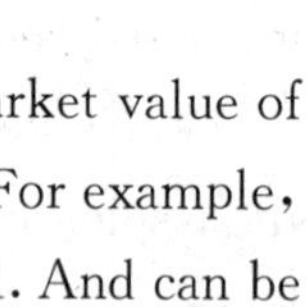

可转换债券的可转换价值随着股价的变化而变化，股价越高，转换价值越大。

Conversion Premium

Conversion premium is the excess of current market value of a convertible bond over its current conversion value. For example, the 7% convertible bonds are currently quoted at 121. And can be converted to 25 shares per $100 nominal value in five years, the current share price is $3. Conversion value = 25 × $3 = $75. Conversion premium = 121 − 75 = $46 or 46/121 = 38%.

转换溢价

转换溢价指可转换债券的现在市值超出当前转换价值的部分。例如:利率7%的可转换债券,现在报价121,每面值100美元可以转换成25股,现在股票的市价是3美元,则转换价值为25×3=75(美元),转换溢价为121−75=46(美元),或46/121=38%。

【学习提示】

转换溢价越高,可转换债券市价受股价的影响越小。

Coupon Interest (of a bond)

Coupon interest is a periodic interest payment at the coupon rate that the bondholder receives from the issuing company during the time between when the bond is issued and when it matures.

债券的票面利息

债券的票面利息是指从债券发行到债券到期,债券持有人从债券发行公司定期收到的、按照票面利率计算的利息。

【知识点巩固与拓展】

一张票面利率6%、面值100美元的债券,其每年的票面利息是多少?

A 6% bond with a par value of $100, what is its annual coupon interest?

Annual coupon interest per bond = $100 × 6% = $6

Covenants

Covenants refer to terms and conditions in a loan agreement that the borrower must comply with for the purpose of protecting creditors. If the borrower breached the covenants, the loan can be considered in default. There are positive covenants and negative covenants. A positive covenant may say 'the borrower must do something', and a negative covenant may say 'the borrower must not do something'.

债务保护性条款

债务保护性条款是指为了保护债权人的利益，借款方必须遵守的债务合约的条款。如果借款方违反这些债务条款，则构成违约。积极条款往往规定借款方必须做什么，而消极条款往往规定借款方不能做什么。

【知识点巩固与拓展】

在信息不对称的情况下，债权人担心管理层和股东在决策时牺牲自己的利益，在借款时就会要求很高的利率，而如果债务合约里有这些保护性条款，债权人就会适当降低利率，企业的借款成本就降低了。

Credit Rating

Credit rating is grade ratings given by credit rating agencies to a company or a government or to a loan note issued by a company or a government after carefully evaluation of its ability to pay off interest and repay debt. The lower the credit ratings, the higher the cost of debt。

信用评级

信用评级指信用评级机构给某家公司或某个政府以及公司或政府所发行债券的评级。这个评级是根据被评主体的付息还贷能力来分级的。信用评级越低,债务成本越高。

【学习提示】

信用评级越低,企业债务违约的可能性越大,投资者所面临的违约风险越大,投资者要求的回报就越高,因此被投资企业的债务成本就越高。

Creditor Hierarchy

Investors will consider risk-return trade-off. If their investment is of higher risk, they will require higher return to compensate for risk and so the investee will have a higher cost of capital. As creditors face less risk than shareholders, so creditors ask for lower return than shareholders, debt finance is cheaper than equity. Creditors who are offered assets as security face lower level of risk than unsecured creditors, so secured creditors ask for lower return than unsecured creditors and finance from secured creditors is less costly than finance from unsecured creditors.

投资者层级

投资者总是权衡风险和收益。如果一项投资风险较高,作为补偿,投资者就会要求更高的回报,被投资方就会承担较高的资金成本。因为债权人承担的风险低于股东，所以债权人比股东要求的回报低，债务融资比权益融资便宜。有担保的债权人比无担保的债权人承担较低的风险，所以有担保的债权人要求更低的回报，有资产作为担保，企业的借钱成本就会比无资产作为担保时低。

【知识点巩固与拓展】

投资者层级，按照风险由小到大依次为：

(1)有担保的债权人；

(2)无担保的债权人；

(3)优先股股东；

(4)普通股股东。

Creditors' Hierarchy with increasing risk is as follows:

1. Secured creditors;
2. Unsecured creditors;
3. Preference shareholders;
4. Ordinary shareholders.

Crowdfunding

It is a project financing method. A company who has an attractive project raising money from a large number of investors who are attracted by the earning potential of the project and are willing to support the project. Usually the investors and the investee are brought together by an internet platform.

众筹

众筹是一种项目融资方式。公司若有吸引人的项目，则可以从众多看好项目潜力并愿意支持项目的投资者那里获得资金。通常投资者和被投资方通过一个网络平台联系在一起。

Cum-rights

When a rights issue is announced but before the first day of dealings in the newly issued shares, all existing shareholders have the right to subscribe for new shares and so there are rights attached to the existing shares, so these shares are being cum-rights.

含权

当配股方案对外公布，但新股还没有开始交易时，所有的现有股东都有认购新股的权利，所有的现有股票都含认购新股的权利，所以这些股票都是含权的。

D

Debt Finance

Debt finance refers to raising funds through borrowing or issuing of preference shares.

债务融资

债务融资指通过借款或发行优先股筹集资金。

【学习提示】

虽然在 ACCA 的书上，把优先股融资归入债务融资，但大家仍要记住优先股是不同于债券等真正意义上的债务的。其实，优先股是介于债券和普通

股之间的一种融资工具。

Debt Capital

Debt capital refers to long-term funds raised through borrowing or issuing of preference shares. Its book value is long-term debts plus preference share capital (as reported in Statement of Financial Position). Its market value is market value of all long-term debts plus market value of preference shares.

债务资本

债务资本是通过借款或发行优先股筹集的长期资金。账面价值用资产负债表中的长期债务加上优先股股本表示。市场价值用所有长期债务的市值加上优先股市值表示。

【学习提示】

鉴于优先股既不同于普通股，也不同于债券，所以，很多时候，债务资本里面会把优先股融入的资本去掉，仅包含借款融入的资本。

Debt Ratio

It is calculated as total debts divided by total assets. It is one of the measures of financial risk of a business.

债务比率

计算公式：债务比率＝总债务/总资产。它是计量企业的财务风险的指标之一。

【学习提示】

注意区分债务(debts)和负债(liabilities)。债务仅指企业的借款(borrowing),不包括应付账款、递延所得税负债、预提费用以及递延收益等。因此,债务比率不同于资产负债率。

Debentures

Debentures are unsecured bonds, which are long-term unsecured debt instruments used by large companies to borrow money.

无担保债券

无担保债券是指大型企业用来借入资金的一种无担保长期债务凭证。

Deep Discounted Bonds

Deep discounted bonds refer to bonds issued at a price at a large discount to the nominal value of the bond, and which offer a low coupon payment and will be redeemed at par (or above par) at the maturity date. The main income for deep discounted bond investors is the deep discount, not interest.

深贴现债券

深贴现债券指以远远低于债券票面价值的高折扣价发行的债券。一般其票面利息较低,在到期日会以票面价值或高于票面价值赎回。此类债券的投资者的主要收入来源是发行公司给予的高折扣,而非利息收入。

【学习提示】

因为深贴现债券给予投资者高折扣，所以投资者所要求的票面利率比一般债券低，甚至可以为0。票面利率为0的深贴现债券为零息债券。

Dividend Policy

Dividend policy is an important financial management decision to decide on the policy of dividend distribution out of the distributable earnings.

股利决策/分红政策

股利决策是一项重大财务管理决策，决定可分配收益中有多少可用来发放股利。

【知识点巩固与拓展】

股利决策需要考量很多因素，包括：

(1)企业的可分配收益；

(2)企业目前和将来的资金状况；

(3)关于公司分红的法律规定；

(4)关于涉及分红的合约条款；

(5)企业以前的分红政策；

(6)股东的反应(信号效应)。

Factors that should be taken into account in making dividend policy:

1. Distributable earnings;

2. Current and future cash position of the business;

3. Legal requirements;
4. Contractual restrictions;
5. Previous dividend policy;
6. The reactions of shareholders (signalling effect).

E

Equity Shares

Equity shares are also called ordinary shares. The holders of this class of shares have voting rights in AGM. And the company can not distribute dividends to them only if the preference shareholders have got dividends.

权益股

又称普通股。此类股票的持有者在年度股东大会上有投票权。只有优先股股东得到股利后,公司才可以向普通股股东派发股利。

Equity Finance

Equity finance refers to raising funds from its owners through selling equity shares or use funds internally generated.

权益融资

权益融资指通过销售权益股份从企业所有者那里筹集资金或使用企业内部产生的资金。

Equity Capital

Equity capital refers to long-term funds from its equity shareholders. Its book value is ordinary share capital plus reserves (as reported in Statement of Financial Position). Its market value is market value of ordinary shares outstanding.

权益资本

权益资本是指来自权益股东的资金。账面价值用资产负债表中的普通股股本加上所有的公积获得。市值是发行在外的普通股的市值。

【学习提示】

权益资本不包括优先股。

Ex-rights

After the new rights issue shares dealing in the stock market, the existing shares will be traded without the rights to subscribe for the new rights issue shares. So these shares are being ex-rights.

除权

随着配售的新股在股票市场上交易，此时买进原先的股票就不再含有可以认购新配售的股票的权利。这些股票已除权。

F

Fixed Rate Loan

Fixed rate loan is a loan that charges interest at a fixed rate, eg. 5%.

固定利率贷款

固定利率贷款指按固定利率(比如5%)来计息的贷款。

Financial Gearing

It measures the degree of financial risk exposed in holding equity shares of a company, in other words, measures the volatility of earning attributable to ordinary shareholders in response to the change in PBIT. It can be calculated as debt capital divided by equity capital or debt capital divided by total capital employed (ie. Debt capital + equity capital). The higher the proportion of debt capital in total capital employed, the more highly geared of the company.

财务杠杆

它计量持有权益股份所面临的财务风险的程度,换句话说,它计量相对息税前利润的变动,普通股股东可享收益的波动幅度。一般用债务资本除以权益资本或债务资本除以所用总资本(即债务资本+权益资本)来计算财务杠杆。债务资本在所用总资本中所占的比例越高,企业的财务杠杆越高。

【学习提示】

杠杆，ACCA 书上用 gearing，美国的书上用 leverage。高杠杆，ACCA 书上用 highly geared，美国的书上用 highly levered.

【知识点巩固与拓展】

下面这些比率可以计量一家企业的财务杠杆：

（1）债务资本比权益资本；

（2）债务资本比权益资本与债务资本之和；

（3）利息费用除以息税前利润；

（4）每股收益变动百分比除以息税前利润变化百分比。

The following ratios can measure financial gearing of a company：

1. Debt capital/equity capital；

2. Debt capital/(debt capital＋equity capital)；

3. Interest cost/*PBIT*；

4. ％ change in *EPS*/％ change in *PBIT*.

另外，前面两个公式，可以账面价值计量，也可以市场价值计量。

Floating Rate Loan

Floating rate loan is a loan that charges interest at a variable rate，eg. base rate ＋2％.

浮动利率贷款

浮动利率贷款指按变动利率（比如，基准利率＋2％）来计息的贷款。

Floor Value（of a convertible bond）

Floor value refers to the minimum market price of a convertible bond, it will be the price of a straight bond with the same coupon rate as the convertible bond.

（可转换债券的）最低限值

最低限值指可转换债券的最低市价。它是与可转换债券票面利率相同的普通债券的价格。

Flotation

Flotation refers to a company becoming listed and selling shares to the public for the first time.

公司上市

指一家公司被允许上市并首次向公众发售股票。

I

Islamic Finance

Islamic finance refers to financing methods consistent with the principles of sharia law and based on the concept of sharing risk and reward between the investor and the investee. Charging of interest (Riba) is immoral and is forbidden.

伊斯兰融资

伊斯兰融资是与伊斯兰教旨一致，基于投资者和被投资者共享收益、共担风险的融资方法。在这种融资方式下，收利息是不道德的，是被禁止的。

Ijara

The Islamic equivalent of a lease.

伊斯兰租赁

这是伊斯兰融资方式之一，相当于租赁。

Interest Coverage Ratio(Interest Cover)

It measures how many times of PBIT can cover interest cost. It indicates the safety of interest payment and financial risk of a business. It is calculated as PBIT divided by interest cost.

利息保障倍数

它计量息税前利润占利息费用的倍数。它反映了企业支付利息的安全性和企业财务风险。计算公式：利息保障倍数＝息税前利润÷利息费用。

【知识点巩固与拓展】

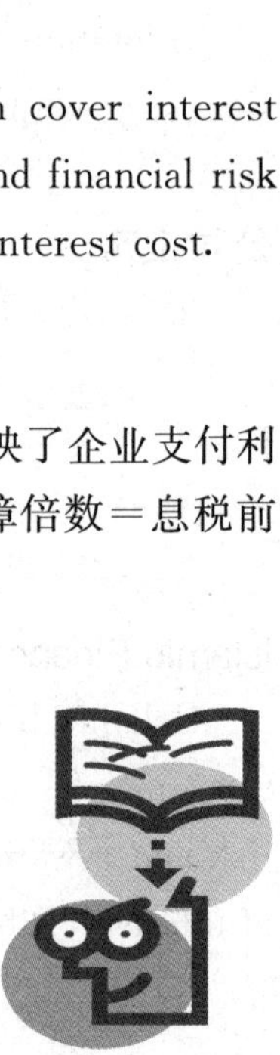

利息保障倍数的倒数是计量财务杠杆的方法之一。利息保障倍数越高，财务杠杆越低，财务风险就越低。

The reciprocal of interest cover measures financial gearing. The higher of interest cover, the lower of financial gearing, the lower of financial risk.

Introduction

The existing shares of a company which are already widely held, are granted a quotation for the first time in a stock market. There are no new issues of shares and no new funds raised by the company. It is one of the means for a unquoted company to become listed.

纳入股市报价

这是指企业已发行的股票(这些股票已经被广泛持有)首次在股市获得公开报价。没有发行新股,企业也没有筹集到任何资金。这是未上市公司寻求上市的一种方式。

【学习提示】

公司上市的方式有:首次公开发行(IPO)、定向发售(placing)、纳入股市报价(introduction)。

Irrelevancy Theory

According to Modigiani and Miller, in a perfect capital market, shareholders are indifferent between dividend and capital gains, so the change in dividend policy will not affect the share price of the company.

(股利政策)无关论

根据 M&M 的观点,在一个完美的资本市场,股东对于获得股利还是资本利得是无偏好的,所以公司改变股利政策不会影响公司的股价。

L

Loan Stock/Notes

Loan stock refers to a type of fixed interest debt instruments, acknowledging a loan that is made to a company. The term is often used interchangeably with bond.

债券

债券是指固定利息的债务凭证,证明借款给发行企业。该术语经常与 bond 交换使用。

M

Management Buyout

Management buyout is a transaction where the management of a company purchase of all or parts of a company from the owners. Many venture capitalists would like to invest in management buyouts.

管理层收购

管理层收购是指一家公司的管理层从业主手里买走企业部分或全部的股权。许多风险资本愿意为管理层收购提供资金支持。

Mortgage Loan

It is a loan that is secured by the collateral of a specified real estate property. Mortgages are usually used by businesses and individuals to purchase real estate without the need to pay a large sum of money immediately. Should the property buyer default on paying the loan, the bank has a claim on the underlying property secured.

抵押贷款

抵押贷款是指用特定不动产做抵押担保的贷款。企业和个人购买不动产时，用抵押贷款无须马上支付一大笔资金。如果不动产买方将来不能履行还款义务，银行就有权处理担保的资产来偿还剩余债务。

【知识点巩固与拓展】

如果企业手里有不动产，则融资方式可以选抵押贷款，也可以用销售回租。

If a company has a property, it can raise funds by means of either mortgage loan or sale and lease back.

Mudaraba

Mudaraba is a partnership contract under which one partner contributes capital and the other contributes the management skill and expertise. Any profits will be shared between the partners and any losses are solely borne by the investor. It is a kind of Islamic finance.

利润分享、损失自担协议

这是一种合伙协议，一方出资，另一方负责经营，有利润一起分享，有损失由投资方自己承担。它是伊斯兰融资方式之一。

Musharaka

A partnership contract under which all partners bring a share of the capital as well as expertise to the business or project. Any profits will shared according to the agreed ratios and any losses are borne by the partners in proportion to capital contributions. It is a kind of Islamic finance.

股本参与协议

这是一种合伙协议，双方都既出资又出技术，利润按照事先规定的比例分享，而损失按出资比例承担。它是伊斯兰融资方式之一。

Murabaha

It is a deferred payment sale. In addition to the normal price of the goods, a mark-up is charged by the seller for the convenience of paying later given to the buyer. It is a kind of Islamic finance.

延期付款销售协议

除了货物的正常价格外，卖方还因向买方提供可以延期付款的便利而另外再加收一部分费用。它是伊斯兰融资方式之一。

O

Ordinary Shares

Ordinary shares are also called equity shares. The holders of this class of shares have voting rights in AGM. And the company can not distribute dividends to them only if the preference shareholders have got dividends.

普通股

普通股又称权益股。此类股票的持有者在年度股东大会上有投票权。只有优先股股东得到股利后，公司才可以向普通股股东派发红利。

Overdrafts

The payments from a current account exceed receipts to the account for a very short period, the excess is the finance provided by the bank, called overdrafts.

Overdrafts are one of the most important sources of short-term finance available to a business. Usually, the bank set a limit on the overdraft facility, the business should not exceed the limit. Also the bank charges interest on overdrawn amount, and technically overdrafts should repayable on demand.

银行透支

短期内，企业基本账户的支出超出了收入，超出的部分由银行提供融资，叫透支。透支是最重要的企业短期融资方式之一。一般银行给企业的透支设一个额度限制，企业不能超过这个限额。另外，透支部分银行要收利息，而且从技术上说，银行可以在任何时候要求返还透支资金。

【知识点巩固与拓展】

银行透支和银行短期借款都是企业筹集短期资金的工具。银行透支的利率一般较高，但透支企业有灵活性，在需要资金的时候就透支，不需要的时候就偿还，这样，总的利息费用可以降低。而银行短期借款，在借款期内都要支付利息。银行短期借款，在没到期前都不需要偿还；而银行透支，银行在任何时候都有权要求企业偿还。

短期融资工具有银行透支、短期借款、供货商提供的商业信用以及短期租赁等。

Both bank overdrafts and short-term bank loans are means of short-term finance. The interest rate of bank overdrafts is higher, but the company has flexibility as to the repayment of bank overdrafts, that is the bank balance is overdrawn if the business needs money, and the bank overdrafts will be paid off if the business have surplus funds. So the total interest cost is lower. However, interest must be paid during the terms of short - term bank loans. Short-term bank loan will not be asked to be paid off before the maturity, but the overdraft is repayable on demand.

Short-term sources of finance include bank overdrafts, short-term bank loans, trade credited offered by supplier and short-term lease etc.

Operational Gearing

It measures the degree of business risk that a company exposed to. The business risk reflects volatility of PBIT in response to changes in contribution (or sales). It can be calculated as contribution divided by PBIT. The higher the proportion of fixed operating cost in total operating cost, the more highly geared of the company.

经营杠杆

它计量了一个企业所面临的经营风险的程度。经营风险反映了息税前利润相对于贡献毛益(或销售收入)变动的波动幅度。通常用贡献毛益除以息税前利润来计算。固定运营成本在总运营成本中占的比例越高,经营杠杆就越大。

【知识点巩固与拓展(一)】

经营杠杆可用以下方式计量:

(1)贡献毛益除以息税前利润;

(2)固定经营成本除以总的经营成本;

(3)固定经营成本除以变动经营成本;

(4)息税前利润变化百分比除以销售额变化百分比。

Operational gearing can be measured as follows:

1. Contribution/PBIT;
2. Fixed operating cost/total operating cost;
3. Fixed operating cost /variable operating cost;
4. Percentage change in PBIT/percentage change in sales.

【知识点巩固与拓展(二)】

经营杠杆一般由企业所处的行业和商业模式所决定。而财务杠杆一般由企业自己的融资决策所决定。

Operational gearing is usually determined by the industry and business model of the company. But financial gearing is determined by the financing decisions of the company.

P

Placing

Placing is one of the means of issuing shares whereby the shares of an issuing company are sold to a small number of institutional investors.

定向发售

定向发售是发行股票的方式之一。发行公司把股票卖给少数几个机构投资者。

Preference Shares

Is is a financial instrument that offers fixed dividend rate to shareholders. Preference shareholders have a preference right to dividends. That is, the issuing company must pay preference dividend before distribute any dividends to ordinary shareholders. Also, upon liquidation, preference shareholders also have a preference right in claims to the net assets of a business before ordinary shareholders can get any liquidation dividends.

优先股

优先股是给予股东固定股息的一种金融工具。优先股股东有优先被派发股利的权利,即在优先股没被派发股利之前,企业不能给普通股派发股利。另外,在企业破产清算时,优先股股东也有优先获得清算股利的权利。

Prior Charge Capital

It is another name for debt capital. These capital providers have a right to receipt of interest or of preferred dividends before ordinary shareholders can claim any dividends out of distributable earnings.

优先偿付资本

这是债务资本的另一个名称。在企业从可分配收益中派发红利给普通股股东前,这些资本的提供方有权要求企业优先支付利息和优先股股息。

Public Offer

It is one of the means of issuing shares. The issuing company offers for sale of the shares to the public at large.

公开发售股票

这是发行股票的方式之一。发行公司向社会公众发售股票。

【学习提示】

首次公开发售股票，被称为 IPO (initial public offer)；后续增发，被称为 SEO(seasoned equity offer)。

R

Redemption

Redemption refers to the act of an issuer repay a bond at par or at a premium price, at or before maturity.

赎回

赎回是指债券的发行企业在到期日或到期日之前以面值或高于面值清偿债券的行为。

Rights Issue

Rights issue is offering for sale of shares to exiting shareholders in proportion to their shareholdings, usually at a price lower than the current market price.

配售股票

配售股票是指根据现有股东的持股比例向他们销售股票，发行价格通常不高于市价。

【知识点巩固与拓展】

企业向现有股东配售股票，现有股东可以有以下选择：一是认购所有配给自己的股票，二是出售认购所配售股票的权利，三是什么也不做。只有认购所有配给自己的股票，现有股东的股权才不会被稀释，其他的选择都会稀释现有股东对企业的控制权。第一和第二种选择，现有股东的财富都没有损失，但第三种选择会导致现有股东的财富减少。

When a rights issue is offered, the existing shareholders have the following options:

1. Take up all the rights.

2. Sell all the rights to others.

3. Do nothing.

The first choice will not dilute control, but the other two options will.

The first and second choice will not decrease the existing shareholder's wealth, but the third choice will.

Redemption Value

It is the price at which the issuing company may choose to repay a bond at or before its maturity date.

赎回价值

赎回价值是指发行公司在到期日或之前清偿债券的价格。

Retained Cash

It is surplus cash available for future re-investment after paying operating costs, interest costs, tax charges, capital expenditures, meeting working capital requirements and paying cash dividends.

留存资金

留存资金是指企业在支付了经营成本、财务成本、税收支出、资本性支出，满足企业营运资本需求并且支付了现金股利之后，所剩余的可用于未来再投资之需的资金。

【学习提示】

注意区分留存资金(retained cash)与留存利润(retained earnings)。

Residual Theory

Dividends are paid out only when there are no profitable investment opportunities any more. That is, dividends are the residual amount of net profits after all funds for positive-NPV projects are set aside.

股利剩余论

只有当不再有有利可图的投资项目时，企业才会发股利。也就是说，股利是企业把净现值为正的投资项目所需要的资金留足后，其净利润所剩下的余额。

Reverse Factoring

It is a method of trade receivables financing by suppliers by selling quality invoice to a funds provider at a discount. The funds provider gives advance payment to the supplier on the grounds that they ensure that the buyer is credit worthy and is of low possibility to default. Usually an internet platform will link the supplier, the buyer and the funds provider and make reverse factoring workable. Reverse factoring is one typical form of supply chain finance (SCF).

反向保理

反向保理是一种应收账款融资方式。供货商把优质客户的发票打折卖给资金提供方。资金提供方在确信买方的资信可靠、违约可能性很小的前提下才给供货商提供预付款。通常这一切是通过一个网络平台把卖方、买方以及资金提供方联系在一起而实现的。反向保理是一种典型的供应链融资。

【学习提示】

注意反向保理(reverse factoring)与正向保理(factoring)的区别。反向保理的资金提供方只评估买方的资信,而正向保理的资金提供方主要评估卖方的资信及客户质量。

S

Sale and Lease Back

It is an arrangement in which the business obtain finance by selling its own property to a finance house and renting it back for business use.

售后回租

企业跟一个金融机构签订协议，把自己的财产卖给对方，对方付一笔资金给融资企业，融资企业再从金融机构把该财产租回继续使用。

【知识点巩固与拓展】

售后回租比抵押贷款可以筹集更多的资金。但售后回租企业丧失了对所涉资产的所有权，影响以后的借贷能力。同时，企业把自己锁定在一个租赁合同中。如果这项资产不再需要了，企业就要承担相应的损失。

A company can raise more funds by sale and lease back than using mortgage loan. But under sale and lease back arrangement, the company loses ownership of the underlying property, and thus reduces its future borrowing capacity. Also the company is locked in a lease agreement. In the lease term, if the property is no longer needed, the lessee will bear the loss.

Security

It refers to using assets as collateral for a debt. On the insolvency of the borrower, the lender sell the assets and use the proceeds to repay the loan. Security may either be a fixed charge or be a floating charge.

担保

担保是指用资产为负债作保。一旦借款人不能还款，出借方就可以把该资产卖掉，用所得资金来偿还贷款。担保可以是以特定资产作保(固定担保)，也可以是以一类资产作保(浮动担保)。

Share Repurchase

A company buys back its own shares from the hands of its shareholders.

股票回购

股票回购指一家公司从股东手里买回自己公司的股票。

【知识点巩固与拓展】

如果公司突然有一笔多余的资金，又没有好的投资机会，就会选择回购股票以回报股东。

股票回购的目的：

(1)把多余的资金回报给股东；

(2)抬高股价；

(3)增加每股收益；

(4)避免成为收购的目标。

The purpose of share repurchase:

1. Return surplus funds to shareholders;

2. Raise share price;

3. Increase EPS;

4. Avoid becoming take-over target.

SMEs

They are of smaller size than large companies but bigger than micro businesses. They are usually unquoted private company and owned by a small number of individuals. Many are just family companies.

中小企业

其规模比大公司小但比小微企业大。它们通常是由少数几个个体持有的未上市的私营企业。很多是家族企业。

Stock Split

Each ordinary share is split into several shares, in order to enhance marketability of shares. The number of shares issued and outstanding is increased, and the par value of a share is decreased proportionately.

股票拆分/股票拆细

股票拆分是把一股股票分成很多股，以增强股票的流通性。发行在外的股数增加，则每股股票的面值相应下降。

Scrip Issue

Scrip issue refers to issuing new shares to existing shareholders in proportion to their existing shareholdings at no charge.

送股

送股是指按照现有股东的持股比例向现有股东免费发行新股。

Scrip Dividends

Scrip dividends are dividends paid by the issue of additional shares of the company, rather than cash.

股票股利

股票股利指以给予股东额外的股票的形式发放的股利，而不是发放现金。

【学习提示】

股票股利，美国的书上称为 stock dividends，是不用支付现金而回报股东的方式。股票股利增加发行在外的股数，但不影响权益的账面价值。发行在外的股数增加，会摊薄每股收益，同时增加将来派发股利的压力。

Signalling Effect

As information asymmetry exists, the outside investors have less information about the invested company than the managers. The outside investors get information from the managers decisions, actions and announcement. So the management decisions, actions and announcement will send signals to the investors, and the investors may interpret the signals as good or bad。A bad signal will depress share price and a good signal will raise share price.

信号效应

由于信息不对称的存在，关于被投资公司的信息，外部投资者比管理层获得的要少得多。外部投资者只能通过管理层的决策、行为以及公告来获得信息。因此，管理层的决策、行为以及公告就会向投资者传递信号，投资者会把这些信号理解为好的或不好的。不好的信号会使股价下跌，好的信号会使股价上涨。

Sukuk

Sukuk is the name of the Islamic bond. It is normally linked to an underlying asset. The Sukuk holder owns a proportional share of the underlying asset, and can enjoy the revenues generated by the asset, but he also needs to bear any losses associated with the share of the underlying asset. It is a kind of Islamic finance.

伊斯兰债券

伊斯兰债券一般跟特定资产相联系。债券的持有人根据其所持有债券的份额享受相应的该资产的所有权。可以按持有份额享受该项资产产生的收入；但是该项资产的损失，也要按相应份额承担。

Supply Chain Finance

Supply chain finance refers to raising funds with the support of collaborating business partners in supply chain, using various financial instruments, practices and modern information technology.

供应链融资

供应链融资指利用各种融资工具、融资办法以及现代信息技术，在供应链中各商业合作伙伴的支持下筹集资金。

【学习提示】

经常使用的供应链融资是反向保理。

T

Term Loan

Term loan is a loan for a fixed amount and for a specified period. The interest payment and capital repayment are setting out in an agreement.

定期贷款

定期贷款是指固定期限、固定金额的贷款。付息和还本的具体条款都在协议中注明。

Trade Credit

Trade credit is the credit provided by goods suppliers who allow the buyer to pay money owed to them for the purchasing of the goods at a later date. It is one of the most important sources of short-term finance available to a business. The supplier creditors are usually charge no interest.

商业信用

商业信用是指商品供货商提供的信用。供货商允许买方企业赊购,在将来一定的日期内还款。商业信用是最重要的企业短期融资方式之一。作为供货商的债权人一般不收取利息。

Theoretical Ex-rights Price (TERP)

It can be calculated as: (market value of old shares + cost of take-up new shares)/(number of old shares + number of new shares issued).

For Example, a company announced a 1 for 3 rights issue, the cost of taking up one new share is \$6. Just before the rights issue, the market price per share is \$10.

Theoretical ex-rights price = (\$10×3 + \$6×1)÷(3+1) = \$9

理论上的除权价

计算公式为:理论上的除权价=(现有股票的市值+认购新配股票的成本)÷(现有股票的股数+新配售股票的股数)。

比如,一家公司公告了一项配股方案,每持有三股配售一股,配售价格为6美元。就在配售以前,市场上的股价为每股10美元。则:理论上的除权价=(10×3+6×1)÷(3+1)=9(美元)。

【知识点巩固与拓展】

认购一股新股的认股权的价值=除权价－认购一股新配股票的成本

原先的一股对应的认股权的价值=含权价－除权价

比如，一家公司公告了一项配股方案，每持有三股配售一股，配售价格为 6 美元。就在配售以前，市场上的股价为每股 10 美元。

认购一股新股的认股权的价值＝9－6＝3（美元）

原先的一股对应的认股权的价值＝10－9＝1（美元）

Value of a right to subscribe for one new share

＝*TERP*－Cost of take-up one new share

Value of the right per one existing share

＝cum-rights price－*TERP*

For Example, a company announced a 1 for 3 rights issue, the cost of taking up one new share is ＄6. Just before the rights issue, the market price per share is ＄10.

Value of a right to subscribe for one new share＝＄9－＄6＝＄3

Value of the right per one existing share＝＄10－＄9＝＄1

U

Underwriting

It is a financial arrangement for new issue of securities, under which a financial institution (a underwriter) agrees to buy any securities that are not subscribed for by the investing public. The underwriters bear the risk of being undersubscribed of the new issued securities in exchange for a fixed fee.

承销

承销是发行新证券时的一种金融安排。一家金融机构（承销商）承诺在投资大众没有足额认购所发行的证券时，由承销商自己认购剩下的证券。承销商承担新发行证券认购不足的风险，但会收取一笔固定费用。

V

Venture Capital

It refers to financial capital provided to startup firms and small businesses with perceived long-term growth potential, usually for an equity stake.

风险资本

风险资本是指提供给有长期增长潜力的新建企业和小企业的金融资本，一般投资方会要求拥有该企业一定的股份。

【知识点巩固与拓展】

风险资本的投资方除了要求一定的股份外，还会要求企业提供一份详细的投资计划说明书，其中说明企业的盈利前景，以及企业在产品、生产、管理、市场以及技术等方面的专长。有些风险资本投资商还会要求加入董事会。

In addition to equity stake, venture capitalists often request a detailed investment plan, being convinced that the investee has strong earning potential and expertise in product, production, management, market or technology. Some venture capital provider may ask for board membership.

Z

Zero Coupon Bonds

Zero coupon bonds are a kind of deep discounted bonds which offer no interest to the investors at all. The only investment income to the bondholder is the deep discount.

零息债券

零息债券是高折扣债券的一种。根本不支付利息。投资者的唯一收益是高折扣。

Module Four

Working Capital Management/营运资本管理

本单元的学习目标：了解营运资本管理的重要性，掌握营运资本管理的目标、基本策略、方法，并且了解其中容易出现的问题。

学生学习时应注意：(1)对基本概念、财务比率以及公式和模型的理解与运用；(2)重点掌握营运资本管理的总体策略；(3)重点掌握应收账款、存货和现金的管理。

A

Aged Accounts Receivable Listing(Accounts Receivable Aged Analysis)

It classifies and lists accounts receivables of a business according to the length of overdue time in order to analysing collectability of accounts receivables and monitoring accounts receivable management.

账龄分析

把企业的应收账款根据其拖欠时间长短进行归类并列出清单，以便分析应收账款的可回收性以及监督企业的应收账款管理。

Advances against Collections

When an exporter receives a bill of exchange or cheque from a customer, it can ask a bank to help handle the collection of payment and to make an advance payment to the exporter.

托收预付款

当一家出口商从客户那里收到汇票或支票时，它可以要求一家银行帮忙收款并预先提供所收款项的一定比例的预付给出口商。

Aggressive Strategy

(1) An aggressive approach in working capital investment aims to keep the money tided up in inventory and accounts receivable to a minimum and reduce the financing cost and increase profitability by cutting the investment in current assets to as low as possible. This approach will expose the business to high system breakdown risk, that is, running out of inventory, customer going elsewhere, and suppliers withholding supplies etc.

(2) An aggressive approach in working capital financing aims to reduce financing cost by relying more on short - term finance. That is, even some long-term assets are financed by short-

term funds. But businesses who use this approach will face an increased risk of liquidity.

(营运资本管理的)激进型策略

(1)在营运资本管理的投资方面,激进型策略是通过降低流动资产的投资来达到把投入到存货和应收账款的资金降到最低,从而减少资金成本、增加盈利的目的。但是这种方法会使企业面临较高的系统崩溃风险,即缺货、客户流失以及供货商拒绝供货。

(2)在营运资本管理的融资方面,激进型策略是通过更多地依赖短期资金来达到降低资金成本的目的。一些长期资产的投资也使用短期资金。但这种方法会增加企业的流动性风险。

【学习提示】

提到营运资本的激进型策略或稳健型策略,应该明确是营运资本的投资策略还是营运资本的融资策略。营运资本的投资策略主要是解决流动资产投入多少资金的问题,而营运资本的融资策略主要是解决所投入流动资产的资金来源的问题。企业有可能实行激进的营运资本投资策略和稳健的营运资本融资策略,或者稳健的营运资本投资策略和激进的营运资本融资策略,不一定投融资都激进或者都稳健。

Assessing Creditworthiness

Assessing the financial status, ability to pay-off debts and possibility of default of a potential or current customer to decide on whether the customer is worthy to be provided with credit and then the amount of credit. Creditworthiness assessment is an ongoing activity, not only the creditworthiness of a new customer needs to be assessed, but also that of an old customer.

资信评估

资信评估是评估潜在客户或现有客户的财务状况、还债能力以及违约可能性，以决定是否给予信用，然后决定给予多少信用。资信评估是一项持续的活动，不仅仅评估新客户的资信，而且老客户的资信也要评估。

Average Inventory

It is the average level of inventory held in stores. It can be calculated as follows:

Average inventory = buffer inventory + order-quantity/2

If there is no buffer inventory, the formula is:

Average inventory = order-quantity/2

平均存货量

平均存货量指仓库存货量的平均值。计算公式为：

$$平均存货量=缓冲库存量+\frac{订货量}{2}$$

如果没有缓冲库存，则计算公式为：

$$平均存货量=\frac{订货量}{2}$$

【学习提示】

注意平均存货量的计算，是两点的平均数，即新订购货物刚入库时的库存量加上本批订购货物用光时的库存量的平均数。有缓冲库存与无缓冲库存的

计算公式是不同的。有缓冲库存时,新订购货物刚入库时的库存量为缓冲库存量加上订购量之和,本批订购货物用光时的库存量为缓冲库存量。无缓冲库存时,新订购货物刚入库时的库存量为订购量,本批订购货物用光时的库存量为0。

【知识点巩固与拓展】

红星公司所处上海的一处物料A仓库的订购政策如下:每批订购量为10 000吨,缓冲库存量为500吨。那这处仓库的平均存货量为多少?

平均存货量=(10 000+500)/2=5 250(吨)

后来,红星公司的这处仓库的订购政策改成:每批订购量11 000吨,不留缓冲库存,那其平均存货量为多少?

平均存货量=(11 000+0)/2=5 500(吨)

One of Redstar Co's warehouses of Materials A has the following policy: re-order quantity is 10 000 tonnes, buffer inventory is 500 tonnes. What's the average inventory?

Average inventory=(10 000+500)/2=5 250(tonnes)

Later, its policy is changed as follows: re-order quantity 11 000 tonnes, and no buffer inventory. What's the average inventory then?

Average inventory=(11 000+0)/2=5 500(tonnes)

Annual Percentage Cost of a Settlement Discount

It refers to an annual percentage rate of a settlement discount policy. It can be calculated as: $\left(1+\frac{\text{discount}}{1-\text{discount}}\right)^{365/\text{days saved}}-1$.

现金折扣的年化利率

计算公式：

$$现金折扣的年化利率=\left(1+\frac{折扣率}{1-折扣率}\right)^{365/缩短的天数}-1$$

【学习提示】

这个计算需要学生理解 APR(annual percentage rate)，即在复利情况下年化利率的计算。比如：一项 1 000 美元的投资，每季度回报 10 美元，则其实际年化利率(APR)为$\left(1+\frac{10}{1\ 000}\right)^4-1=4.06\%$。

【知识点巩固与拓展】

红星公司给客户的信用条款如下：2/30，净 90，则其现金折扣的年化利率为多少？

$$现金折扣的年化利率=\left(1+\frac{2}{98}\right)^{\frac{365}{60}}-1=12.89\%$$

The credit terms offered by Redstar Co. to its customers are as follows: 2/30, net 90. Calculate annual percentage cost of the settlement discount.

Annual percentage cost of the settlement discount $=\left(1+\frac{2}{98}\right)^{\frac{365}{60}}-1=12.89\%$

The Baumol Model

It is a cash management model. It based on the assumption

that the amount of cash requirements over a future period is steady and can be predicted with certainty and the business holds adequate marketable securities that can be sold to raise cash. The optimal amount of cash to be raised each time is calculated using the following formulae:

$$Q=\sqrt{\frac{2CS}{i}}$$

C: the transaction cost per sale of securities.

S: the total amount of cash required in each period.

i: the cost of holding cash, ie. the interest rate of short-term borrowing less the interest rate of short-term investment (eg. deposit).

Baumol 模型

一种现金管理模型，假设将来一定时期现金的需求量是稳定且可以准确预测的，并且企业持有足够的有价证券，则在企业需要资金时，即可通过变卖一部分证券来达到融资的目的。每次最佳筹集资金量可通过以下公式计算得出：

$$Q=\sqrt{\frac{2CS}{i}}$$

C：每次变卖证券的交易成本。

S：每期需要的资金总量。

i：持有资金的成本，即短期借款利率减去短期投资（比如存款）利率。

【学习提示】

比照 EOQ 公式$\left(EOQ=\sqrt{\dfrac{2C_oD}{C_h}}\right)$，体会两者的异同。

Baumol 模型把现金管理等同于存货管理，既然存货有最佳订货量，那现金管理就应该有一个最佳筹集资金量。就像存货的最佳订货量取决于一个期间企业对存货的需求量、每次订货所发生的固定成本以及一单位存货持有一期的持有成本，最佳筹集资金量取决于一个期间企业对资金的需求量(S)、每次卖出证券筹集资金的交易成本(C)，以及借款利率与投资利率之差(i)。Baumol 模型假设企业在资金多时就投资有价证券，在资金短缺时就通过卖出手里的有价证券来筹集资金 。

【知识点巩固与拓展】

红星公司今年的资金需求量大约为 100 万美元，卖出有价证券的每次平均交易成本约为 3 000 美元，短期借款利率为 5.2%，短期投资利率为 2.8%，则根据 Baumol 模型，每次最佳筹集资金量为多少？

$$每次最佳筹集资金量=\left(\frac{2\times 3\,000\times 1\,000\,000}{5.2\%-2.8\%}\right)^{0.5}$$
$$=500\,000(美元)$$

Redstar Co. needs about \$1 000 000 of funds this year. Assume Redstar Co. has sufficient investments in marketable securities. Average transaction cost per sale of marketable securities is \$3 000. Interest rate for short-term borrowing is 5.2%, interest rate for short-term investment is 2.8%. According to Baumol Model, what's the optimal amount of funds raised each time by Redstar Co.?

$$Q=\left(\frac{2\times \$3\ 000\times \$1\ 000\ 000}{5.2\%-2.8\%}\right)^{0.5}=\$500\ 000$$

Bill of Exchange

A bill of exchange is a written order by one party (the drawer) to another (the drawee) to pay a certain sum to a third party (the payee), either immediately (a sight bill) or on a fixed date (a term bill).

汇票

汇票是由出票人签发给付款方，要求其向收款人无条件支付一定款项的票据。或者见票即付（即期汇票），或者在将来某个固定的日期支付（远期汇票）。

【学习提示】

汇票是货币市场上广泛使用的一种融资工具。

Buffer (Safety) Inventory

It refers to inventory held to meet the unexpected demand in lead time and to reduce stock-outs. It is the minimum inventory level beyond which stock-outs are possible. It acts as a warning to management that inventories are reaching a dangerously low level. Buffer inventory = re-order level − average usage × average lead time.

缓冲库存(安全库存)

缓冲库存是指为应对意料之外的需求和减少缺货而持有的存货。这是最低的存货量,少于这个量,就会有缺货现象存在,它提醒管理者存货已到了非常危险的水平。缓冲库存量=再订货库存量-平均前置时间×单位时间平均货物需求量。

【学习提示】

缓冲库存应定在什么水平,企业应权衡缺货成本和缓冲库存的持有成本。

Bulk Discounts

Bulk discounts refer to the discounts given to customers by suppliers if customers buy goods in larger quantity.

大宗采购折扣

因客户大量购买商品而由供货商给予客户的折扣。

C

Cash Flow Forecast

It is a forecast of expected cash receipts and cash payments during a specific future period. It is a useful and widely used tool of cash management. It is prepared to show when the business will be lack cash and when the business will have surplus cash to ensure sufficient but excessive cash available to meet future business needs.

现金流预测

现金流预测是指预测未来某个期间的预计现金流入和现金支出。这是被广泛使用的一种有用的现金管理工具。编制现金流预测可以使企业了解何时缺钱、何时有盈余资金，以便保证企业保留足够但不过多的资金去满足企业经营需求。

Cash Operating Cycle

It refers to the length of time that elapses from the point of paying out cash to suppliers for the purchase of goods to the point of collecting cash back from customers. It indicates how long the money invested in current assets is tied up. It is calculated as inventory turnover period plus receivable collection period minus payables payment period. In a manufacturing business, the inventory turnover period equals: raw materials holding period + production period + finished goods turnover periods. The longer the cash operating cycle, the more investment in working capital, the more financing cost incurred. Businesses should shorten its cash operating cycle as far as possible without affecting adversely its relationship with suppliers and customers.

现金周期/净营运周期

现金周期就是指从付款给供货商购买存货或原材料，到从顾客那里收回现金这段时间的长度。它表明投资于流动资产的资金被占用了多长时间。用存货周期加应收账款周期减去应付账款周期来计算。在制造业，存货周转期＝原材料持有期＋产品生产期＋产成品周期。企业在不影响与供货商和客户关系的前提下，应该尽量缩短现金周期。

【学习提示】

这是一个重要的概念。除了会计算，学生还要能够理解决定现金周期长短的因素以及现金周期的长短对企业本身意味着什么。另外，注意区分营运周期(operating cycle)和现金周期(cash operating cycle)。营运周期等于存货周期与应收账款周期之和。营运周期减去应付账款周期就得到现金周期或称为净营运周期。

【知识点巩固与拓展】

目前，A 公司给客户的信用期限为 60 天，客户平均 65 天付款，原材料从入库到运到生产线平均历时约 10 天，产品生产约需 15 天，产成品从入库到卖出平均需要 20 天。供货商给 A 公司提供的信用期限平均为 30 天，A 公司平均 32 天付款。则 A 公司目前的现金周期为多少天？

应收账款周期 65 天

存货周期＝10＋15＋20＝45(天)

应付账款周期 32 天

现金周期＝65＋45－32＝78(天)

Currently, credit period offered by Company A to customers is 60 days, it takes customers on average 65 days to pay their debts to Company A. Materials stay in the warehouse for about 10 days. And it takes 15 days to produce a complete goods. The finished goods stay in the warehouse for about 20days on average. Credit period offered by the suppliers is on average 30 days. And Company A pays its debts to the suppliers in about 32 days. Calculate the cash operating cycle.

Trade receivables days 65

Inventory days＝10＋15＋20＝45

Trade payables days 32

Cash operating cycle＝65＋45－32＝78(days)

Cash Holding Motives

Why do organisations hold cash? There are three main reasons for holding cash:(1) transaction motive, a business needs cash to meet its regular operating cash requirements, such as to pay its accounts payable and to pay wages and salaries. (2) precautionary motive, a business needs a safety cash for unforeseen contingencies. (3) speculative motive, a business needs cash to take profitable investment opportunities whenever possible.

企业持有现金的动机

一个组织机构为什么持有现金？主要原因有三个：(1)交易动机，企业需要现金去满足日常经营的资金需求，比如偿付货款、支付员工的薪资等；(2)预防动机，企业需要现金以应对不时之需；(3)投机动机，企业需要现金去尽可能抓住有盈利的投资机会。

【学习提示】

这三个动机中真正需要现金的是交易动机。而预防动机和投资动机只需要企业保持足够的流动性就可以了，即在需要时能快速筹集资金来处理紧急事件或抓住有利的投资机会。很多企业通过持有有价证券投资来充分运用短期多余的资金，而在需要资金时，则在市场上把这些证券卖出去以回笼资金。

Conservative Strategy

(1) A conservative approach in working capital investment aims to keep a stable amount of money invested in inventory and accounts receivable and reduces the potential for liquidity problem. This approach may result in too much money tied up in inventory and accounts receivable, thus leads to higher financing cost and lower profitability.

(2) A conservative approach in working capital financing aims to reduce cash shortage risk by relying more on long-term finance. That is even some short-term assets are financed by long-term funds. But this approach will lower profits.

(营运资本管理的)稳健型策略

(1)在营运管理的投资方面，稳健策略是通过保持存货和应收账款等稳定的资金投入来降低流动性问题发生的可能性。但这种方法会导致太多的资金投入，从而增加资金成本、降低盈利能力。

(2)在营运资本管理的融资方面，稳健策略的目的是通过更多地依赖长期资金来降低资金短缺风险。也就是说，即便是一些短期资产的投资，也占用长期资金。但这种方法会减少企业盈利。

【知识点巩固与拓展】

营运资本的投资策略如何判断呢？一般用销售收入/净营运资本这个比率来与同行或者企业的前几期进行比较。如果这个比率偏大，则说明企业营运资本的投资策略偏激进；如果这个比率偏小，则说明企业营运资本的投资策略偏稳健。

营运资本的融资策略如何判断呢？一般用流动负债/流动资产或者营运资本/流动资产这两个比率来比较。流动负债/流动资产比率偏高，营运资本/流动资产比率偏低，则说明企业用更多的短期资金来支持流动资产投资，企业营运资本的融资策略偏激进。如果流动负债/流动资产比率偏低，营运资本/流动资产比率偏高，就说明企业用更多的长期资金来支持流动资产投资，企业营运资本的融资策略偏稳健。

How to asses working capital investment strategy? Usually the ratio of sales/net working capital is compared with that of industry average or previous periods. If the ratio is lower, the business has a more aggressive working capital investment policy. And if the ratio is higher, its working capital investment policy is more conservative.

How to assess working capital financing strategy?

The ratios of current liabilities/current assets and/or net working capital/current assets are compared with those of previous periods. If current liabilities/current assets is higher, and net working capital/current assets is lower, the business relies more on short-term funds to funding current assets than before, and it adopts a more aggressive working capital financing policy. And if current liabilities/current assets is lower, and net working capital/current assets is higher, the business relies more on long-term funds to funding current assets than before, and it adopts a more conservative working capital financing policy.

【知识点巩固与拓展】

红星公司 2020 年的年报披露了以下信息：

销售收入 600 万美元；

流动资产 1 500 万美元；

流动负债 1 000 万美元；

销售收入/净营运资本比率的行业平均值为 2；

上一年度，流动负债/流动资产＝50％。

请判断 2020 年红星公司采用了何种营运资本策略，是激进型还是稳健型。

(1)营运资本的投资策略

2020 年销售收入/净营运资本＝6/(15－10)＝1.2

其值小于行业平均值 2，所以，企业采用了比同行更稳健的营运资本投资策略。

(2)营运资本融资策略

2020 年流动负债/流动资产＝10/15＝67％

其值比 2019 年的 50％高，所以，与 2019 年相比，红星公司的营运资本融资策略更加激进。

Financial statements for Year 2020 of Redstar Co. shows the following information.

Sales revenue ＄6m

Current assets ＄15m

Current liabilities ＄10m

And the industry average for sales/net working capital is 2.

Current liability/current assets is 50％ last year.

What working capital strategy did Redstar follow in Year 2020, aggressive or conservative?

1. Working capital investment strategy

Sales /net working capital for Year 2020=6/(15−10)=1.2

It is less than industry average 2.

So Redstar Co. followed a more conservative working capital investment policy in the industry.

2. Working capital financing strategy

Current liabilities/current assets for Year 2020 = 10/15 = 67%

It is greater than 50% of Year 2019.

So compared with last year, Redstar Co. followed a more aggressive working capital financing policy.

Counter Trade

Counter trade refers to exchanging goods or services which are paid for with other goods or services, rather than with money.

对销贸易

对销贸易是指用另一种货物或服务，而不是货币，去购买一种商品或服务。

Credit Control

Credit control is the management of accounts receivable. It involves making credit policy, assessing credit-worthiness of customers, control credit limits, collecting cash due from customers and chasing overdue debts.

信用控制

信用控制是企业对应收账款的管理。一般需要制定信用政策、评估客户资信、控制客户信用限额、从客户那里收回账款以及追讨拖欠款项等。

Credit Analysis

It involves analysing the effectiveness and efficiency of credit control using tools such as customer history analysis, in-house credit rating, credit utilization report, aged listing of accounts receivable, bad debts ratio, accounts receivable collection period and some statistical data.

信用分析

信用分析就是运用一些工具来分析信用控制的成效。这些工具有客户交易历史分析、企业内部的客户信用评级、客户信用额度使用情况报告、账龄分析、坏账率、应收账款回收期以及一些统计数据等。

Credit Worthiness

It refers to the financial status, ability to pay-off debts, possibility of default and whether a business is worthy to be provided with credit.

资信

资信是指企业的财务状况、偿债能力、违约可能性以及是否值得为其提供信用。

Cost-benefit Analysis

It is a financial analysis method to assist in decision-making, where benefits and costs are compared. If benefits exceed costs, there is a net benefit, the proposal should be accepted. And if costs outweigh benefits, there is a net cost, the proposal should be rejected. Decision makers will consider non-financial costs and benefits as well as financial costs and benefits.

成本效益分析

成本效益分析是通过比较成本和效益来帮助决策的一种财务分析方法。如果效益超过成本，产生净效益，则提议的方案应该接受；相反，如果成本超过效益，产生净成本，则提议的方案不应该采纳。决策者既要考虑财务成本和效益，也要考虑非财务成本和效益。

【学习提示】

企业营运资本管理有很多决策，比如是否改变营运资本管理策略、是否改变信用政策、是否给客户结算折扣、是否接受供货商的折扣、是否改变存货订购政策等。这些决策都可以用成本效益分析法来辅助决策。决策者往往重视财务的成本和效益而忽略非财务的成本和效益，重视可以量化的成本和效益而忽视很难量化的成本和效益。要做出正确决策，则所有的成本和效益都应考虑在内。

Customer History Analysis

It involves analysing an individual customer's payment records of accounts receivable in order to monitor individual accounts receivable control.

客户历史还款记录分析

分析单个客户的应收账款还款记录以便对每位客户的应收账款控制情况进行监督。

Credit Utilization Report

It is a report to show the extent to which the total credit limits offered to individual customers are being utilized in order to assess the tightness of the credit policy and to monitor accounts receivable management.

信用使用情况报告

这个报告分析每一个客户对企业所给予的信用额度的使用程度，以便评估企业信用政策的松紧以及对应收账款管理进行监督。

D

Discounting Bills of Exchange

A company who receives a bill of exchange from a customer may approach a bank before the bill is due for payment and ask the bank to buy the bill at a discount to its face value.

汇票贴现

一家公司收到客户付的汇票，在汇票未到期之前，可以去联系一家银行，把汇票以低于面值的价格卖给银行。

Documentary Credits (Letter of Credit)

In order to reduce the bad debts risk in foreign trade, the exporter usually requires for the payment through a letter of credit. The importer approaches a bank in its country for issuing a documentary credit. The issuing bank actually guarantees the payment. Once the L/C is issued, the bank becomes the first who is liable to the payment for the goods traded.

信用证

在外贸中,出口商为了降低坏账风险,一般要求进口商通过信用证付款。进口商向其所在国的银行申请开立信用证。开证行实际上为进口商的付款做了担保。一旦开立信用证,开证行即变成付款第一责任人。

【学习提示】

为了进一步降低坏账风险,出口商会要求进口商开具不可撤销的(irrevocable)、由另一家银行担保(guaranteed)或承兑(accepted)的信用证。

E

Economic Order Quantity (EOQ)

EOQ is the optimal order quantity for an item of inventory which minimizes the total inventory costs. The formula is:

$$EOQ=\sqrt{\frac{2C_oD}{C_h}}$$

C_o: fixed cost of placing an order.

C_h: holding cost of one unit for one period.

D: units of demand for one period.

经济订货量

经济订货量是指某种货物的最佳订货量。这个订货量可以使存货总成本达到最低。公式是：

$$EOQ=\sqrt{\frac{2C_oD}{C_h}}$$

C_o:每次订货的固定成本。

C_h:每一期间单位存货的持有成本。

D:一个期间的货物需求量。

【知识点巩固与拓展】

红星公司的仓库B对物料A的年需求量为10 000吨，每个订单发生的固定成本为500美元，每吨货物在仓库一年的持有成本为200美元，则每单最佳订货量应为多少？

$$每单最佳订货量=\sqrt{\frac{2\times500\times10\ 000}{200}}$$

$$=224(吨)$$

Annual demand for Material A in Redstar Co.'s Warehouse B is 10 000 tonnes. The fixed cost per order is \$500, and the annual holding cost per tonne is \$200. Calculate the EOQ.

$$EOQ=\sqrt{\frac{2\times\$500\times10\ 000}{\$200}}=224\ (\text{tonnes})$$

Export Factoring

It refers to the factoring of foreign accounts receivable by an overseas factor.

出口保理

出口保理指由国外保理商所提供的针对国外应收账款的保理服务。

Export Credit Insurance

It refers to the insurance against the bad debts risk of foreign accounts receivable.

出口信用保险

出口信用保险指针对国外应收账款坏账风险的保险。

F

Factoring

Factoring refers to a financial arrangement to have receivables managed by a factor company. The factor company usually provides any combinations of three types of service: (1) advances a proportion of the debts owed by the customers; (2) administers the debts on the clients' behalf; (3) provides bad debts insurance. For with-recourse factoring, the factor does not provide bad debts insurance, the business itself bears the bad debts expense. For non-recourse factoring, it is the factor, not the business, who bears the bad debts risk.

保理

保理是指把应收账款转包给保理公司管理的一种财务安排。一般保理公司常可提供三种服务:(1)给客户一定比例的预付款;(2)帮客户管理应收账款;(3)提供坏账保险。对于有追索权的保理服务,保理公司不提供坏账保险,企业自己承担坏账费用。对于无追索权的保理服务,是保理公司而不是企业最终承担坏账风险。

【学习提示】

企业可以利用应收账款进行短期融资,有保理(factoring),也可以利用应收账款作担保来借款(loans secured by accounts receivable)以及单张或部分发票贴现(invoice discounting)。

Forfaiting

It is a method of medium-term export financing. It has normally been used for export sales of capital goods. The minimum bill size is usually over \$250 000, but only in the major convertible currencies. The forfaiter buys from a company a selection of the foreign accounts receivable at a discount, usually obtaining a guarantee or a letter of credit from a bank in the importer's country, and takes on all the credit risk of these receivables.

包买票据(票据买断、福费廷)

包买票据是一种出口融资,期限一般为 3～5 年。一般在资本性商品(如机器设备)的出口销售中用得较多。一般应收金额至少为 250 000 美元,但仅接受几种主要的流通货币。买断方一般在得到进口方所在国银行的担保或开立的信用证后,折价买断一家公司的部分国外应收账款并承担这些应收款的所有坏账风险。

【知识点巩固与拓展】

国外应收账款管理的几种特殊方法:

(1)信用证;

(2)银行预付或议付;

(3)汇票贴现;

(4)出口保理;

(5)包买票据;

(6)投保出口信用险。

The following are specific means of managing foreign accounts receivables:

1. Letter of credit;

2. Advances against collections or negation of bills;

3. Discounting bills of exchange;

4. Export factoring;

5. Forfaiting;

6. Take out export credit insurance。

H

Holding Cost

Holding cost refers to the cost incurred for holding inventory or accounts receivable. The holding cost of inventory include financing cost of money tied up in inventory, warehousing and storage costs, physical deterioration and technical obsolescence and other loss of inventory etc. The holding cost of accounts receivables include financing cost of money tied up in accounts receivable and bad debts.

持有成本

持有成本是持有存货或者应收账款的成本。存货的持有成本包括投到存货的资金成本、仓储成本，还有物理损坏和技术过时以及其他原因导致的存货损失等。应收账款的持有成本包括投入应收账款的资金成本以及坏账损失等。

Invoice Discounting

It is a financing arrangement to have a selection of high quality invoices sold to an invoice discounter, and get advances. The invoice discounter does not take over the administration of the client's debts and does not provide bad debts insurance.

发票贴现

这是把一部分高质量的发票所代表的应收账款卖给贴现商并获得预付款的一种融资安排。贴现商不代管债务，不提供坏账保险。

【学习提示】

发票贴现是利用应收账款融资的方式之一。

Inventory Costs

Inventory costs are costs incurred by a business as a result of holding an inventory. There are four types of inventory costs. That is, purchase cost, procuring (ordering) cost, holding cost and inventory shortage cost. Less of holding cost means more of inventory shortage cost, and vice versa.

存货成本

存货成本是指企业因为拥有存货而发生的成本。存货成本有四类,分别是采购成本、订购成本、持有成本和缺货成本。存货的持有成本与缺货成本、持有成本与订购成本是此消彼长的关系,即存货越多,持有成本越高,但缺货成本和订购成本越少。

【学习提示】

学生应掌握不同存货管理政策下存货成本的计算。

【知识点巩固与拓展】

红星公司的仓库B对物料A的年需求量为12 000吨,每个订单发生的固定成本为500美元,每吨货物在仓库一年的持有成本为200美元。其采购政策是每月采购一次。缓冲库存量为30吨。平均采购价格为每吨5 000美元。计算现行政策下的年存货总成本(因为从没发生缺货现象,所以缺货成本忽略不计)。

存货总成本＝采购成本＋订购成本＋持有成本

采购成本＝12 000×5 000＝60 000 000(美元)

订购成本＝12×500＝6 000(美元)

年持有成本＝(30＋1 000/2)×200＝106 000(美元)

年存货总成本＝60 000 000＋6 000＋106 000

＝60 112 000(美元)

Annual demand for Material A in Redstar Co.'s Warehouse B is 12 000 tonnes. The fixed cost per order is $500, and the annual holding cost per tonne is $200. Currently it orders each month. Buffer inventory is 30 tonnes. Average purchase price is $5 000 per tonne.

Calculate total annual inventory cost. As no shortage of inventory has ever happened, inventory shortage cost is negligible.

Total inventory cost ＝purchase cost ＋ ordering cost ＋holding cost ＋ shortage cost

Purchase cost ＝12 000× $5 000＝ $60 000 000

Ordering cost ＝12× $500＝ $6 000

Holding cost ＝(30＋1 000/2)× $200＝ $106 000

Total annual inventory cost ＝ $60 000 000＋ $6 000＋ $106 000＝ $60 112 000

【知识点巩固与拓展】

年采购成本＝年需求量×单位采购价格

年订购成本＝一年发生的订单数×每份订单所发生的平均固定成本

年持有成本＝平均存货水平×单位存货年持

有成本

缺货成本很难量化。

Annual purchase cost = annual demand quantity × unit purchase price

Annual ordering cost = number of orders per year × fixed cost per order

Annual holding cost = average inventory × unit holding cost per year

Inventory shortage cost is difficult to quantify.

J

JIT(Just-in-time) System

JIT is a system that a business employs to manage its inventory, under which the business obtains goods from suppliers when they are needed and manufactures products to order, so avoid to carry inventory. Its successful operation relies heavily on the accurate production projection and close collaboration with business partners in the supply chains, especially with suppliers. It reflects TQM(total quality management) philosophy.

实时制存货管理/准时制存货管理

这是企业管理存货的一种机制，货物在需要的时候购买，并且根据订单生产产品，因此企业可以避免持有存货。它的成功运行在很大程度上依赖企业精确的生产规划以及与供应链各合作伙伴特别是与供货商间的紧密合作。它体现了全面质量管理的理念。

【知识点巩固与拓展】

虽然准时制存货管理可以大大降低存货的持有成本,其全面质量管理的理念也会给企业带来效率和质量提高的好处,但是如果供应链不畅,其缺货成本是很大的。在某些不能冒任何缺货风险的行业,准时制存货管理是不合适的。

Although JIT system reduces greatly holding cost of inventory,and TQM philosophy improves efficiency and quality of the business,but the inventory shortage cost will be large if the supply chain doesn't operate well. If it cannot take any risks of inventory shortage for an industry, JIT system should not be employed.

L

Lead Time

It refers to the length of time elapsed from placing a new order to the delivery of ordered goods to stores.

前置时间

前置时间是从企业下新订单到此订单所订货物运抵仓库的这段时间。

【学习提示】

为了避免缺货,企业在货物用完之前,需提前一段时间订购货物。

Liquidity

It refers to the ability of a business to pay off short-term debts. The business needs adequate liquid resources for day-to-day smooth running of business. Adequate liquidity of a business ensures its survival. Lack of liquidity will cause business failure.

流动性

它是指企业偿付短期债务的能力。企业需要足够的流动资产来维持企业日常的顺利运行。充足的流动性确保了企业的生存，而流动性不足会使企业倒闭。

【学习提示】

分析企业流动性的财务比率有流动比率(current ratio)、速动比率(quick ratio)以及现金比率(cash ratio)。

Long-term Assets

Both non-current assets and permanent current assets are long-term assets. The funds invested in long-term assets are tied up for long-term.

长期资产

长期资产包括非流动资产和流动资产的永久性投资部分。投入长期资产的资金都是长期绑定的。

【学习提示】

区分非流动资产和长期资产。非流动资产属于长期资产，而长期资产包括非流动资产和永久性的流动资产。

Long-term Finance

It refers to sources of funds that is long-term, including long-term debt finance and equity finance. Bonds, preference shares and ordinary shares are all long-term financial instruments.

长期融资

长期的资金来源，包括长期债务融资和权益融资。债券、优先股和普通股都是长期融资工具。

M

Maximum Inventory Level

It is the inventory level that reaches maximum. It can be calculated as: re-order level + re-order quantity − minimum usage × minimum lead time.

存货最高水平

存货最高水平是存货量达到的最大值。其计算公式为：

存货最高水平＝再订货库存量＋订购量－单位时间最低消耗量×最短前置时间

Minimum Inventory Level

It is the inventory level that reaches minimum. It is buffer inventory level. It can be calculated as: re-order level－average usage×average lead time.

存货最低水平

存货最低水平是存货量的最小值。它就是缓冲库存水平。其计算公式为：

存货最低水平＝再订货库存量－单位时间平均消耗量×平均前置时间

Miller-Orr Model

It is a more realistic cash management model based on the assumption that cash balance varies daily and the business should keep the variation to its lower and upper limits set by this model.

The decision rule is as follows: (1) if the cash balance reaches its upper limit, the business should buy in marketable securities at cash, which amounts to upper limit minus return point. (2) if the cash balance reaches its lower limit, the business should sell marketable securities to raise cash, which amounts to return point less lower limit. For example, if upper limit is ＄60 000, return point ＄40 000, the lower limit is ＄30 000. If the cash balance reaches ＄60 000, the amount of cash that needs to be spent on marketable securities is ＄20 000. If the cash balance reaches ＄30 000, the amount of cash that needs to be raised through selling marketable securities should be ＄10 000.

Miller-Orr 模型

它是一个更实用的现金管理模型,基于现金余额每天都在波动,企业应该把现金余额控制在这个模型所设定的上限和下限之间的假设。

决策方法如下:(1)如果现金余额到达上限,企业就应该投资一部分资金去购买有价证券,投出的资金量等于资金量上限减资金量回归点;(2)如果现金余额到达下限,企业就应该出售所持有的有价证券去筹集一定量的资金,筹集的资金量等于资金量回归点减资金量下限。例如,上限是 60 000 美元,回归点是 40 000 美元,下限是 30 000 美元。如果现金余额到达 60 000 美元,企业就应该投资 20 000 美元去购买有价证券。如果现金余额到达 30 000 美元,企业就应该卖出所持有价证券去筹集 10 000 美元的资金。

Maturity Matching Principle

Long-term assets should be funded by long-term finance, and short-term assets should be funded by short-term finance.

期限匹配原则

该原则要求:长期资产的投资需用长期资金,而短期资产的投资需用短期资金。

【学习提示】

这是企业融资决策的一个重要原则。购买固定资产和永久性流动资产的资金来源应是长期的,这样可以避免频繁融资,并且避免承担不必要的风险。对于季节性波动引起的临时性流动资产的增加,其资金来源则应是短期的，以保证一定的灵活性和降低资金成本。更进一步，如果要投资购买使用年限预计为 5 年的一套设备，则所筹集的资金使用年限，比如借款期限，最好也是 5 年。

Moderate Strategy

(1)For a moderate approach in working capital investment, a business manages to be in the middle way of aggressive approach and conservative approach, that is, its working capital investment level is close to industry average.

(2) For a moderate approach in working capital financing policy, a business conforms with maturity matching principle, that is, long-term assets are supported by long-term funds and short-term assets supported by short-term funds.

居中型策略

(1)对于居中型的营运资本投资策略，企业走的是激进型投资策略和稳健型投资策略的中间路线，即企业的营运资本投资接近行业平均水平。

(2)对于居中型的营运资本融资策略，企业严格遵照期限匹配原则，即长期资产的投资用长期资金来支持，而短期资产的投资用短期资金来支持。

【学习提示】

对于营运资本的投资策略，如果流动资产的投资比行业平均水平偏低，实行偏紧的信用政策，保留偏少的库存，企业采用的就是激进型投资策略。如果流动资产的投资比行业平均水平偏高，实行偏松的信用政策，保

留较多的库存，企业采用的就是稳健型投资策略。

对于营运资本的融资策略，如果企业用短期资金来支持部分长期资产的投资，则融资偏激进；如果用长期资金去支持部分短期资产的投资，则融资偏稳健。

N

Net Working Capital

The value of current assets less current liabilities. It indicates requirements for long-term funds to finance the investment in current assets.

净营运资本

净营运资本是指流动资产减去流动负债所得的值。它是指流动资产投资需要多少长期资金的支持。

【知识点巩固与拓展】

净营运资本强调流动资产减去流动负债的净值。流动资产的资金来源分短期(短期负债)和长期(净营运资本)。两者的相对比例反映了企业的营运资本的融资策略。比如：一家公司目前流动资产 5 000 万美元，流动负债 3 000 万美元，则净营运资本 2 000 万美元。流动资产有 60％由短期资金支持(3 000/5 000＝60％)，有 40％由长期资金支持(2 000/5 000＝40％)。这家公司更多地依赖短期资金，融资策略偏激进。

Net working capital is current assets net of current liability. Financing for current assets include both short-term funds(represented by current liability in the statement of financial position) and long-term funds (represented by net working capital). The relative proportion of short-term and long-term finance reflect s the company's working capital financing strategy.

For example, a company, currently has current assets of $ 50 million, current liability of $ 30 million. Its net working capital is $ 20 million. So short-term finance accounts for 60% of current assets investment funds(3 000/5 000 = 60%) and long-term finance accounts for 40%(2 000/5 000=40%). The company relies more on short-term finance, its working capital financing policy is conservative.

Negotiation of Bills of Exchange or Cheques

When an exporter receives a bill of exchange or cheque from a customer payable outside the exporter's country, it can ask a bank to help handle the collection of payment and to make an advance payment to the exporter.

议付

当出口商从客户那里收到汇票或支票时，并且汇票或支票要求国境外支付，出口商可以要求一家议付行帮忙收款并预先提供所收款项的一定比例的预付款给出口商。

【学习提示】

议付和银行预付是相似的，不同之处在于议付的汇票是要求在国境外支付。

O

Objectives of Working Capital Management

Working capital management has two objectives, one is liquidity, the other is profitability. First, the business must have sufficient liquid resources for smooth running of business, that is to have sufficient inventory to meet customer needs, to offer credit to customers to attract customers and to have sufficient cash to meet day-to-day business needs. Second, the business main objective is to increase its profitability.

Liquidity and profitability are not in conflict. Sufficient liquid resources will maintain and boost sales, thus maintain and increase profits. Cutting excessive inventory and receivables will release money tied up in these assets, thus liquidity is improved. Also cutting excessive inventory and receivables will reduce holding cost of these assets, thus profitability is improved.

But sometimes, liquidity and profitability are in conflict. If cutting inventory and receivables to an unacceptable low level, customers will go elsewhere, profitability will be worsened although liquidity improved.

营运资本管理目标

营运资本管理有两个目标:一是流动性,二是盈利能力。首先,企业要顺利运营就必须有足够的流动资源,即要有足够的库存来满足客户需求,要给客户信用以吸引客户,要有足够的现金来满足日常商业支出。其次,企业的主要目标是增加盈利。

流动性和盈利能力这两个目标目前并不冲突。有足够的流动资源才能保证或者增加销售，也就能保证或增加盈利。削减过量的库存和应收账款，就会把困于这两项资产的资金释放出来，从而提高企业的流动性。另外，削减过量的库存和应收账款，还会降低这两项资产的持有成本，从而提高盈利。

但有时，这两者又是冲突的。比如削减过量的库存和应收账款到不可接受的过低水平，虽然流动性提高了，但会丢失客户，从而影响盈利。

【学习提示】

关于营运资本管理的两个目标，要注意两者的对立与统一，不能过分强调两者的对立冲突。

Ordering Cost

It is procuring cost or re-ordering cost incurred for placing a new order.

订货成本

订货成本是订立一份新的订单而产生的成本。

Over-trading

It is also called under-capitalization. The excessive expansion of business with too little long-term funds puts excessive pressure on cash flows of a business. Signs of over-trading include:

(1)sales soar.

(2)over-reliance on short-term funds.

(3)worsened liquidity ratios.

(4)sales/net working capital ratio rises.

Overtrading may also lead to worsened profitability.

If a business let overtrading go unresolved for a period of time, finally the business will fail due to lack of liquidity.

In order to solve overtrading problem. The business need find ways to improve liquidity. It can raise new funds, cut or delay expenditures, tighten control of working capital, slow down the growth or even curtail activities.

过度交易/过度扩张

又称营运资本不足。长期资金不足的企业过度扩张业务会给现金流带来过度压力。主要的标志有:(1)销售收入猛增;(2)过度依赖短期资金;(3)流动性比率恶化;(4)销售收入/净营运资本比率增大。

过度扩张还会使企业的盈利能力下降。如果一家企业不及时解决过度扩张带来的问题,最终企业就会因为缺乏流动性、资金断链而倒闭。为了解决过度扩张带来的问题,企业需要想办法改善流动性。比如,企业可以筹集新的资金,可以削减或推迟各项支出和费用,收紧对营运资本的管理控制,放慢增长速度,甚至压缩业务规模。

【学习提示】

过度交易和营运资本不足是问题的两个表现,确切地说应该是因果关系,即因为过度交易和扩张导致营运资本不足。

Over-capitalization

Working capital is excessive compared to the sales level. There are excessive inventories, accounts receivable and cash, and very few accounts payable. The money invested in current assets is too much. Signs of over-capitalization are:

(1) sakes/net working capital falls.

(2) too high liquidity ratio.

(3) too long cash operating cycle.

Over-capitalization will increase financing cost of current assets and harm profitability. The business needs to optimize working capital management. Management of receivables, inventory and payables should be improved.

营运资本过多

对目前的销售水平而言，营运资本过多。即有过多的存货、过多的应收账款以及非常少的应付账款。投资到流动资产的资金过多。主要的迹象有：(1) 销售收入/净营运资本比率降低；(2) 太高的流动比率；(3) 太长的现金周转期。营运资本过多，会增加流动资产的资金成本，从而损害企业的盈利能力。企业需要优化营运资本管理，改善应收账款、存货以及应付账款的管理。

【学习提示】

过度扩张会导致营运资本不足，进而导致公司资金链断裂，最终使企业倒闭。而营运资本过多，只会影响企业的盈利，短期不会使企业倒闭。

P

Procuring Cost

It is re-ordering cost incurred for placing a new order.

订货成本

订货成本是订立一份新的订单而产生的成本。

R

Reorder Level(ROL)

ROL refers to the level of inventory left in the stores at which a new order should be placed. It indicates the timing of re-order. If both the lead time and the demand in lead time are certain, the re-order level is equal to the demand in lead time. If the lead time or the demand in lead time is uncertain, ROL＝average demand in lead time ＋buffer inventory, or ROL＝maximum usage × maximum lead time.

再订货库存量

再订货库存量是指应下新订单时仓库中所剩下的存货量。它表示再订货的具体时间。如果从下订单到货物运达的时间长短能够确定，而且这段时间内对该货物的需求量也可以确定，则再订货库存量就等于从下订单到货物运达这段时间内对该货物的需求量。如果以上两个因素中有任何一个不能确定，则：

再订货库存量＝从下订单到货物运达这段时间的平均需求量＋缓冲库存量

或者：

再订货库存量＝从下订单到货物运达的最长时间×单位时间的最大需求量

【学习提示】

在存在不确定性的情况下，如果缺货的后果很严重，企业就会用最多法来定再订货库存量，即最长的前置时间乘以单位时间的最大需求量。如果企业缺货的后果不是很严重，企业就可用平均法来定再订货库存量，即根据过去的统计计算前置时间的平均存货需求量，再加上一定量的缓冲库存。

S

Sales Revenue/Net Working Capital Ratio

Sales revenue/(current assets－current liabilities) or sales revenue/(trade receivables＋inventory－trade payables) shows the level of working capital that supports sales. If the ratio rises, it may indicate that the working capital may not keep in line with the sales growth or indicate that the business pursue a more aggressive working capital management strategy. If the ratio falls, it may indicate that the working capital is increased more quickly compared to the sales or indicate that the business pursue a more conservative working capital management strategy.

销售收入除以净营运资本(营运资本周转率)

销售收入除以流动资产和流动负债之差或者销售收入除以(应收账款+存货−应付账款),说明支持销售的营运资本水平。如果这个比率提高了,则可能是因为营运资本没有跟上收入的增长或是因为企业本身采用了更激进的营运资本投资策略。如果这个比率降低了,则可能是因为营运资本的增长比销售增长更快或者因为企业采用了更保守的营运资本投资策略。

【学习提示】

这是判断企业营运资本投资情况的非常重要的一个比率。企业的营运资本应该随着业务量(由销售收入反映)的增加而成比例地增加。

Settlement Discount

Cash discounts offered to customers for payment made within certain days of invoicing being sent. It is employed by businesses to speed up the collection of debts, reduce investment in accounts receivable, and thus reduce cost of capital.

结算折扣(现金折扣)

企业给予那些在发票开出一定日期之内付款的客户的现金折扣。企业一般用其加快债务的回收、降低应收账款的投资,以降低资金成本。

【知识点巩固与拓展】

供货商给客户结算折扣,对供货商是否划算呢?这需要做成本和效益的对比:如果效益大于成本,则供货商给客户结算折扣是划算的;如果效益小于成本,就是不划算的。成本就是给客户的折扣,效益就是客户提前付款而给企业节约的资金成本以及因流动性改善而抓住的投资机会。

那供货商提供结算折扣,客户是否应该接受呢?客户也要做成本和效益对比。成本就是提前付款的资金成本,效益就是得到的折扣。同样,效益大于成本,则接受折扣;反之,则拒绝折扣。

通常有两种方法去比较成本和效益。

一是绝对金额法,即看一年的成本是多少金额,效益是多少金额。

二是年化利率法,即把折扣换算成年化利率,与资金成本的年利率进行比较。

Is it financially acceptable to a supplier to offer a settlement discount to customers? Costs and benefits should be analysed. If benefits exceed costs, it is acceptable to offer settlement discounts. If costs exceed benefits, it is not worthwhile to offer discounts. Costs are discounts given and benefits are financing cost saved by collecting funds earlier.

If a company is offered a settlement discount by its supplier, is it worthwhile to accept the discount? The company also needs to analyse costs and benefits. Benefits are discounts offered and costs are financing cost for paying debts earlier. If benefits exceed costs, it is acceptable to accept settlement discounts. If costs exceed benefits, it is not worthwhile to accept discounts.

There are two methods of cost-benefit analysis. One is absolute value method. That is, absolute currency value of cost and benefits are compared. The other method is annual percentage rate method. Compare annual percentage cost of discount with cost of capital.

Shortage Costs (of Inventory)

It is also called Stock-out costs. Shortage costs refer to costs incurred as a result of running out of inventory. Shortage costs include loss from lost production and sales, extra cost of emergency inventory.

缺货成本

缺货成本是指因为货物用完而产生的成本。它包括因缺货而导致生产停工、丢失销售的损失以及紧急调货的额外成本。

Short-term Assets

Fluctuating current assets are short-term assets. Funds invested in short-term assets are tied up for short term.

短期资产

流动资产的投资波动部分。投入短期资产的资金是短期绑定的。

Short-term Finance

It refers to funds that cannot be used for more than one year. It is cheaper than long-term funds because of lower default risk to investors. And it is more flexible as it can be raised when needed and repaid when not needed. But it is riskier, since its cost of capital will change with the prevailing interest rate and businesses may find that it is difficult to renew.

短期融资

短期融资是指使用期限不超过一年的资金来源。与长期资金相比较,它的资金成本更低,因为投资者承担的违约风险比长期资金的小。它更加灵活,企业可以在需要资金的时候就去筹集而在不需要的时候就偿还。但是短期资金的风险更大,因为它的资金成本会随着当前的利率水平的波动而波动,有时企业会发现资金再续存在困难。

System Breakdown Risk

It refers to the type of risk faced by a business if it has too little working capital for its everyday operations, that is, there are increasing chances of shortage of inventory and losing of customers and loss of goodwill with suppliers.

系统崩溃风险

系统崩溃风险是一家企业因支持日常运营的营运资本过少而要面临的一种风险,即缺货、失去客户以及跟供货商关系恶化的概率增加。

Surplus Cash

It refers to temporarily available cash that will be needed soon. Surplus cash can be invested with the following criteria in mind:

1. liquidity—the investment should be converted to cash immediately if the company needs funds.

2. safety—the risk of a capital loss should be avoided.

3. profitability—if both liquidity and safety criteria are satisfied, the investment should earn a good return.

暂余现金

暂余现金是指临时剩余、在不久就要被使用的现金。暂余现金可以按照以下原则去做一些短期投资:

(1)流动性——在企业需要资金时,所投资金能及时回笼。

(2)安全性——应避免资金损失。

(3)盈利性——在流动性和安全性两个原则得到保证的前提下,尽量取得好的回报。

【知识点巩固与拓展】

暂余现金可以投资的金融工具有短期银行存款、国库券、大额存单、银行承兑汇票等。

Surplus cash can be invested in short-term bank deposit, treasury bills, certificates of deposit, and bank accepted bill of exchange.

T

Treasury Management

It refers to the corporate handling of all financial matters, including the generation of external and internal funds for business, the management of currencies and cash flows, and the complex strategies, policies and procedures of corporate finance. (Association of Corporate Treasures)

Treasury management mainly involves management of liquidity, management of funding, risk management and advising on corporate finance issues.

资金管理

资金管理就是指处理公司所有的财务事项，包括筹集企业外部和内部的资金，管理现金和现金流，以及公司理财的战略、政策和具体措施的制定与实施。（公司财务协会的定义）

资金管理主要有流动性管理、筹资管理、风险管理，以及就一些财务事项提出建议。

【学习提示】

集团公司的资金管理分集中管理（centralized management）和分散管理（decentralized management）。集中管理可以使公司的资金统筹安排，提高资金使用效率，降低资金成本。但各分部或者子公司缺乏资金使用的独立自主性，不能及时满足资金需求和投资需求。

Treasury Bills

Treasury bills are short-term (with a term of less than one year, typically 91 days to maturity) debt obligations issued by the government to promise to pay a certain amount to the holder on maturity. They are short-term government bonds.

国库券

国库券是政府发行的短期国债，承诺在到期日支付给持票人一定金额的债务凭证，期限一般不超过一年，以到期期限为 91 天的居多。

Trade Credit

It refers to the convenience a supplier given to the buyer to allow it a credit period and pay the debts due later. Suppliers offer trade credit charges no interest.

商业信用

商业信用是供货商给客户提供的一种便利，给客户一个账期，允许其之后偿付货款，并且在此期间供货商不收任何利息。

W

Working Capital

Working capital is long-term funds required for everyday operations.

Net working capital＝current assets－current liabilities

营运资本

营运资本是企业日常运营所需要的长期资金。

净营运资本＝流动资产－流动负债

Working Capital Management

It refers to short-term financial management activities involving management of current assets and current liabilities.

营运资本管理

营运资本管理是短期财务管理活动，涉及流动资产和流动负债的管理。

Working Capital Management Strategy

It refers to the approach employed by a business in working capital investment and financing aspects. Both working capital investment strategy and working capital financing strategy have three approaches, that is, aggressive strategy, moderate strategy and conservative strategy.

营运资本管理策略

营运资本管理策略是企业在营运资本的投资和融资方面所分别采取的管理方式。不管是营运资本的投资策略还是营运资本的融资策略，都包含三种策略，即激进型策略、居中型策略和稳健型策略。

【学习提示】

短期财务管理首先要确定营运资本管理策略。营运资本管理策略分投资策略和融资策略。

Working Capital Investment Strategy

It refers to the approach employed by a business in working capital investment aspect. A business who employs an aggressive working capital investment strategy keeps a lower working capital investment level, that is, compared with industry average, it has a lower level of inventory, give customers more stringent credit policy and try to get longer credit period given by supplies. An aggressive working capital investment strategy will reduce financing cost by cutting money tied up in current assets, and thus will improve profitability. But system breakdown risk increased through more running out of inventory and more dissatisfied customers and suppliers. The opposite is right with conservative strategy.

营运资本投资策略

营运资本投资策略是一家企业在营运资本投资方面所采用的管理方式。采用激进型营运资本投资策略的企业，一般维持较低的营运资本水平，即与行业平均水平相比，企业库存水平较低，给客户较严格的信用政策以及向供货商争取较长的信用期限。由于削减了绑定在流动资产的资金量，企业的融资成本下降，盈利能力上升。但是由于缺货更频繁，不满意的客户和供货商更多，企业将面临更高的系统崩溃风险。稳健型的策略正好相反。

Working Capital Financing Strategy

It refers to the approach employed by a business in working capital financing aspect. A business who employs a moderate financing policy will conform with maturity matching principle. A business who employs an aggressive working capital financing policy will rely more on short-term finance, that is, not only fluctuating current assets are supported by short-term funds, but part of permanent current assets are also funded by short-term funds. A business with an aggressive working capital financing policy will have lower financing cost and higher profitability, but increased liquidity risk. A business who employs a conservative working capital financing policy will rely more on long-term finance, that is, not only long-term assets are supported by long-term funds, but some fluctuating current assets are also supported by long-term funds. Businesses will have lower liquidity risk, but higher financing cost and lower profitability.

营运资本融资策略

营运资本融资策略是一家企业在营运资本融资方面所采用的管理方式。采用居中型营运资本融资策略的企业严格遵照期限匹配原则。与居中型企业相比，采用激进型营运资本融资策略的企业更多地依赖短期资金，除了流动资产的浮动部分用短期资金来支持外，流动资产的持久部分也部分地用短期资金来支持。企业的融资成本较低，盈利能力提升，但是流动性风险增大。与居中型企业相比，采用稳健型营运资本融资策略的企业更多地依赖长期资金，除了长期资产用长期资金来支持外，流动资产的浮动部分也部分地用长期资金来支持。企业面临较低的流动性风险，但是融资成本增加，盈利能力下降。

Module Five

Cost of Capital and Capital Structure/资本成本和资本结构

本单元的学习目标：

(1)掌握投资者所要求的回报与资本成本之间的关系，以及融资工具风险的变化对资本成本的影响。

(2)理解并掌握各种资本成本的计算公式。

(3)理解并掌握加权平均资本成本(WACC)的计算。

(4)熟悉特定项目资本成本(project-specific cost of capital)或者折现率(discount rate)的计算方法。

(5)探讨企业是否能找到最佳资本结构(optimal capital structure)。

A

Arbitrage

It refers to making profit by purchasing at a lower price in a market and selling at a higher price in another market and through taking advantage of the price difference between the markets.

套利

套利是指在一个市场以低价买进而在另一个市场以高价卖出，通过利用市场间的价差来盈利。

Asset Beta（Ungeared Beta）

It is the beta coefficient of an ungeared firm, which is dependent only on the business risk of the firm. The asset beta is not affected by the capital structure of a firm, therefore, with all else equal, the asset beta will remain the same no matter the firm's level of debt.

资产 β（无杠杆 β）

资产 β 就是一家无杠杆公司的 β 系数，其大小只受企业的经营风险影响。公司的资本结构不会影响资产 β，即在其他条件不变的前提下，不管公司的债务水平如何，资产 β 都将保持不变。

【学习提示】

一家无杠杆的公司，即债务为零、全部为权益融资的公司。公司只有经营风险，没有财务风险。其 β 系数只反映经营风险。

资产 β 也可以看成由权益和负债组成的投资组合的 β，而投资组合的 β 是各项投资的 β 的加权平均数。

资产 β＝权益市值/(权益市值＋负债市值) ×权益 β＋负债市值/(权益市值＋负债市值) ×负债 β

Agency Cost of Debts

It refers to the cost incurred as a result of protective action taken by debt providers as the gearing level of a company becomes higher and higher. As the gearing level increases, there is more chance for the management and shareholders to act at the expense of creditors to pursue their own interests, so debt providers impose debt covenants and require more monitoring of the management in order to protect their own interests.

债务的代理成本

债务的代理成本是指随着公司的杠杆水平越来越高，因债务资本的提供方为了自保而采取的某些措施给公司带来的成本。随着杠杆水平的提高，管理层和股东有更多机会牺牲债权人的利益而追求自己的利益，所以债务资本的提供方就会增加一些债务合约的限制条款，并要求加强对管理层的监管，从而保护债权人的利益。

【学习提示】

债务增加，即财务杠杆增加，一方面，利息费用增加可使企业少缴税（tax relief of interest payment），另一方面，债务增加也增加了财务困境成本（包括破产成本和债务的代理成本）。另外，如果企业的应纳税所得不足，利息费用的增加就不再起到节税的效应，即发生税盾耗尽（tax exhaustion）现象。

After-tax Cost of Debt（Post-tax Cost of Debt）

If before-tax cost of debt is K_d, the corporation tax rate is t, after-tax cost of debt is $K_d \times (1-t)$, because interest cost of debt is tax deductible, the tax relief of interest payment will reduce the cost of debt.

税后债务成本

如果税前债务成本是 K_d，企业所得税税率为 t，则税后债务成本为 $K_d \times (1-t)$。因为利息成本可以在计算企业所得税时作为费用扣除，从而使企业少缴企业所得税，故而降低了企业债务的成本。

B

Bankruptcy Cost

With the level of financial gearing increasing, there is an increasing risk of the firm going bankrupt and being unable to meet its debt obligations, so the shareholders will require a higher rate of return in compensating for the higher bankruptcy risk and the cost of capital of the firm increases. The increased cost of capital is bankruptcy cost.

破产成本

随着公司财务杠杆水平的提升,公司走向破产、不能偿付债务的风险也在增加,所以,股票投资者会要求更高的回报率来弥补所增加的破产风险,因而企业融资成本增加。由此而增加的融资成本就是破产成本。

【学习提示】

这是一种间接的破产成本。另外,直接的破产成本还包括债务纠纷所产生的法律成本和管理成本,间接的破产成本还包括因为债务违约而给企业经营带来的负面影响。

Beta Factor (Beta Coefficient)

It measures the systematic risk of a risk investment. The average systematic risk of a stock market investments has a beta of 1. A beta of less than 1 or more than 1 means the risk investment has a lower than or higher than average systematic risk.

β 系数

它衡量一项风险投资的系统风险。股票市场各项投资的平均系统风险用 $\beta=1$ 表示。如果 $\beta<1$,则表示该项投资的系统风险低于市场平均水平;如果 $\beta>1$,则表示该项投资的系统风险高于市场平均水平。

【知识点巩固与拓展】

$\beta=0$，只意味着系统风险为0，并不意味着无风险，因为除了系统风险外，还有非系统风险。

β的大小受企业收入的周期性、经营杠杆（经营风险）以及财务杠杆（财务风险）等因素影响。

A zero beta only means there is no systematic risk, and it does not mean there is no risk, because risks include both systematic risk and unsystematic risk.

Beta coefficient is affected by such factors as cyclity of revenues, operating gearing (business risk) and financial gearing (financial risk).

Book Value

It is the value as shown in the statement of financial Position a company.

账面价值

账面价值是指公司资产负债表上所列示的价值。

C

Capital Asset Pricing Model (CAPM)

In common sense, the required rate of return by investors on a risk investment is equal to risk-free rate of interest plus risk premium. Risk premium is the premium for bearing average risk of the whole market and the excess of the systematic risk of the investment over the average market risk. CAPM explicitly explains the relationship between risk and return in the following formula:

$$E(r_i)=R_f+\beta_i[E(r_m)-R_f]$$

资本资产定价模型

根据常识，一项风险投资的投资者所要求的回报率等于无风险利率加上风险溢价。而风险溢价就是因为承担市场平均风险水平以及承担高于市场平均水平的风险所需要的额外报酬。资本资产定价模型用如下公式清楚明了地解释了风险和回报之间的这种关系：

权益投资者所要求的回报率＝无风险利率＋该项投资的 β 系数×(市场平均回报率－无风险利率)

【学习提示】

资本资产定价模型是计算权益资本成本的方法之一。计算公式如下：

$$K_e=E(r_i)=R_f+\beta_i[E(r_m)-R_f]$$

【知识点巩固与拓展】

资本资产定价模型由三部分组成：一是无风险利率，即货币的时间价值；二是承担市场平均风险的风险溢价，即市场平均回报率与无风险利率的差额；三是承担高于市场平均风险或低于市场平均风险的调整系数，即该项投资的 β 系数。

资本资产定价模型的假设前提是一个完美的资本市场和充分多样化的投资者。并且，在实际运用中，无风险利率、市场风险溢

价以及 β 系数都很难精确估计。β 系数会随时间而改变。

CAPM model has three components. Firstly, risk-fee rate (R_f), it represents the pure time value of money. Secondly, the market risk premium[$E(r_m)-R_f$], it represents the return for bearing average market risk. Thirdly, Beta coefficient (β), it is an adjusting factor to market risk premium for bearing lower or higher than average market risk.

CAPM model assumes a perfect capital market and well-diversified investors. And it is difficult to estimate risk-free rate, market risk premium and beta factor in practice. Also, Beta factor changes over time.

Company Value (Business Value)

It refers to the market value of a company, usually reflecting the net present value of all future cash flows of the company.

公司价值(企业价值)

公司价值是指一家公司的市场价值,通常反映公司未来现金流的现值。

【学习提示】

注意公司价值与加权平均资本成本(WACC)之间的关系。一般用公司的加权平均资本成本作折现率计算公司价值,所以,加权平均资本成本越高则公司价值越低,而加权平均资本成本越低则公司价值越高。

Conversion Value

It is the value of convertible debt if converted to ordinary shares. For example, if a \$100 convertible bond can be converted to 30 ordinary shares at maturity, and the current share price is \$10 per share. The conversion value of a \$100 convertible bond is $30 \times \$10 = \$300$.

转换价值

转换价值是指把可转债转换成普通股的价值。例如，一张面值 100 美元的可转债在到期时可转换成 30 股普通股，现在股票的市值为每股 10 美元，则这张面值 100 美元的可转债的当前转换价值为 30×10=300(美元)。

Cost of Capital

It is the cost of finance raised, usually expressed in the form of annualized interest rate. For example, a business borrows a lump sum of money from a bank at an annual interest rate of 8%. The cost of capital of this borrowed money is 8%. In order to raise finance successfully, the firm needs to satisfy the requirements of the investors. So the cost of capital of a firm is equal to the required rate of return by investors of the firm. The cost of capital is an opportunity cost of capital, it is the returns sacrificed by the investors for not investing somewhere else.

资本成本

资本成本就是所筹集资金的成本，一般用年利率的形式表示。

比如一家企业向银行以8%的年利率借入一笔款项,这笔款项的资金成本就是8%。为了成功融资,企业需要满足投资者的要求。所以企业的资金成本就等于投资者所要求的回报率。资金成本是一种机会成本,是投资者投资于企业某一融资工具却没有投资别处而牺牲的回报。

【学习提示】

企业的资本成本=投资者要求的回报。所以,估算企业的资本成本,实际是估算投资者投资该项融资工具所要求的回报。投资者权衡风险与收益。一项融资工具对投资者的风险越大,则投资者要求的回报越高,企业的资本成本也越高。

Cost of Equity

It refers to the cost of equity capital raised by a company. It is the return required by the ordinary shareholders currently. It is usually higher than cost of debt due to its higher risk to investor.

权益资本成本

权益资本成本是指企业所筹集的权益资本的成本。它是现时普通股股东所要求的回报。由于它对于投资者风险较高,因此它一般高于债务资本的成本。

【学习提示】

权益投资对投资者来说是风险最高的一项投资,所以投资者要求的回报最高,高于债务投资所要求的回报。

计算权益资本成本的方法有两种：一种是股利模型(dividend growth model)，另一种是资本资产定价模型(CAPM model)。

Cost of Debt

It refers to the cost of debt capital raised by a company, it is the return required by debt providers currently.

债务资本成本

债务资本成本指企业所筹集的债务资本的成本，是现时债务资本的提供方所要求的回报。

【学习提示】

计算债务的资本成本时，首先要看债务是属于不可赎回债务、可赎回债务还是可转债，然后选择正确的估算方法。

Cost of Irredeemable Debt

It is the return required by irredeemable debt providers, which is the cost of capital borne by the issuing company of the irredeemable debt. If interest is paid yearly, the formula is: $K_d = i/P_0$ (i is annual interest paid, P_0 is current market price of the irredeemable debt). If interest is paid n times per year, the formula is: $K_d = (1 + i/P_0)^n$ (i is interest paid per period, P_0 is current market price of the irredeemable debt).

不可赎回债务的资本成本

这是不可赎回债务资本的提供方所要求的回报，是发行公司所要承担的资本成本。如果利息一年一付，则计算公式为：$K_d = i/P_0$（i 是年度利息，P_0 是该不可赎回债务目前的市价）。如果利息一年付 n 次，则计算公式为：$K_d = (1+i/P_0)^n$（i 是每次支付的利息，P_0 是该不可赎回债务目前的市价）。

【学习提示】

这里的 K_d 是税前资本成本(before-tax cost of capital)。如果所得税税率为 t，则税后资本成本(after-tax cost of capital)为 $i(1-t)/P_0$ 或 $[1+i(1-t)/P_0]^n$。

【知识点巩固与拓展】

一面值为 100 美元、年利率为 8%的债券，当前市价为 102 美元，所得税税率为 20%。请估算其税后资本成本。

A 8% bond, par value $100, current market value $102, corporation tax rate 20%. Calculate after-tax cost of debt.

这是不可赎回的债务，因为没有到期日。

税后资本成本(after-tax cost of debt)

$=8(1-20\%)/102=6.27\%$

如果每半年计一次利息(if interest is paid half yearly)，则：

税后资本成本(after-tax cost of debt)

$=[1+4(1-20\%)/102]^2-1=6.37\%$

Cost of Redeemable Debt

The return required by redeemable debt providers, which is the cost of capital borne by the issuing company of the redeemable debt. It is the current market yield to maturity of the redeemable debt. The cost of redeemable debt can be estimated using IRR method.

可赎回债务成本

这是可赎回债务资本提供方所要求的回报，即该可赎回债务发行公司所要承担的资本成本。也就是现时市场上该债务的到期收益率。可用 IRR(内部收益率)法来估算可赎回债务成本。

【知识点巩固与拓展】

一面值为 100 美元、年利率为 8%的债券，5 年后到期，当前市价为 102 美元，所得税税率为 20%。用 IRR 法来估算其税后资本成本。

A 8% bond, par value $100, redeemable at par in five years, market value 102, corporation tax rate is 20%. Calculate after-tax cost of debt using IRR method.

年份	变量	$	6%折现系数	现值
0	市价	(102)	1	(102)
1～5	利息	6.4	4.212	26.96
5	赎回价值	100	0.747	74.70
	NPV			−0.34

年份	变量	$	5%折现系数	现值
0	市价	(102)	1	(102)
1～5	利息	6.4	4.329	27.71
5	赎回价值	100	0.784	78.40
	NPV			4.11

税后资本成本(after-tax cost of debt)＝*IRR*＝5%＋(6%－5%)×[4.11/(4.11＋0.34)]＝5.92%

Cost of Floating Rate Debt

It refers to the cost of capital borne by the issuing company of the floating rate debt. As the interest charged for floating rate debt is variable, so the cost of capital should be estimated by referring to the cost of an equivalent fixed interest debt with a similar term to maturity in a firm of similar standing.

浮动利率的债务成本

这是指浮动利率债务发行公司所要承担的资本成本。因为其利率是变动的，所以其资本成本一般参考与该浮动利率债务到期时间相同、发行公司状况相当的固定利率债务的资本成本来估算。

Cost of Convertible Debt

It refers to the cost of capital borne by the issuing company of the convertible debt. It can be estimated using IRR method, but its calculation depends on whether or not conversion is likely to happen.

可转债的资本成本

这是指发行可转债公司所要承担的资本成本。可用 IRR 方法来估算,但其计算要首先判断投资方把可转债转换成普通股的可能性大不大。

【学习提示】

计算可转债的资本成本,首先要判断投资者在到期时,是选择转换成普通股,还是选择获得赎回价值。

【知识点巩固与拓展】

一面值为 100 美元、年利率为 8%的可转换债券,5 年后到期,可转换成 35 股普通股或者以面值赎回。该债券当前市价为 102 美元,所得税税率为 20%,普通股股价目前为每股 2.5 美元,预计股价每年以 3%的增长率增长。用 IRR 法来估算其税后资本成本。

A 8% bond, par value \$100, redeemable at par in five years or converted into 35 ordinary shares. Current market value of the bond is \$102, corporation tax rate is 20%. Current share price is \$2.5 and it is expected that the annual growth rate of the share price is 3%. Calculate after-tax cost of debt using IRR method.

首先判断 5 年后投资者是选择转换成普通股还是选择获得赎回价值。

5 年后的股价预计为 $2.5\times(1+3\%)^5=2.90$(美元)

转换价值$=35\times2.90=101.50$(美元)

因转换价值大于赎回价值 100，故投资者会选择转换成普通股。

年份	变量	$	6%折现系数	现值
0	市价	(102)	1	(102)
1～5	利息	6.4	4.212	26.96
5	转换价值	101.5	0.747	75.82
	NPV			0.78

年份	变量	$	8%折现系数	现值
0	市价	(102)	1	(102)
1～5	利息	6.4	3.993	25.56
5	转换价值	101.5	0.681	69.12
	NPV			−7.32

税后资本成本(after-tax cost of debt) $= IRR = 6\% + (8\% - 6\%) \times [0.78/(0.78+7.32)] = 6.19\%$

Cost of Preference Shares

It refers to the cost of capital borne by the issuing company of the preference shares, that is the return required by the preference shareholders. The formula is: $K_P = d/P_0$ (d is annual dividend per share, P_0 is current share price).

优先股资本成本

这是发行优先股融资的公司所要承担的资本成本，也就是优先股股东所要求的回报。计算公式为 $K_P = d/P_0$（d 是每股年度股利，P_0 是当前每股股价）。

【知识点巩固与拓展】

一股息 6%、面值 10 美元的优先股，目前其股价为 9 美元。计算其资本成本。

A 6% $10 preference shares, current share price is $9. Calculate the cost of these preference shares.

该优先股的资本成本(the cost of these preference shares)=10×6%/9=6.67%

Cost of a Bank Loan

The before-tax cost of a bank loan is the annualized interest rate(i) charged by the bank. If corporation tax rate is t, the post-tax cost of a bank loan=$i(1-t)$.

银行贷款的资本成本

银行贷款的税前资本成本就是银行收取利息的年化利率。如果企业所得税税率为 t，则银行贷款的税后资本成本=贷款的年化利率×(1－税率)。

【知识点巩固与拓展】

一笔本金为 100 万美元，年利率为 6%的银行贷款，所得税税率 20%，计算其税后的资本成本。

A $1 million bank loan, annual interest rate is 6%, corporation tax rate is 20%, calculate after-tax cost of the bank loan.

该笔贷款的税后资本成本(after-tax cost of the bank loan)=

6%×(1－20%)＝4.8%

Cost Structure

If refers to the relative proportion of fixed cost and variable cost for a business. It affects the operating gearing and thus business risk of a company.

成本结构

成本结构是指一家企业的固定成本与变动成本相对的比例。成本结构影响一家公司的经营杠杆和经营风险。

Creditor Hierarchy

Upon liquidation, the order of the claims of the creditors being paid off before equity is dictated by the creditor hierarchy. Normally, secured creditors come first, followed by unsecured creditors, and then come preference shareholders.

债权人层级

在企业破产清算时，债权人层级决定了在权益所有者之前，债权人的债务被清偿的先后顺序。一般有担保的债务首先清偿，其次是无担保债务，最后是优先股。

Creditors with Fixed Charge

Creditors with fixed charge are debt capital providers who have a specific fixed assets as security. During the debt term, the debtor cannot dispose the assets without the consent of the creditors. If the debtor defaults, the creditors can sell the secured assets to settle the debt.

固定资产作担保的债权人

即有某项特定固定资产作为担保的债务资本的提供方。在债务存续期间,未经债权人同意,债务人不可以处置该项资产。如果债务人违约,债权人就可以变卖这项担保的资产来偿还债务。

Creditors with Floating Charge

Creditors with floating charge are debt capital providers who have a class of current assets as security. As long as the debtor does not default, the debtor can dispose the assets without the consent of the creditors. Once the debtor defaults, the debtor will not be allowed to dispose the secured assets any longer and the creditors will sell the secured assets to settle the debt.

流动资产作担保的债权人

即有一类流动资产作为担保的债务资本的提供方。只要债务人不违约,就可以不经债权人同意而随意处置该类资产。一旦违约,债务人就不可以再随意处置担保资产,而债权人则通过变卖担保资产来清偿债务。

D

Diversified Portfolio

It refers to the investment mix that includes a diversification of investment opportunities with different risk and return trade-off. A well-diversified portfolio will diversify away unsystematic risk, but systematic risk will not be diversified away.

多样化投资组合

这是包含不同风险收益组合的多样化投资机会的投资组合。一个充分多样化的投资组合，其非系统风险会被削减至零，但投资多样化不会削减系统风险。

【学习提示】

资本资产定价模型(CAPM model)假设投资者都拥有充分多样化的投资组合(well-diversified portfolios)，故它只考虑系统风险，而忽略非系统风险。这也是该模型的一个缺陷，因为现实世界中，投资者很难通过多样化投资策略把非系统风险完全消除。

Dividend Valuation Model

If the future annual dividend per share is expected to be constant, the cost of equity under dividend valuation model is $k_e = d/P_0$ (d is the annual dividend per share, P_0 is the current ex-dividend price).

股利估值模型

如果预计未来每年派发的每股股利(红利)是保持不变的，则权益资本的成本公式为 $k_e = d/P_0$(d 是每年派发的每股股利，P_0 是股票的当前除息价)。

【学习提示】

这是股利增长模型的一个特例，即假设股利增长率为0。

Dividend Growth Model

If the future annual dividend per share is expected to grow at a constant rate in perpetuity, the cost of equity can be calculated as $k_e=\frac{d_0(1+g)}{p_0}+g$ or $k_e=\frac{d_1}{P_0}+g$ (d_0 is the current dividend per share, d_1 is the next dividend per share, g is the expected annual growth rate of dividend payments, P_0 is the current ex-dividend price).

股利增长模型

如果预计将来每年派发的每股股利(红利)是以固定的年增长率永续增长，则权益资本的成本计算公式为 $k_e=\frac{d_0(1+g)}{p_0}+g$，或者 $k_e=\frac{d_1}{P_0}+g$(其中 d_0 是当前派发的每股股利，d_1 是下次派发的股利，g 是所派发股利的年增长率，P_0 是股票的当前除息价)。

【知识点巩固与拓展】

股利增长模型实际运用起来较简单，但只适用于那些派发股利的公司。并且它没有非常显性地把风险和资本成本之间的关系在公式中描述出来。另外，股利增长率很难精确估计。

Using dividend growth model to estimate

cost of equity is simple in practice, but it is only applicable to companies who pay out dividends. And it does not explicitly explain the relationship between risk and cost of capital. Also, the dividend growth rate is difficult to estimate accurately.

【学习提示】

股利增长模型是除资本资产定价模型之外，计算权益资本成本(cost of equity)的另一种方法。

E

Equity Risk Premium(Market Risk Premium)

It is the excess of the expected rate of return on market portfolio over risk-free rate of return. Equity risk premium$=E(r_m)-R_f$.

权益风险溢价(市场风险溢价)

权益风险溢价是市场投资组合的平均回报率超过无风险回报率的部分。权益风险溢价=市场平均回报率－无风险利率。

【知识点巩固与拓展】

红星公司刚刚每股派发了 2 美元的股利。公司的股利政策是以每年 2%的增长率派发股利。当前的股价为每股 30 美元。用股利增长模型来计算权益资本成本。

Redstar Co. just paid a dividend of ＄2 per

share. The company's dividend policy is to pay out dividends at an annual growth rate of 2%。Current share price is $30 per share. Calculate the cost of equity using dividend growth model.

权益资本成本 $=2\times(1+2\%)/50+2\%=8.8\%$

Equity Beta(Geared Beta)

It is the beta of a firm with financial gearing. As the firm increases its proportion of debts in capital structure (ie. financial gearing), its equity beta increases as well.

权益 β(有杠杆 β)

权益 β 是指有财务杠杆的公司的 β 值。随着公司资本结构中债务资本比例(即财务杠杆)的增加,权益 β 值也在增加。

【知识点巩固与拓展】

红星公司目前的权益 β 为 1.5,无风险利率为 4%,权益风险溢价为 7%,用资本资产定价模型计算权益资本成本。

The equity beta of Redstar Co. is 1.5, and risk-free rate is 4%, equity risk premium is 7%, calculate the cost of equity using CAPM model.

权益资本成本 $=4\%+1.5\times7\%=14.5\%$

【学习提示】

一家全权益公司的权益 β 等于其资产 β。一家有杠杆公司的权益 β 大于其资产 β。

Ex-interest

The buyer of the ex-interest debt will no longer has the right to receive the interest of this period, so the buyer paid an ex-interest price.

除息

除息后的债务工具的买方不再享有收到本期利息的权利，所以只支付一个除息价。

Ex-interest Market Value

The market value of ex-interest debt.

Ex-interest market value＝cum-interest market value－interest to be paid

除息市值

除息市值是指债务除息后的市值。

除息市值＝含息市值－将要支付的利息

F

Fundamental Theory of Share Valuation

It holds that the market value of a share is the present value of all future cash flows from investing in the shares.

股票估值的基础理论

该理论主张股票的市场价值等于投资股票所得到的所有未来

现金流的现值。

Floating Rate Debt

It refers to the debt which has a variable interest rate.

浮动利率债务

浮动利率债务是指利率变动的债务。

【知识点巩固与拓展】

比如一笔银行贷款，其利率为基准利率加2%。当基准利率为3%时，其利率为5%；当基准利率为4%时，其利率为6%。这笔贷款就是浮动利率的债务。

For example, a bank loan, its interest is charged at base rate plus 2%. If base rate is 3%, its interest rate is 5%, and if base rate rises to 4%, its interest rate rises to 6%. This bank loan is a floating rate debt.

G

Gordon's Growth Approximation

The rate of growth in annual dividend payments can be estimated as $g = br$ (b is the proportion of profits that are retained for future reinvestments, r is the expected rate of return on new investments).

戈登股利增长估计模型

公司派发股利的年增长率可用如下公式估计：$g=br$（b 是指每年公司盈余中留存用来再投资的比例，r 是指新投资的预计回报率）。

【学习提示】

股利增长模型中，股利的增长率(g)是一个关键变量。估算方法有两种：一是根据过去的股利统计数据来估算，二是用戈登股利增长估计模型来估计。

【知识点巩固与拓展】

(1)红星公司的权益回报率平均为 15%，盈利中的 40%留存在企业用来再投资。用戈登股利增长估计模型估计股利增长率。

The average return on equity (ROE) of Redstar Co. is 15%, and it retains 40% of profits earned for future reinvestment. Estimate the annual growth rate of the dividends using Gordon's growth approximation model.

股利年增长率(g)$=15\%\times40\%=6\%$

(2)红星公司过去 5 年的每股股利发放情况如下(Dividends per share for the last five years are as follows)：

2016 年：$ 2.00

2017 年：$ 2.12

2018 年：$ 2.24

2019 年：$ 2.35

2020 年：$2.48

估计股利的年增长率(Estimate the annual growth rate of the dividend)。

估算如下：

$2.00\times(1+g)^4=2.48$

股利的年增长率 $g=5.5\%$

Geared Beta

It is also called equity beta. It is the equity beta of a geared company and reflects both financial risks and business risks of the company.

有杠杆 β

它又叫权益 β，是一家杠杆公司的权益 β，既反映公司的财务风险，又反映公司的经营风险。

【知识点巩固与拓展】

在有税的情况下，资产 $\beta=\frac{Ve}{Vd(1-t)}\times$ 权益 $\beta+\frac{Vd(1-t)}{Ve+Vd(1-t)}\times$ 负债 β，Ve 为权益的市值，Vd 是债务的市值，t 是所得税税率。

一般负债的系统风险可忽略不计，即假设负债 β 为 0，则：

$$资产\ \beta=\frac{Ve}{Ve+Vd(1-t)}\times 权益\ \beta$$

$$权益\ \beta=\frac{Ve+Vd(1-t)}{Ve}\times 资产\ \beta$$

If corporation tax is taking into account, $\beta_a=\frac{Ve}{Ve+Vd(1-t)}\times\beta_e+\frac{Vd(1-t)}{Ve+Vd(1-t)}\times\beta_d$, β_a is asset beta, β_e is equity beta, β_d is debt beta, Ve is market value of equity, Vd is market value of debts, t is corporation tax rate. The systematic risk of debts is negligible, so β_d is assumed to be 0, then

$$\beta_a=\frac{Ve}{Ve+Vd(1-t)}\times\beta_e$$

$$\beta_e=\frac{Ve+Vd(1-t)}{Ve}\times\beta_a$$

I

Irredeemable Debt

It is a debt that has no maturity date and the issuer do not need to redeem it but needs to pay interest in perpetuity.

不可赎回债务

不可赎回债务是没有到期日、发行公司无须赎回但必须永续支付利息的债务。

IRR Approach

It is a method to estimate the cost of redeemable debt or convertible debt. The cost of redeemable debt or convertible debt is the required return by the debtholders, which is the IRR of the investment in the debt with the aim of holding to maturity.

内部收益率法

这是估算可赎回债务或可转债的资本成本的一种方法。可赎回债务或可转债的资本成本就是投资者所要求的回报，即持有至到期债务投资的内部收益率(IRR)。

M

Market Risk

It is also called systematic risk. It is the risk to which all risky investments in the market are exposed, which is brought about by macro-economic factors. A well-diversified investors cannot be protected against it.

市场风险

市场风险又称系统风险，是市场上所有风险投资都要面临的风险，一般是由宏观经济因素所导致的风险。即使是一个充分多样化的投资者，也不能规避此项风险。

Market Return

It refers to the average return of the risky investments in a market.

市场回报

市场回报指某个市场中风险投资的平均回报。

Market Risk Premium

It is also called equity risk premium. It is the excess of the expected rate of return on market portfolio over risk-free rate of return. Market risk premium $=E(r_m)-R_f$.

市场风险溢价

市场风险溢价又称权益风险溢价。它是市场投资组合的平均回报率超过无风险回报率的部分。权益风险溢价＝市场平均回报率－无风险利率。

Market Portfolio

It refers to an investment portfolio that includes all the risk investments in the financial market, with each weighted in proportion to its total presence in the market.

市场投资组合

市场投资组合囊括金融市场上所有风险投资产品的投资组合,并且每种投资产品在组合中所占的比重跟这种投资产品在整个市场上所占的比重是相同的。

Market Imperfections

One or more conditions of a perfect capital market do not exist in the real world. Investors tend to act irrationally. The information that investors get is not the same, and different investors have different risk attitudes and thus different expectations. There are tax and transaction costs.

市场的不完美

在现实世界中，关于完美资本市场存在的条件不成立。投资者的行为往往是非理性的。投资者得到的信息是不同的，不同的投资者对风险的态度是不同的，因此他们的期望也是不同的。还有税收和交易成本。

Marginal Cost of Capital

It indicates the cost of financing one more dollar of capital investment.

边际资本成本

它是指资金每增加一个单位而增加的成本。

【学习提示】

边际资本成本比加权平均资本成本更能体现项目投资所带来的新的风险状况，更适合用作项目投资评估的折现率。

【知识点巩固与拓展】

红星公司原本的资本结构如下：权益——市场价值1 000万美元，票面利率为8%的债券——市场价值200万美元，年利率为6%的银行贷款——市场价值100万美元。

权益资本成本12%，债券的税后资本成本为9%，银行贷款的税后资本成本为4.8%。

现在有一个新的投资项目，投资到全新领域，需要资金400万美元，红星公司准备200万美元权益融资，另外200万美元发行新的债券。考虑到新的项目投资到全新领域以及财务杠杆的增加，权益资本成本增加到13%，新的债券的税后资本成本为9.5%。求新项目的边际资本成本。

边际资本成本＝[(1 200×13%＋200×9%＋200×9.5%＋100×4.8%)－(1 000×12%＋200×9%＋100×4.8%)]÷400＝13.75%

The current capital structure of Redstar Co. is as follows:

Equity—market value ＄10 million

8%bonds—market value ＄2 million

6%bank loan—market value ＄1 million

The cost of equity is 12%, after-tax cost of 8% bonds is 9%, after-tax cost of the bank loan is 4.8%.

A new capital investment project in totally different business area, needs funds of ＄4 million. Redstar Co. is planning to raise ＄2 million equity capital and ＄2 million debt capital by issuing new bonds. As the new business area investment and the increased financial gearing, the cost of equity increases to 13%, and the after-tax cost of new bonds is 9.5%. Calculate the marginal cost of capital for the new project.

Marginal cost of capital＝[(1 200×13%＋200×9%＋200×9.5%＋100×4.8%)－(1 000×12%＋200×9%＋100×4.8%)]÷400＝13.75%

Market Value

The value that is measured by the current market price.

市值

市值是由当前市场价格所计量的价值。

Modigliani-Miller(MM) Theory (Net Operating Income View)

According to this theory, ignoring taxation, a company's capital structure would have no effect on its WACC and business value. The WACC and the business value are only determined by two factors: (1) the total earnings of the company; (2) the business risk level. As the level of financial gearing increases, the WACC keeps constant.

MM 理论(净营业收益观)

根据该理论,如忽略税收因素,一家公司的资本结构不会影响其加权平均资本成本和企业价值。加权平均资本成本和企业价值只受两个因素影响:一是公司的总的盈利水平,二是公司本身的经营风险水平。随着财务杠杆水平的不断提高,加权平均资本成本保持不变。

【学习提示】

MM(无税)理论认为,除了企业本身的盈利能力和经营风险外,其他因素不会影响企业的价值和企业的资本成本。所以资本结构不会影响企业的价值,也不会影响企业的资本成本。因此,找不到一个最佳的资本结构可以使企业价值最大而资本成本最低。

MM(有税)理论认为,增加财务杠杆可以使企业获得更多的因利息费用增加而带来的节税。因此,杠杆越高,企业价值越大,资本成本越低。

MM(有税)理论忽略了因财务杠杆增加而带来的负面效应,比如破产成本和债务代理成本的增加以及可能出现税盾耗尽的现象。

N

Net Operating Income View

That is MM theory(ignoring tax).

净营业收益观

净营业收益观即 MM(无税)理论。

Nominal Value

The par value or face value of a bond or loan note.

名义价值

名义价值是一张债券或借款票据的面值。

O

Optimal Capital Structure

The capital structure where the weighted average cost of capital (WACC) reaches the lowest and the business value reaches the maximum.

最佳资本结构

最佳资本结构是使企业加权平均资本成本(WACC)达到最低而企业价值达到最大的资本结构。

【学习提示】

财务杠杆增加,一方面,在资本结构中,便宜的债务资本所占的比例增加,这拉低了总的资本成本;另一方面,财务杠杆的增加意味着财务风险的增加,权益投资者要求更高的回报率,这拉高了总的资本成本。根据传统理论(traditional view),在财务杠杆较低时,第一项拉低资本成本的作用大于第二项拉高资本成本的作用,所以加权平均资本成本(WACC)随着财务杠杆的增加而降低。等到财务杠杆到达某一临界点,第一个效应与第二个效应相抵,WACC 达到最低点。越过这一点,第二个效应大于第一个效应,WACC 随着杠杆的增加而提高。因此,WACC 的最低点的财务杠杆就代表着最佳的资本结构。

P

Pecking Order Theory

According to this theory, in real world the businesses prefer one source of finance to the other, the order of preference is as follows: retained cash, straight debt, convertible debt, preference shares and ordinary shares.

优序理论(啄序理论)

根据该理论,现实世界中,企业在选择资金渠道时有优先顺序,企业选择资金渠道的先后顺序如下:留存资金、普通债务、可转换债、优先股和普通股。

【学习提示】

企业在融资时,会优先选择内部融资(即留存资金),这个选项的成本和其他负面效应最小。然后选择外部融资。在外部融资渠道中,企业优先选择资本成本低的普通债务,最后选择资本成本最高的权益融资。

Perfect Capital Market

In a perfect capital market, all investors are rational and homogeneous, there is information symmetry, there are no tax or transaction costs, and so there are no arbitrage opportunities. Homogenous investors mean all the investors have the same attitude to risks and they have the same expectations about the same financial assets. Information symmetry refers to all investors get the same information due to the complete transparency in the capital market.

完美资本市场

在完美资本市场里,投资者是理性的、同质的,信息是对称的,没有税收和交易成本,因而也没有任何套利机会。投资者同质意指所有投资者对风险的态度是相同的,因此,对于同一种金融产品,他们的期望也是相同的。信息对称是指由于资本市场的完全透明，投资者得到的信息都是相同的。

Pool of Capital

Funds of a company can be viewed as a pool of financial resources from different sources.

资本池

一家企业的资金可以看作来自不同渠道的财务资源的集中池。

Post-tax Cost of Debt

It refers to after-tax cost of debt.

税后债务成本

税后债务成本是指债务的税后成本。

Portfolio Theory

As the number of securities in an investment portfolio increases, the total risk of the portfolio decreases.

投资组合理论

随着投资组合中所投资的证券数量的增加，投资组合的总体风险下降。

Project-specific Cost of Capital

Cost of capital raised specifically for the project, it should reflect both the new capital structure and the business risk of the new project.

项目的特定资本成本

为特定项目所筹集的资本的成本，它既反映新的资本结构，也反映新项目的经营风险。

【学习提示】

项目的特定资本成本，可以用边际资本成本(marginal cost of capital)计算，也可以用CAPM模型计算。在充分考虑新项目的风险后，先计算项目的权益成本，再计算新的WACC。

【知识点巩固与拓展】

红星公司原本的资本结构如下：权益——市场价值1 000万美元，票面利率为8%的债券——市场价值200万美元，年利率为6%的银行贷款——市场价值100万美元。

权益资本成本12%，债券的税后资本成本为9%，银行贷款的税后资本成本为4.8%，权益β为1.05。

现在有一个新的投资项目，投资到全新领域，需要资金400万美元，红星公司准备200万美元权益融资，另外200万美元发行新的债券。新的项目融资改变了企业目前的资本结构。新的权益β为1.16，新的债券的税后资本成本为9.5%。无风险利率为5%，权益风险溢价为7%。计算项目的特定资本成本。

首先，利用CAPM模型去计算新的权益资本成本：

$5\%+1.16\times7\%=13.12\%$

其次，计算新的WACC，即项目的特定资本成本：

(12×13.12%+2×9%+2×9.5%+1×4.8%)÷(12+2+2+1)=11.72%

The current capital structure of Redstar Co. is as follows:

Equity—market value $10 million

8% bonds—market value $2 million

6% bank loan—market value $1 million

The cost of equity is 12%, after-tax cost of 8% bonds is 9%, after-tax cost of the bank loan is 4.8%, the equity beta is 1.05.

Redstar Co. is planning to invest in a new capital project which is in totally different business area. The project needs funds of $4 million. Redstar Co. is planning to raise $2 million equity capital and $2 million debt capital by issuing new bonds. The new funding will change its current capital structure.

The new equity beta is 1.16, and the cost of new bonds is 9.5%. Risk-free rate is 5%, equity risk premium is 7%. Calculate the project-specific cost of capital.

First, using CAPM to calculate project-specific cost of equity.

New cost of equity=5%+1.16×7%=13.12%

Second, calculate new WACC.

Projcct-specific cost of capital=(12×13.12%+2×9%+2×9.5%+1×4.8%)÷(12+2+2+1)=11.72%

R

Redeemable Debt

It refers to a debt that has a maturity date and must be redeemed at this date by the issuing company.

可赎回债务

可赎回债务是有到期日且发行公司必须在此日期赎回的债务。

Risk-free Securities

They refers to Securities that exposed to negligible risk of default by securities issuer. Usually, government bonds, especially treasury bills, are assumed to be risk-free.

无风险证券

无风险证券是指发行方违约风险几乎可以忽略不计的证券。通常,政府债券,特别是国库券,被认为是无风险的。

Risk-free Rate of Return

It is the rate of return required by investors of risk-free securities.

无风险回报率

这是无风险证券的投资者所要求的回报率。

Risk Premium

It refers to a premium above the risk-free rate of return which is required by the investors of a risky investment for bearing more risk. The higher the risk, the higher the risk premium.

风险溢价

风险投资的投资者因为要承担较高的风险，在无风险回报率之上所要求增加的溢价就是风险溢价。风险越高，风险溢价越高。

S

Systematic Risk

It is a risk that influences a large number of assets in a stock market, each to greater or lesser extent. Because systematic risks have market - wide effects, they are sometimes called market risks. It is the risk that can not be eliminated by diversification.

系统风险

系统风险是指对股票市场上的投资产品或多或少都会有影响的风险。由于系统风险的影响范围是整个市场，因此系统风险又叫市场风险。它是投资者通过投资多样化不能消除的风险。

T

Tax Exhaustion

It refers to a situation where a business incurs enough tax allowable expenses and losses but it has no enough taxable income to enjoy the tax relief of these expenses and losses.

税盾耗尽

它是指如下情形:企业发生了足够多的计税时允许扣减的费用和损失,但因企业缺乏足够的应纳税所得而无法享受这些费用和损失所能带来的税收减少的实惠。

Tax Relief

It is the tax benefits enjoyed by the debtor for paying interest because the interest payment is tax deductible in calculating corporation tax.

税盾

税盾就是债务人因支付利息而少交的所得税。因为所付利息在计算企业所得税时是作为费用在税前扣除的。

Traditional View (of Capital Structure)

The traditional view of capital structure states that there is an optimal capital structure at which WACC is lowest and the business value is highest. With the rising of financial gearing level, WACC falls initially and then begins to increase. It assumes the company can change financial gearing immediately and incur no transaction cost. It also assumes constant business risk and expected earnings.

资本结构传统观

传统观认为企业可以达到最佳资本结构,这时加权平均资本成本最低而企业价值最大。随着企业财务杠杆水平的提高,加权平均资本成本起初下降，等达到最低点后开始增加。这种观点是基于如下假设：公司可以随时改变财务杠杆而不会发生任何交易成本，且企业经营风险和期望收益不变。

U

Ungeared Beta

Also called asset beta.

无杠杆 β

它又称资产 β。

【学习提示】

如果两家公司除了资本结构外，其他各方面都相似，特别是属于相同的行业，在相同的地理区域经营，那么这两家公司的资产 β 或者无杠杆 β 就相同，因为它们的经营风险相同。

【知识点巩固与拓展】

如果已知一家经营风险相似的公司的权益 β 值，我们就可以利用公式 $\beta_a = \frac{Ve}{Ve+Vd(1-t)} \times \beta_e$ 求出所投项目的资产 β。再利用公式 $\beta_e = \frac{Ve+Vd(1-t)}{Ve} \times \beta_a$ 求出企业自己的新的权益 β。

If a proxy company who has similar business risk as the new

project, and its equity beta is known, we can use the formula $\beta_a = \frac{Ve}{Ve+Vd(1-t)} \times \beta_e$ to get asset β of the new project. And then using the formula $\beta_e = \frac{Ve+Vd(1-t)}{Ve} \times \beta_a$ to calculate the new equity beta of the business.

【知识点巩固与拓展】

红星公司投资一个新项目，与以前的经营领域完全不同。A公司是新的经营领域的一家平均水平的公司，其权益β为1.24，以市值表示的资本结构为40%的债务、60%的权益。新的项目融资后，红星公司以市值表示的资本结构为50%的债务、50%的权益。企业所得税税率为20%。计算红星公司新的权益β。

首先，把A公司的权益β剔除财务杠杆因素，得到资产β。

$$\beta_a = \frac{Ve}{Ve+Vd(1-t)} \times \beta_e = 60/(60+40\times 0.80) \times 1.24 = 0.81$$

其次，重新考虑红星公司的新的财务杠杆，利用资产β求出新的权益β。

$$\beta_e = \frac{Ve+Vd(1-t)}{Ve} \times \beta_a = (50+50\times 0.80)/50 \times 0.81 = 1.46$$

Redstar Co. has a new project, which is in totally different business area.

Company A is an average company in the new business area, its equity beta is 1.24, and its market value based capital structure is 40% debt, 60% equity.

After the new project finance, Redstar's new market value

based capital structure is 50% debt and 50% equity. Corporation tax rate is 20%. Calculate the new equity beta of Redstar Co..

First, degear β_e of Company A to get β_a.

$\beta_a = Ve/[Ve+Vd(1-t)]\times\beta_e$

$=60/(60+40\times0.80)\times1.24$

$=0.81$

Second, regear β_a to get new β_e of Redstar Co.

$\beta_e = [Ve+Vd(1-t)]/Ve\times\beta_a$

$=(50+50\times0.80)/50\times0.81$

$=1.46$

Unsystematic Risk

It is also called unique or asset-specific risk. It is a risk that affects at most a small number of assets in a stock market, which is brought about by factors specific to an industry or a company. It is the risk that can be eliminated by diversification.

非系统风险

非系统风险也称独有风险或某种投资产品的特有风险，是只影响股票市场上一小部分投资产品的风险，是由只影响特定行业和特定公司的因素所导致的。它是投资者通过投资多样化可以消除的风险。

Unique Risk

Another name for unsystematic risk.

特有风险

特有风险是非系统风险的另一种叫法。

V

Variable Rate Debt

That is floating rate debt. The lender charges an interest rate which varies with the prevailing interest rate.

变动利率债务

变动利率债务即浮动利率债务。借款方收取的利率根据市场当前的利率波动而变动。

W

Weighted Average Cost of Capital（WACC）

It is the average cost of the funds raised by a company, weighted according to the proportion of each source of finance in the total pool of capital.

加权平均资本成本

这是企业筹集资金的平均成本，根据每种来源的资本在企业总资本中所占的比例为权数计算出来的加权平均数。

【学习提示】

建议用以下模板来计算加权平均资本成本。

sources	cost of capital	market value	cost of capital×market value
equity			
debt			

【知识点巩固与拓展】

红星公司原本的资本结构如下：权益——市场价值 1 000 万美元，票面利率为 8%的债券——市场价值 200 万美元，年利率为 6%的银行贷款——市场价值 100 万美元。

权益资本成本 12%，债券的税后资本成本为 9%，银行贷款的税后资本成本为 4.8%。

计算红星公司目前的加权平均资本成本。

资金来源	资本成本	市值(百万美元)	资本成本×市值(百万美元)
权益	12%	10	1.2
票面利率为8%的债券	9%	2	0.18
年利率为 6%的银行贷款	4.8%	1	0.048
总　计		13	1.428

加权平均资本成本=1.428/13=10.98%

The current capital structure of Redstar Co. is as follows:

Equity—market value \$10 million

8% bonds—market value \$2 million

6% bank loan—market value \$1 million

The cost of equity is 12%, after-tax cost of 8% bonds is 9%, after-tax cost of the bank loan is 4.8%.

Calculate the current WACC.

sources	cost of capital	market value (\$m)	cost of capital × market value (\$m)
equity	12%	10	1.2
8% bond	9%	2	0.18
6% bank loan	4.8%	1	0.048
total		13	1.428

$WACC = 1.428/13 = 10.98\%$

Unsecured Creditors

Lenders that lend money to the debtor without any assets as security.

无担保债权人

无担保债权人就是没有任何资产作为担保而借款给债务人的借款方。

Module Six

Business Valuation/企业估值

本单元的学习目标：熟悉和掌握权益估值与债务估值的影响因素以及估值方法，了解各种估值方法的优缺点。

A

Asset Valuation Bases

Valuing business based on the worth of assets. It is appropriate for valuing the business whose value comes mainly from the assets.

基于资产的估值

基于资产的价值对企业进行估值。它适合那些价值主要来自资产的企业。

【知识点巩固与拓展】

有些资产没有市场价值，另外一些企业的有价值的资源，比如品牌价值、人力资源的价值、渠道价值、社会关系的价值以及创新能力等没有在资产负债表里列示。这些都没包含在基于资产的估值中。

Some assets do not have a market value, and other valuable economic resources such as brand name, human resources, business channels, social relationship and innovation potential are not shown in the statement of financial position. These are all excluded from asset-base valuation.

Allocative Efficiency

Funds allocation in the financial market are directed to the most productive use of them. This kind of financial market is allocatively efficient.

资本配置的有效性

金融市场的资金配置导向是资金产出效率高的项目优先。这种金融市场的资本配置就是有效的。

B

Behavioural finance

It is an alternative view to EMH, which proposes to use psychology-based theories to explain financial market anomalies and suggests that psychological factors do affect investor decisions and investors may not always be rational.

行为金融学

行为金融学是不同于有效市场假设的另一种金融领域的观点，它建议使用基于心理学的理论来解释金融市场的异常现象，并且认为心理因素确实会影响投资者的决策，投资者并不是一直都保持理性。

【学习提示】

行为金融学可以很好地解释金融市场对信息的过度反应、价格异常波动以及股票市场的泡沫与崩盘等。

Business Valuations

Putting a value on a business or on shares of a business.

企业估值

企业估值是对整个企业或企业的股权进行估值。

【学习提示】

关于估值，一定要区分是对整个企业进行估值还是对企业的股权进行估值。企业总的价值(business value)等于其股权价值(share value)加上债权价值(debt value)。对股权进行估值时，要区分是对控制权益(controlling interest)进行估值还是对非控制权益(non-controlling interest)进行估值。

C

Cash Flow Based Valuation Models

Valuing business or shares based on future cash flows obtained from the business or share investment. It bases on the idea that the business value comes mainly from cash flows created by it.

基于现金流的估值方法

这是一种根据从企业或股票投资中获得的现金流来对企业或股票进行估值的方法。它的基本理念是企业价值主要来自其所创造的现金流。

【学习提示】

股利估值模型和折现现金流估值法都属于基于现金流的估值方法。基于现金流的估值方法一般是投资者把投资预计获得的未来现金流用自己所要求的回报率进行折现而估算出现值。除了股票和企业价值可以基于现金流来估值外,优先股和债务的估值也都可以用这种方法。

Coupon Rate

Stated interest rate on a debt, usually expressed in a percentage of nominal value of the debt. For example, for a 6% bond, its coupon rate is 6%.

票面利率

票面利率是某项债务的指明的利率，一般以票面价值的一定百分比来表示。比如，对于6％的债券，其票面利率为6％。

Charting or Technical Analysis

A method of predicting share price, which attempts to predict share price by studying past price movements and assuming there are regular price patterns in share price movements and past price patterns will repeat in future.

K线分析或技术分析法

这是预测股价的一种方法，通过研究股价在过去的变动情况来预测未来的股价，往往假设股价的波动是有规律可循的，而且过去的股价变化模式在将来还会重复。

Collateral

Physical assets or marketable securities that pledged as security for a debt.

担保品

作为某项债务的担保品而被抵押或质押的有形资产或者有价证券。

D

Discounted Cash Flow Method of Share Valuation

A method of valuing shares whereby the cash flows of the target company in the foreseeable future are discounted at an appropriate discount rate to get a present value. This method may be appropriate when one company intends to acquire the target company.

现金流折现估值法

这是一种股票估值法，把目标公司在可预见的未来的现金流用一个合适的折现率折现来得到现值。一家企业想收购目标企业时，此方法也可适用。

【知识点巩固与拓展】

现金流折现估值法有两种。一是减去利息和税后的现金流，是属于普通股股东的现金流，用普通股股东要求的回报率（权益资本成本）来折现算出现值，即股权的估值。二是未减去利息的现金流，是属于所有投资者的现金流，应该用加权平均资本成本来折现算出现值，即企业总的价值，减去债务价值后得到股权估值。

1. If cash flows are after interest payments and tax, these cash flows are attributable to ordinary shareholders and should be discounted at cost of equity. The present value is the valuation of

shares.

2. If cash flows are before interest payments, these cash flows represent cash flows to all investors (including shareholders and lenders) and should be discounted at weighted average cost of capital (WACC). The present value is the total business value. The debt value needs to be deducted from the business value to get the value of equity.

Dividend Valuation Model of Share Valuation

The share price that an investor is willing to pay now is the present value of future expected income (such as dividends) from the share. If a constant dividend per year is assumed, the model can be expressed as follows: $MV = D/k_e$ (D is constant annual dividend, k_e is shareholder's required rate of return or cost of equity).

股利估值模型

投资者目前愿意支付的股价是其所投资的股票未来预期收益(比如股利)的现值。如果假设股东每年得到的股利是固定不变的,则该模型可用下面的公式表示股票市值:$MV = D/k_e$(D 指固定不变的年股利,k_e 指股东所要求的回报率或指权益资本的成本)。

【学习提示】

股利估值模型适合对少数股权(非控制权益)进行估值。假设投资者是理性的,投资者的期望是一致的,市场上的信息是对称的,且企业维持稳定的、可预

测的股利政策。因为股票的市值不会低于0,所以必须有 $k_e>g$。

Dividend Growth Model of Share Valuation

The price that an investor is willing to pay now is the present value of future expected income (such as dividends) from the share. If annual dividend is assumed to grow at a constant annual rate, the model can be expressed as follows: $MV=D_0(1+g)/(k_e-g)=D_1/(k_e-g)$ (D_0 is current year's dividend, g is annual growth rate in dividends, D_1 is expected dividend of next year, ke is shareholder's required rate of return or cost of equity).

股利增长模型

投资者目前愿意支付的股价是其所投资的股票未来预期收益(比如股利)的现值。如果假设股东每年得到的股利的年增长率是固定的,则该模型可用如下公式表示:股票市值$=D_0(1+g)/(k_e-g)=D_1/(k_e-g)$($D_0$ 是当年度的股利,g 是股利的固定不变的年增长率,D_1 是下一年度的预计股利,k_e 指股东所要求的回报率或指权益资本的成本)。

【知识点巩固与拓展】

红星公司拟购买蓝天公司的一小部分股权,现用股利估值模型来对蓝天公司的股权进行估值。有关信息如下:蓝天公司上一年度派发的股利为每股5美元,蓝天公司多年来一直维持年平均增长率为2%的股利政策。蓝天公司的权益资本成本为14%。蓝天公司发行在外面值为1美元的普通股股票有1 000万股。

用股利增长模型来估值。

蓝天公司的每股价值＝5×(1＋2%)/(14%－2%)＝42.5(美元)

蓝天公司的股权总价值＝42.5×1 000万＝42 500万(美元)

Redstar Co. plans to acquire a small proportion of Bluesky Co. 's shares and dividend valuation model is used to value shares of Bluesky Co. The following information is available:

—Last year, Bluesky Co. distributed a dividend of $5 per share.

—For years, Bluesky Co. maintains a stable dividend policy with an average annual growth rate of 2%.

—The cost of equity is 14%.

—Bluesky Co. has 10 million of outstanding $1 ordinary shares.

Using dividend growth model.

Value per share= $5×(1+2%)/(14%−2%)= $42.5

Total equity value= $42.5×10m= $425 million

E

Earnings Yield (EY) Valuation Method

If a constant annual earnings of the target company is assumed, MV = earnings/EY or MV = earnings/K_e (EY is earnings yield, K_e is cost of equity); if a constant growth rate for annual earnings of the target company is assumed, MV = earnings$(1+g)/(EY-g)$ or MV = earnings$(1+g)/(K_e-g)$ (EY is earnings yield, K_e is cost of equity, g is annual growth rate of earnings).

股票盈利收益率估值法

如果假设目标公司的每年盈利是固定不变的，则其股票的市值＝每年盈利/盈利收益率，或者，股票市值＝每年盈利/目标公司的权益资本的成本；如果假设目标公司的盈利每年呈固定的增长率，则股票市值＝本年盈利×(1＋年增长率)/(盈利收益率－年增长率)，或者，股票市值＝本年盈利×(1＋年增长率)/(权益资本成本－年增长率)。

【知识点巩固与拓展】

红星公司要收购蓝天公司的股权，拟用盈利收益率法来估值。蓝天公司目前的盈利收益率为4%，上一年度的每股收益为3美元，蓝天公司发行在外1 000万股。(1)预计蓝天公司的归属于股东的盈利每年维持在5 000万美元；(2)预计蓝天公司的归属于股东的盈利每年以1%的增长率增长。

股权估值如下：

(1)每股价值＝3/4%＝75(美元)，股权总价值＝75×1 000万＝75 000万(美元)

(2)每股价值＝3(1＋1%)/(4%－1%)＝101(美元)，股权总价值＝101×1 000万＝101 000万(美元)

Redstar Co. is planning to acquire a proportion of Bluesky Co.'s shares. Earnings yield valuation method is used to value shares.

—Currently, the earnings yield of Bluesky Co. is 4%.

—Last year, its EPS is \$3.

—Bluesky Co. has 10 million of outstanding ordinary shares.

(1) If earnings attributable to ordinary shares per year maintains $\$50$ million.

(2) If earnings attributable to ordinary shareholders grows at an annual rate of 1%.

(1) Value per share $=3/4\%=75$

Total value of equity $=\$75\times 10\text{m}=\$750\text{m}$

(2) Value per share $=\$3(1+1\%)/(4\%-1\%)=\$101$

Total value of equity $=\$101\times 10\text{m}=\$1\,010\text{m}$

Efficient Market Hypothesis (EMH)

The hypothesis that share prices in the stock market have reflected all available information and no investors can consistently achieve returns in excess of average market returns. Efficiency refers to information processing efficiency in the stock market. EMH takes three forms: weak form efficiency, semi-strong form and strong-form efficiency.

有效市场假说

假设股票市场的股价已反映所有可得信息，没有任何投资者的获利可持续超过市场平均回报率。有效是指股票市场的信息处理有效。有效市场假说有三种形式的假设：弱型有效、半强型有效、强型有效。

F

Floor Value

The minimum value.

最低值

最小值。

H

Historical Basis (Net Book Value)

One of assets valuation basis, on which assets are valued on historical cost basis, that is on book value basis.

历史成本计价基础(账面净值)

这是资产计价的基础之一,资产以历史成本为基础计价,即以账面价值为计价基础。

【学习提示】

以历史成本为计价基础很难正确地反映资产的真实价值,因此,在以资产为基础的估值方法中,历史成本计价基础被弃用。

|

Income-based Valuation Bases

Valuing business based on income earned by the company. It is based on the idea that business value comes mainly from the earning power of the business.

基于收益的估值方法

基于公司所赚得的收益来对企业进行估值。它的基本理念是企业的价值主要来自其盈利能力。

【学习提示】

基于收益的估值方法，有市盈率法(P/E method)和盈利收益率法(earnings yield method)。

估值中用到的收益最好是未来可持续收益的预估值。

Interest Yield

The rate of return to debt investors at the form of coupon interest. It can be calculated as coupon interest per bond/market price per bond.

票息收益率

票息收益率是以票息形式给予债权投资人的回报率。计算公式为:票息收益率=每张债券的票息÷每张债券的市价。

【学习提示】

新的债权投资者，以当前市价买进一张债券，这是其投资成本，票息是每年获得的票面利息，因此，用票息除以投资成本，就算出了票息形式的年投资回报率。

Inside Information

Material information about a company that has not been made available to the public and that is known only by the insiders.

内部信息

这是关于公司的重大信息，还没有对公众披露，只有公司内部人知晓。

Information Processing Efficiency

The efficiency of a stock market to process information available. The market price of securities reflects all the available information quickly and fairly.

信息处理的有效性

即股票市场处理信息的有效性。证券的价格对所有可得的信息进行快速而公允的反映。

【学习提示】

有效市场假说（EMH）中的“有效市场”就是指信息处理的有效性（information processing efficiency）。

L

Liquidity of Shares

It refers to how easy it is to buy and sell shares without significant change in share prices. The market for a share is said to be liquid if the shares can be rapidly sold and the act of selling has little impact on the share price.

股票的流动性

股票流动性是指在没造成股价重大波动的情况下买卖股票的难易程度。如果某股票可以被快速卖掉而对股价影响甚微,那就可以说这种股票的流动性好。

M

Marketability of Shares

A measure of the transferability of a share from one investor to another. If there is an active marketplace for a share, it has good marketability. Marketability is similar to liquidity, except that liquidity emphasizes no big change in share price.

股票的可交易性

该指标衡量股票从一个投资者转给另一个投资者的难易程度。如果该股票有活跃的交易市场,它就有好的可交易性。可交易性类似于流动性，只不过流动性强调交易后股价无重大变动。

Management Buyout

A transaction where the management team of a company takes over controlling interest or acquires all the assets and operations of the business, after which the management team becomes the controlling shareholders of the company.

管理层收购

这是指管理层收购公司的控股权或者购买公司的所有资产和经营业务的交易。自此，管理层变成公司的控股股东。

【学习提示】

管理层收购，也需要对公司或公司的股权进行估值。

Market Capitalization

The total market value of a company's shares.

股票总市值

一家公司的股票的总市值。

【知识点巩固与拓展】

蓝天公司发行在外的面值为 1 美元的普通股有 1 000 万股，当前市价为每股 50 美元。求蓝天公司目前的股票总市值。

蓝天公司目前股票总市值＝1 000 万×50＝

50 000 万(美元)

Bluesky Co. has 10 million of outstanding $1 ordinary shares, current market price is $50 per share. What is market capitalization of the equity?

Market capitalization of the equity = 10 million × $50 = $500 million

Market Imperfections

Various types of anomalies exist in the stock market, such as overreaction to some events, share price rising or falling at a particular time of the year, week or day etc.

市场的非完美性

这是指股票市场存在的各种异常现象,比如对某些事件的过度反应,在一年、一周或者一天内某个时刻股价的上涨或下跌等。

Merger

A business combination of two or more firms on roughly equal terms into one new legal entity.

兼并

两家或多家企业在平等条款的基础上合并成一个新的法律实体。

【学习提示】

兼并,也需要对企业或企业的股权进行估值。

N

Net Asset Method of Share Valuation

A method of share valuation based on the net asset value of the whole business. The total equity value is equal to the total asset value net of total liabilities of a company. Usually, assets are valued on a realizable basis, the net asset valuation provides a 'floor value' for a business that is up for sale and acts as a measure of the asset backing value for shares of a business.

净资产估值法

这是基于企业的净资产价值的一种股票估值方法。企业的权益总值等于企业的总资产价值减去企业的总债务价值。通常，资产以可实现净值计价。此净资产估值是被购并企业能接受的最低出价，同时，又是购并企业股票投资的资产担保价值。

【学习提示】

净资产估值法的思路是会计等式，即资产＝负债＋权益，则权益＝资产－负债。净资产估值法有两种资产的计价基础：一是可实现净值，二是重置成本。

Noise Trader

A trader who buys and sells shares emotionally and irrationally, often based on information he or she believes to be well-founded and will give him or her a better return but in reality not.

噪音交易者

感性且非理性地买卖股票的交易者。其交易往往基于他或她认为的有充分根据且会带来更好收益的信息，而现实并非如此。

【学习提示】

噪音交易者的存在是对有效市场假说的挑战，印证了市场中非完美性和非理性因素的存在。

O

Operational Efficiency

Transaction costs in a financial market are kept very low, as there is open competition and pricing transparency. This kind of financial markets are operationally efficient.

市场运转的有效性

由于存在公开竞争和定价的透明，因此某金融市场的交易成本维持在较低水平。这样的金融市场就具备市场运转的有效性。

P

P/E Ratio Method of Share Valuation

A method of share valuation. The total equity value = P/E

ratio of a target company ×the expected total annual earnings of the target company. It is the market appraisal of share value of a business.

股票估值的市盈率法

这是股票估值的一种方法。权益总值=目标公司的市盈率×年盈利。它是市场对企业股票价值的估计。

【学习提示】

这是基于收益的一种股票估值方法。其估值要确定两个因素:一是合适的市盈率(P/E ratio),二是恰当的收益值(earnings)。这两个因素的确定都带有主观性。市盈率一般参照行业平均市盈率或者与被购并企业各方面相当的上市公司的市盈率。同时,考虑不同企业的成长性和风险水平,做一些适当的调整。收益值可以参考被购并企业过去的平均收益值,也可以采用基于一定假设的预测值。

【知识点巩固与拓展】

红星公司目前正考虑购买蓝天公司的股权。蓝天公司是一家非上市公司,其所在行业上市公司的平均市盈率为20,蓝天公司过去5年的平均收益为5 000万美元。用市盈率法对蓝天公司的股权进行估值。

行业上市公司平均市盈率为20,因为蓝天公司是非上市公司,又因其盈利较稳定,所以其市盈率可适当下调为20×2/3=13。

蓝天公司股权价值=5 000万×13=65 000万(美元)

Redstar Co. is planning to acquire a significant proportion of shares of Bluesky Co.. Bluesky Co. is an unquoted company. Average P/E ratio of listed companies in the same industry as Bluesky Co. is 20. The average earnings attributable to ordinary shareholders in the past five years is \$50 million. Calculate the equity value of Bluesky Co. using P/E ratio method.

Average P/E ratio of listed companies in the same industry as Bluesky Co. is 20. As Blusky Co. is an unquoted company and its earnings are stable in past years, so its P/E ratio $=20\times2/3=13$.

The value of equity $=$ \$50 million $\times13=$ \$650 million

Pricing Anomalies

A price distortion on a financial market that seems to contradict the efficient market hypothesis, such as January effect.

定价异常

金融市场里与有效市场假设相悖的价格扭曲，比如一月效应。

Projection

A well-informed plan based on estimates of future amounts.

规划

基于充分信息，根据对未来数据的预估来制订的计划。

R

Random Walk Theory

The actual share price of a company fluctuates around the intrinsic value. The intrinsic price depends on the fortunes of the company and the market expectations of prospects of the company. Share prices in future evolve according to a random walk and thus cannot be predicted.

随机游走理论

实际的股价围绕企业内在价值上下波动。内在价值是由企业的财富和市场对该企业前景的预期来决定的。股价是随机游走的,无法预测。

Realizable Basis

The assets are valued at a net realizable value on a break-up basis. That is, the business is assumed to be liquidated, the proceeds from selling assets are used to pay off liabilities first, and the remaining is to be distributed to equity shareholders.

可实现净值计价基础

假设企业将要倒闭,资产以可实现净值计价。即,假设企业要破产清算,变卖资产的收入在清偿债务后的剩余部分则属于普通股股东。

【学习提示】

这是企业最糟糕的情况下股权的估值,是卖方企业可以接受的最低价。

【知识点巩固与拓展】

蓝天公司净资产的账面价值为 5 000 万美元。商誉的账面价值为 150 万美元。固定资产的可实现净值比账面价值高 200 万美元，存货的可实现净值比账面价值高 50 万美元，应收账款的可实现净值比账面价值低 75 万美元。请用净资产估值法(可实现净值计价基础)对蓝天公司的股权进行估值。

股权总价值＝5 000－150＋200＋50－75＝5 025 万(美元)

The net assets value (book value) of Bluesky Co. is ＄50 million. The carrying amount of Goodwill is ＄1.5 million. The NRV of tangible non-current assets is ＄2 million greater than the book value. The NRV of inventory is ＄0.5 million greater than the book value. The NRV of accounts receivable is ＄0.75 million lower than the book value. Calculate the value of equity using net assets valuation (realizable basis) method.

Value of equity＝＄50－＄1.5＋＄2＋＄0.5－＄0.75＝＄50.25(million)

Replacement Cost Basis

The assets are valued at current replacement cost, that is the cost of net assets if the same business is established from scratch.

重置成本计价基础

资产以当前重置成本计价，即重新建立一家一模一样的企业所需要的净资产的成本。

【学习提示】

这是从零开始建立一家相同的企业所要耗费的成本。它是买方企业能够接受的最高价。

【知识点巩固与拓展】

蓝天公司净资产的账面价值为 5 000 万美元。商誉的账面价值为 150 万美元。固定资产的重置成本比账面价值高 1 000 万美元，存货的重置成本比账面价值高 100 万美元。请用净资产估值法(重置成本计价基础)对蓝天公司的股权进行估值。

股权价值＝5 000－150＋1 000＋100＝5 950 万(美元)

The net assets value (book value) of Bluesky Co. is $50 million. The carrying amount of Goodwill is $1.5 million. The current replacement cost of tangible non-current assets is $10 million greater than the book value. The current replacement cost of inventory is $1 million greater than the book value. Calculate the value of equity using net assets valuation (replacement basis) method.

Value of equity＝$50－$1.5＋$10＋$1＝$59.5(million)

S

Semi-strong Form Efficiency

Under semi-strong form efficiency hypothesis, the current share price reflects not only information about past share price movements but also publicly available information.

半强型有效假说

在半强型有效假说下，当前的股价不仅反映关于过去股价变动的信息，而且反映当前所有已公布的信息。

Strong Form Efficiency

Under strong-form hypothesis, the current share price reflects all information including inside information.

强型有效假说

在强型有效假说下，当前股价反映所有信息，包括内部信息。

Speculation

Sell when most investors are buying and buy when most investors are selling in order to take advantage of unexpected opportunities and obtain abnormal profits.

投机

等大部分投资者在买进的时候卖出而在大部分投资者卖出的时候买进，目的是抓住意外的机会而获得超额利润。

T

Takeover

The acquisition of one company's controlling interest by another. If the target company is publicly traded, the acquiring company will make an offer for the outstanding shares.

股权收购

股权收购就是指一家公司购买另一家公司的控股权。如果目标公司是上市公司，则收购公司一般会对其发行在外的股票进行要约收购。

【学习提示】

股权收购，需要对收购企业的股权进行估值。

V

Valuation of Debt

Putting a value on a debt of a company.

债务估值

对一家公司的债务进行估值。

Valuation of Shares

Putting a value on a company's shares or equity.

股票估值/股权估值

对一家公司的股票或权益进行估值。

W

Weak-form Efficiency

Under the weak-form efficiency hypothesis, all available information about past share price changes is reflected in current share prices.

弱型有效假说

在弱型有效假说下,所有关于过去股价变动的可得信息都已在当前股价中反映。

Window Dressing of the Accounts

The act of manipulating financial data in order to make financial statements appear better to outside investors.

粉饰报表

为了使报表对外部投资者来说看起来更好而操纵财务数据的做法。

Module Seven

Risk Management/风险管理

本单元的学习目标：

（1）掌握影响汇率的因素；

（2）掌握外汇风险的种类；

（3）掌握管理外汇风险的方法和工具；

（4）掌握影响利率和利率期限结构的因素；

（5）掌握利率风险的种类；

（6）掌握管理利率风险的方法和工具。

A

Ask Price

It is also called offer price. It is the exchange rate at which the bank sells foreign currency and importers buy foreign currency.

银行卖出价

银行卖出价就是银行卖出外币即进口商买进外币的汇率。

B

Basis(Futures)

The difference between spot price and futures price of a specific asset.

基差(期货)

基差是指某资产的现货成交价与交易所期货价的价差。

Basis Risk(Interest Rate Risk Management)

The risk exposed by the imperfect correlation between base rates across different interest rate markets for similar maturities. For example, a bank funding loans whose payments are based on U. S. Treasury rates with deposits based on LIBOR rates is exposed to the risk of unexpected changes in the spread between these base rates

基准风险(利率风险管理)

相同期限的贷款或存款在不同的利率市场上所用的利率基准是不完全相关的,由此给企业带来的风险被称为基准风险。例如:一家银行的存款利率基准为伦敦同业拆借利率而其所支持的贷款利率基准为美国国债利率,那这家银行将面临这两种不同利率基准之间的基准差的突然变化给其带来的风险。

Bid Price

The exchange rate at which the bank buys foreign currency and exporters sell foreign currency.

银行买进价

银行买进价就是银行买进外币即出口商卖出外币的汇率。

C

(Currency) Call Option

The option to buy a specified quantity of one specified currency at a specified exchange rate on or before a specified future date.

看涨(货币)期权

看涨期权就是在指定的未来某个日期或之前,以指定汇率购买指定数量的指定货币的选择权。

Closing Out (of Forward Exchange Contracts)

If a customer cannot satisfy a forward exchange contract, the bank will force the customer to fulfil the contract. If according to the forward contract, the customer should sell a certain amount of a foreign currency, the bank will sell the same amount of the foreign currency to the customer at spot rate first. And if according to the forward contract, the customer should buy a certain amount of a foreign currency, the bank will arrange to buy the same amount of the foreign currency first.

终结(远期外汇合约)

如果一远期外汇合约的客户如期不能履约,银行就会强制这个客户履行合同。如果根据远期合约,客户需卖出一定数量的某种外币,银行就将首先以即期汇率卖给这个客户相同数量的该种外币。如果根据远期合约,客户需买进一定数量的某种外币,银行就会首先以即期汇率从这个客户处买进相同的该种外币。

Currency Futures

A standardized, exchange-traded contract to buy or sell a specified amount of a foreign currency at the futures rate at a specified future date.

货币期货

这是一种标准化的、在期货交易所交易的合约,确定在未来某一特定日期以期货市场报出的汇率买进或卖出特定数量的外币。

【学习提示】

因为期货是在交易所买卖的(Exchange-traded),所以交易活跃,定价透明(pricing transparency),交易成本(transaction costs)较低。但期货是标准化合约(standardized contract),不管从时间上还是金额上,都很难按照企业自己的需求量身定制(tailored to the exact requirements),因而难以完美对冲风险(perfect hedging),且只有有

限的货币期货产品。

Currency of Invoice

The currency in which the invoice value is denominated and thus the currency in which settlement is made.

开票货币

开票货币是确定发票金额所用的货币，即结算所用的货币。

【学习提示】

为了规避外币交易风险，外贸中尽量争取用本国货币来开票和结算。

Currency Option

A right of an option holder to buy or sell a specified amount of foreign currency at a specific exchange rate at a specified future date.

货币期权

这是期权的持有方在未来某一特定日期以特定的汇率购买或出售特定数量外币的选择权。

【学习提示】

货币期权既可以使企业规避不利的汇率变动对其形成的不利影响，又可以使企业充分利用有利的汇率变动对其形成的有利影响。且能损失的最大金额就是购买期权的期权费(premium)。但期权费是购买期权的必需成本。

【知识点巩固与拓展】

有两种期权：一种是跟银行柜台商定的期权，另一种是在交易所交易的期权。

There are two kinds of options available: one is negotiated options, the other is Exchange-traded options.

Currency Swap

A formal agreement whereby two parties agree to exchange of debt from one currency to another.

货币互换

这是交易双方同意交换不同币种的债务的正式合约。

【学习提示】

相比远期外汇合约、货币期货等，货币互换可以对冲相对较长期限的汇率变动风险，它也是从他国获取融资的一种方式。

D

(Financial) Derivatives

Financial instruments that derive value from a specific financial instrument or an indicator or acommodity. For example, futures, options and swaps etc.

金融衍生工具

价值派生于标的金融工具、标的指标或标的商品价值的金融工具,如期货、期权、互换等。

E

Exchange Rate

The price at which one currency is exchanged for another currency.

汇率

汇率就是一种货币换成另一种货币的价格。

【学习提示】

汇率有两种表示形式:

一种是一个单位的本币等于多少外币。比如一家英国的企业,本币是英镑,英镑兑美元的汇率为 1 英镑=1.388 2 美元。

另一种是一个单位的外币等于多少本币。比如一家中国的企业,本币是人民币,美元兑人民币的汇率为 1 美元=6.510 4 元人民币。

在外币折算时,注意这两种不同的汇率表示方式的区别。

【知识点巩固与拓展(一)】

银行报出的汇率有两个:一个是企业买进价(银行卖出价),另一个是企业卖出价(银行买进价)。

比如,英镑兑美元:1.387 3～1.388 2 美元/英镑。对于一家英国的企业,1 英镑=1.387 3 美元是美元的买进价,1 英镑=1.388 2 美元是美元的卖出价。

再如,美元兑人民币:6.508 8～6.510 4 元人民币/美元。一家中国企业,美元的买进价是 1 美元=6.510 4 元人民币,美元的卖出价是 1 美元=6.508 8 元人民币。

There are two exchange rates quoted by banks, one is for companies to buy foreign currencies (for the bank to sell foreign currencies, offer price), the other is for companies to sell foreign currencies (for the bank to buy foreign currencies, bid price). For example, one day the exchange rates between sterling and dollars are quoted as follows: \$1.387 3－\$1.388 2 per £. For a UK company, if it wants to buy dollars, the applicable exchange rate is £1=\$1.387 3, and if it wants to sell dollars, the applicable exchange rate is £1=\$1.388 2.

Another example, the quoted exchange rates between dollars and CNY is 6.508 8－6.510 4 CNY per dollar. The exchange rate for a China's company to buy dollars is \$1=6.510 4 CNY, and the exchange rate for a China's company to sell dollars is \$1=6.508 8CNY.

【知识点巩固与拓展(二)】

蓝天公司从英国出口货物到美国。美国客户马上要支付 9 000 万美元给蓝天公司。汇率为 1.387 3～1.388 2 美元/英镑。则这笔收入的英镑价值是多少？

蓝天公司需要卖出美元。适用汇率为 1 英镑＝1.388 2 美元。故英镑收入＝90 000 000/1.388 2＝64 832 157(英镑)。

Bluesky Co. exports from UK to USA. A customer will pay it \$90 million shortly. The exchange rates are：\$1.387 3—1.388 2 per. What is the sterling revenue from this customer?

Bluesky Co. needs to sell dollars. The applicable exchange rate is \$1.388 2 per £. The sterling revenue = 90 000 000/1.388 2 = £64 832 157.

【知识点巩固与拓展(三)】

红星公司在中国运营。最近该公司从美国进口了一批成本为 600 万美元的材料。结算日的汇率报价为 6.508 8～6.510 4 人民币/美元。则这批材料的人民币成本为多少？

红星公司需要买进美元，适用的汇率是 1 美元＝6.510 4 元人民币，故人民币成本＝600 万×6.510 4＝3 906.24 万(元)。

Redstar Co. operates in China. It imported some materials costing \$6 million from America recently. The exchange rate quoted at settlement date is 6.5088 ～ 6.5104 CNY per dollar. What is the CNY cost of the materials?

Redstar Co. needs to buy ＄6 million dollars, so the applicable exchange rate is ＄1=6.510 4 CNY.

The CNY cost=6×6.510 4=39 062 400

Exercise Price

The price at which the option is exercised. For currency option, it is the specified exchange rate at which the specified quantity of one specified currency is bought or sold on or before the option's expiry rate.

行权价

行权价是期权最后的执行价格。对于货币期权，指在指定行权日或之前指定数量的指定货币买进或卖出的执行价格。

Economic Risk

The effect of exchange rate movements on the long-term value or competitiveness of a company.

经济风险

经济风险是指汇率变动给企业的长期价值或竞争力带来的影响。

【学习提示】

经济风险会对进口商或出口商的长期现金流出或流入产生影响。经济风险很难规避，但企业可通过出口客户或进口供应商的多币化来减少此类风险。

Expectation Theory (FX Market)

The difference between forward and spot rates equals expected changes in spot rate. This relationship can be expressed in the following formula: $F_0 - S_0 = S_1 - S_0$ (F_0, forward rate; S_0, spot rate; S_1, expected spot rate).

期望理论(外汇市场)

远期汇率与即期汇率的差异等于即期汇率的预计变动额。这种关系可用如下公式表示:远期汇率－即期汇率＝预期即期汇率－即期汇率。

Exposure

Being open or exposed to a certain type of risk.

(风险)敞口

面临某种风险。

F

Floating Interest Rate

Interest rate that varies with the base rate.

浮动利率

浮动利率是随基准利率的变化而改变的利率。

Forward Rate

An exchange rate quoted now for the exchange of two currencies at a future date. For example, for one month forward rate, it is the exchange rate that will be used to settle the debt in one month.

远期汇率

远期汇率是指现在报出的在未来某个固定日期交换两种货币的汇率。比如,一个月的远期汇率是一个月后结算的汇率。

Forward Rate Agreements(FRAs)

An formal agreement entered into with a bank to specify a fixed rate of interest (FRA rate) on a notional amount of loan for a specified period of time. The bank pays interest on this loan at actual interest rate and receives interest on this loan at FRA rate. If the actual interest rate has risen above the FRA rate, the bank pays the company the difference. The amount paid=(actual rate−FRA rate)×the notional amount×(days/365days). If the actual interest rate has fallen below the FRA rate, the company pays the bank the difference. The amount paid=(FRA rate−actual rate)×the notional amount×(days/365days).

远期利率合约

远期利率合约是企业与银行之间签订的一种正式合约,合约中规定指定期限内的名义贷款额的固定利率。银行按实际利率支付该贷款的利息,并按协议利率收取该贷款的利息。如果实际利率高于协议利率,则银行支付差额。所支付的差额=(实际利率—协议利率)×贷款名义金额×(指定期限天数/365 天)。如果实际利率低于协议利率,则企业支付差额。所支付的差额=(协议利率—实际利率)×贷款名义金额×(指定期限天数/365 天)。

【学习提示】

远期利率合约的作用是把预计的短期借款的利率固定下来,为银行当日报出的 FRA 利率。

【知识点巩固与拓展】

红星公司在三个月后需要一笔期限为九个月、金额为 100 万美元的借款。当前的 FRA 利率为 6%。假设三个月后的市场利率为 7%。如果红星公司现签订一项远期利率合约,那么,三个月后,它应该向银行支付还是银行向它支付?金额是多少?

因为市场利率大于 FRA 利率,所以银行向红星公司支付,金额为 1 000 000×(7%—6%)×9/12=7 500(美元)。

Redstar Co. will need a nine-month borrowing of \$1m in three months' time. The FRA rate is 6% now. If after three month, the prevailing interest rate is 7%. What is the payment or receipt to the bank by Redstar Co. if it signs a FRA now?

The prevailing interest rate is greater than FRA rate, so the bank will make a payment to Redstar Co.. The amount is \$1 000 000×(7%—6%)×9/12=\$7 500.

Forward Exchange Contract

An immediate binding contract between a bank and a customer whereby the customer agrees to buy or sell a certain amount of specific foreign currency at the current forward exchange rate at a specified future period of time.

远期外汇合约

远期外汇合约是银行跟其客户之间签订的立即生效、有法律约束力的一种合同，合同规定客户在未来指定的期限以当前远期汇率从银行购买或出售给银行一定数量的指定外汇。

【学习提示】

远期外汇合约是企业对冲外币交易风险可以借助的外部金融工具之一。其操作简单，可以精确对冲任何时间、任何金额的外币交易风险。但对于远期汇率，企业没有谈判权，只能接受银行的报价。

【知识点巩固与拓展】

英国三岛公司三个月后将从一个美国客户那里收款 50 万美元。当前汇率报价为：

即期汇率 1.387 3～1.388 2 美元/英镑

三个月远期汇率 1.385 0～1.386 6 美元/英镑

三岛公司应该签订一个什么样的远期外汇合约去对冲这笔应收款项的外币交易风险？计算这笔应收款项的三个月后的英镑价值。

三岛公司应该签一项三个月的远期外汇合约，以每英镑 1.386 6

美元的汇率卖出50万美元给银行。三个月后,50万美元的应收款可以换回英镑=500 000/1.386 6=360 594(英镑)。

Threeislands Co. will receive \$500 000 from an American customers in three months' time. Current exchange rates are as follows:

Spot exchange rate \$1.387 3~1.388 2 per £

three-month forward \$1.385 0~1.386 6 per £

What forward exchange contract should be agreed in order to hedge against the transaction risk of the dollar receivables?

Threeislands Co. should sign a three-month forward exchange contract with a bank now, whereby the company sell \$500 000 three-month forward at \$1.386 6 per £. Its sterling value in three months' time = \$500 000/\$1.386 6 per £=£360 594.

Foreign Currency Risk

The risk exposure faced by a business with foreign currency assets and liabilities, as the movements of exchange rates will change the value of foreign currency assets and liabilities.

外汇风险

外汇风险是外币资产和负债给企业带来的风险敞口——因为汇率的变动会改变外币资产和负债的价值。

【知识点巩固与拓展】

外汇风险分为三类:一为交易风险,二为外币折算风险,三为经济风险。

There are three forms of foreign currency

risk, one is transaction risk, the other is translation risk, and the third one is economic risk.

Foreign Currency Derivatives

Financial instruments that derive from underling foreign currency trading, such as currency futures, currency options and currency swaps.

外币衍生品

外币衍生品是从最基本的货币交易衍生出来的金融工具，例如货币期货、货币期权以及货币互换等。

Foreign Exchange Market

A financial market where a large volume of currencies is traded at quoted exchange rates. In addition to foreign exchange dealers (mainly banks), the main participants in foreign exchange market are importers and exporters. Importers need to buy foreign currency at home currency and exporters need to convert foreign currency receipts to home currency.

外汇交易市场

外汇交易市场是大量货币以公开报出的汇率进行交易的金融市场。除了外汇交易商(主要是银行)，外汇交易市场的主要参与者还有进口商和出口商。进口商需要用本币换外币，而出口商需要把收到的外币换成本币。

Fisher Effect

It explains the relationship between the nominal (money) interest rate and real interest rate. It also explains the effect of expected rates of inflation on interest rates. The formula is: 1+nominal interest rate=(1+real interest rate)(1+inflation rate).

费雪效应

费雪效应解释了名义利率与实际利率之间的关系，也解释了预期通货膨胀率对利率的影响。公式如下：

1+名义利率=(1+实际利率)(1+通货膨胀率)

Four-way Equivalence Model

In complete equilibrium, the difference between forward and spot rates, differences in interest rates, expected differences in inflation rates and expected changes in spot rates are equal to one another. That is, there exist interest rate parity, purchasing power parity, Fisher effect, international fisher effect. Also the forward rate is an unbiased predictor of future spot rate.

四路平衡模型

在全面平衡时，远期汇率与即期汇率之间的差异、两个经济体的利率的差异、两个经济体预期通货膨胀率的差异以及即期利率的预期变化应彼此相等。也就是说，利率平价、购买力平价、费雪效应、国际费雪效应成立。另外，当前的远期汇率是对所对应期间的将来即期汇率的无偏差预测。

Futures

A standardized contract between two parties to buy or sell a specified asset of standardized quantity(contract size) and quality for a price agreed upon today(contract price) with delivery and payment occurring at a specified future date(a settlement date or a delivery date). They are traded on a futures exchange.

期货

期货是规定在未来某一特定的时间(结算日或交割日)和地点按照当日达成的价格(合约价)交割一定数量(合约单位)和质量标的物的标准化合约。期货是在期货交易所买卖的。

G

Gap(Interest Rate Risk Management)

The difference between interest-sensitive assets maturing at a certain time or in a certain period and interest-sensitive liabilities maturing at the same time. A negative gap occurs when interest-sensitive liabilities are greater than interest-sensitive assets. A positive gap occurs when interest-sensitive assets are greater than interest-sensitive liabilities.

利率敏感缺口(利率风险管理)

利率敏感缺口是指相同时间或相同期限到期的利率敏感性资产与负债之间的差异。当利率敏感性负债超过利率敏感性资产时,就形成负缺口。当利率敏感性资产超过利率敏感性负债时,就形成正缺口。

【学习提示】

当有负缺口时，利率上涨，企业有风险；当有正缺口时，利率下降，企业有风险。

Gap Analysis

Grouping together interest sensitive assets and interest sensitive liabilities with the same maturity dates and identify whether there is a negative or positive gap in order to manage interest rate risk.

利率敏感缺口分析

把相同到期日的利率敏感资产和利率敏感负债归在一起，确定是负缺口还是正缺口，以便管理利率风险。

Interest Rate Parity

The difference between spot and forward rates reflects differences in interest rates of two countries. It can be depicted by the following formula:

$$F_0/S_0=(1+i_c)/(1+i_b)$$

利率平价

即期汇率与远期汇率之间的差异充分反映了两个经济体之间的利率差异。可用公式描述如下：

$$\frac{\text{远期汇率}}{\text{即期汇率}}=\frac{1+\text{某一经济体的利率}}{1+\text{另一经济体的利率}}$$

Interest Rate Caps

An option which sets an upper limit of interest rate.

利率封顶期权

利率封顶期权就是规定利率上限的期权。

【学习提示】

企业如果担心利率上升，就可以买进利率封顶期权。

Interest Rate Collars

The arrangements to buy an interest rate cap and sell an interest rate floor or to buy an interest rate floor and sell and interest rate cap.

利率领子期权安排

利率领子期权安排就是买进利率封顶期权但同时卖出利率兜底期权，或者买进利率兜底期权但同时卖出利率封顶期权的安排。

【学习提示】

企业如果担心利率上升，就会买进利率封顶期权，但为了节省成本，就会同时卖出一兜底期权。企业如果担心利率下降，就会买进一兜底期权，但为了节省成本，就会同时卖出一封顶期权。

Interest Rate Floors

An option which sets an lower limit of interest rate.

利率兜底期权

利率兜底期权就是规定利率下限的期权。

【学习提示】

企业如果担心利率下降,就会买进利率兜底期权。

Interest Rate Futures

A futures contract to hedge against the adverse movements of interest rate. It is similar to FRAs, except that the terms, amounts and periods are standardized. With interest rate futures, the buyer is entitled to receive interests and the seller promises to make interest payments.

利率期货

利率期货是用来对冲利率的不利变动的一种期货合约。除了合约条款、金额、期限都是标准化的,其他方面都与远期利率合约相似。利率期货的购买方有权收到利息,而期货的出售方承诺支付利息。

Interest Rate Options

An option contract to limit exposure to the adverse interest rate movements but at the same time can take advantage of favourable interest rate movements. The buyer gets the right but not the obligation to deal at the strike rate at a future maturity date. On the date of the expiry, the buyer must decide whether or not to exercise the right.

利率期权

利率期权是一种期权合约，既可以使企业在利率发生不利变动时限制损失，又能使企业充分利用利率的利好变动。购买者有权但没有义务在行权日按照行权利率来交易。期权到期，期权购买方必须决定是否行权。

Interest Rate Risk

The possible loss or gain of a company brought about by movements of interest rate.

利率风险

利率风险就是因利率波动可能给企业带来的损失或收益。

Interest Rate Swaps

An agreement whereby two parties agree to exchange interest payments with each other over an agreed period. It may involve fixed-for-floating swap, fixed-for-fixed swap or floating-for-floating swap.

利率互换

利率互换是双方同意在约定的期限内交换债务利息的一种合约。利率互换有固定利率债务与浮动利率债务互换、不同固定利率的债务互换以及不同浮动利率的债务互换。

International Fisher Effect

It suggests that differences in nominal interest rates of two countries provide unbiased predictor of future changes in spot exchange rate. The currency of countries with relatively high interest rate is expected to weaken against the currency with lower interest rates. Due to the adjustments to spot exchange rate, the real interest rate in different countries will equalize.

国际费雪效应

国际费雪效应认为，两国之间名义利率的差异为即期汇率的未来变化提供了无偏估计。利率相对较高的国家的货币相对于利率较低的国家的货币贬值。由于即期汇率的相应调整，两国的实际利率相等。

L

Leading

Making payments in advance of the due date in order to take advantage of foreign exchange rate movements.

提前支付

为了使汇率变动对己有利，在到期日前提前支付。

Lagging

Making payments beyond the due date in order to take advantage of foreign exchange rate movements.

延后支付

为了使汇率变动对己有利，拖延至到期日后支付。

【学习提示】

根据汇率的走势判断提前支付还是延后支付，这也是外币交易风险管理的基本方法之一。

Liquidity Preference

People usually prefer money now than later and they need compensation for being unable to use money now. The longer the period for waiting to use money, the higher the return they require.

流动性偏好

人们通常喜欢现在而非将来得到现金，如果牺牲现在使用现金的权利，他们就需要补偿。牺牲使用现金的时间越长，则要求的回报越高。

Liquidity Preference Theory

It holds that the required rate of return by bonds investors increases with the length of time for which they are unable to use the invested money. So longer-term yields of bonds are higher than that of shorter-term bonds, and the yield curve slopes upward.

流动性偏好理论

流动性偏好理论认为，债券投资者不能使用所投资金的时间越长，要求的回报就越高。因此，到期期限长的债券的收益率高于到期期限短的债券的收益率，故其收益率曲线向上倾斜。

M

Market Segmentation Theory

It holds that a particular market segment will attract its own particular investor groups and these investor groups will rarely change segments. This explains why there are wiggles in the yield curve.

市场细分理论

市场细分理论认为，某个特定的细分市场会吸引它自己的特定投资群体，这些投资群体一般不轻易改变所投资的细分市场。这解释了为什么收益率曲线是不平滑的。

Matching（Foreign Currency Risk Management）

In order to reduce or eliminate foreign currency transaction risk，a company should match the receipts and payments in a foreign currency，also should match assets and liabilities in a foreign currency.

匹配法（外币风险管理）

为了减少或者完全规避外币交易风险，公司应该把一种外币的收入与其支出相匹配，也应该把一种外币的资产与该外币的负债相匹配。

【学习提示】

匹配法是企业外币交易风险管理最基本的方法之一。一家公司只要在银行开设外币账户，就自然可以做到该外币的收入与支出相匹配。

Matching (Interest Rate Risk Management)

Liabilities and assets with common interest rate base are matched. For example, investments at LIBOR are matched with borrowings at LIBOR.

匹配法（利率风险管理）

把相同利率基准的负债与资产相匹配。例如，把以 LIBOR 为基准的投资与以 LIBOR 为基准的借款相匹配。

【学习提示】

匹配法的目的是使利率敏感缺口接近 0。当有负的缺口时，则担心利率上升；当有正的缺口时，则担心利率下降。当缺口为 0 时，既不怕利率上升，也不怕利率下降，风险自动抵消。

Money Market Hedging

It involves borrowing foreign currency in money market today to hedge against the foreign currency risk of a foreign currency receivable or involves buying in foreign currency at spot rate and putting it on deposit in a bank account to hedge against the foreign currency risk of a foreign currency payable.

货币市场对冲风险

为了对冲外币应收账款的外币风险，今时在货币市场借入外币；或者为了对冲外币应付账款的外币风险，马上以即期汇率买入外币并存入银行。

【学习提示】

货币市场对冲外币交易风险的原理就是外币资产与外币负债的匹配。有外币应收，就应该有外币应付与其匹配，故借入外币。有外币应付，就应该有外币应收与其匹配，故形成外币银行存款。

【知识点巩固与拓展(一)】

一家英国公司欠一家美国供货商 200 万美元，在三个月后支付。另外，还有以下信息：

即期汇率 1.387 3～1.388 2 美元/英镑

英镑三个月借款利率 9%

美元三个月存款利率 8%

用货币市场对冲风险，三个月后的英镑成本为多少？

以 8% 的年利率存入银行三个月的美元金额＝2 000 000÷(1＋8%×3/12)＝1 960 784(美元)

以即期汇率 1.387 3 买进 1 960 784 美元，目前的英镑成本＝1 960 784/1.387 3＝1 413 381(英镑)

三个月后的英镑成本＝1 413 381×(1＋9%×3/12)＝1 445 182(英镑)

A UK company owes an American supplier ＄2 million which is payable in three months' time. The following information is available:

Spot exchange rate ＄1.387 3－1.388 2 per £

Sterling three-month borrowing rate of interest 8%

Dollar three-month deposit rate of interest 6%

What is the sterling cost in three months' time with a money market hedge?

Dollars deposited in a bank account at 8% for three months＝＄2 000 000÷(1＋8%×3/12)＝＄1 960 784

Buy dollars 1 960 784 at spot exchange rate 1.387 3, the sterling cost now＝＄1 960 784/＄1.387 3 per £＝£1 413 381

The sterling cost in three months' time＝£1 413 381×(1＋9%×3/12)＝£1 445 182

【知识点巩固与拓展(二)】

一家英国公司有一笔美国客户所欠的三个月期限的应收账款 600 万美元。另外，还有以下信息：

即期汇率 1.387 3～1.388 2 美元/英镑

美元三个月借款利率 9%

英镑三个月存款利率 8%

如果在货币市场对冲风险，三个月后这笔美元的应收账款的英镑价值为多少？

以年利率 9%借三个月的美元金额＝6 000 000÷(1＋9%×3/12)＝5 867 971(美元)

以即期汇率 1.388 2 把借进的 5 867 971 美元换成英镑，目前

的英镑金额=5 867 971/1.388 2=4 227 036(英镑)

三个月后的英镑价值=4 227 036×(1+8%×3/12)=4 311 577(英镑)

A UK company has a receivable of $6million from an American customer in three months' time. The following information is available:

spot exchange rate $1.387 3~1.388 2 per £

dollar three-month borrowing rate 9%

sterling three-month deposit rate 8%

What is the sterling value of the dollar receipts in three months' time with money market hedge?

Dollars borrowed at 9% for three months=$6 000 000÷(1+9%×3/12)=$5 867 971

Current sterling value if dollars borrowed are converted to sterling at spot rate 1.388 2=$5 867 971/$1.388 2 per £=£4 227 036

Sterling value in three months' time=£4 227 036×(1+8%×3/12)=£4 311 577

N

Netting

Netting off inter-company indebtedness denominated in same foreign currency, only the net amounts are settled, thus transaction costs are saved. For example, subsidiary A of a multinational company owed subsidiary B $1 million, and B owed A

$800 000. After netting off, a net debt of $200 000 owed by A to B is left.

账面轧差

公司内部子公司之间相同外币的应收账款与应付账款相互抵消后，只结算轧差后的净值，以节省交易成本。例如，一家跨国公司的子公司 A 欠子公司 B 100 万美元，而子公司 B 欠子公司 A 80 万美元。账面轧差后，只剩下子公司 A 欠子公司 B 20 万美元。

Negotiated Options

An option that is negotiated with a bank over the counter and is tailor-made to the company's exact requirements.

柜台商定的期权

这是与一家银行在柜台上商定的一种期权，可以根据企业的要求量身定制。

【学习提示】

柜台商定的期权，由于企业缺乏谈判力(lack negotiability)，交易汇率多数只能接受银行的报价。

O

Offer Price

It is also called ask price. It is the exchange rate at which the bank sells foreign currency and importers buy foreign currency.

银行卖出价

银行卖出价就是银行卖出外币即进口商买进外币的汇率。

Option

An option is a contract which gives the buyer the right, but not the obligation, to buy or sell an underlying asset or instrument at a specified price at a specified future date.

期权

期权是一种合同，赋予买方在未来某一特定日期（指欧式期权）以事先规定好的价格向卖方购买或出售特定标的物的选择权利，但买方不承担必须买进或卖出的义务。

P

Purchasing Power Parity

The spot exchange rates adjust over time according to relative price changes of two countries. The currency of the country with higher inflation rate will depreciate against the currency of the country with lower inflation rate. The relationship can be expressed in the following formula:

$$S_1/S_0=(1+h_c)/(1+h_b)$$

购买力平价

即期汇率根据两个国家价格相对变化水平而进行调整。高通货膨胀率国家的货币相对于低通货膨胀率国家的货币贬值。可用公式描述如下：

$$\frac{\text{预计未来即期汇率}}{\text{当前即期汇率}}=\frac{1+\text{某一个国家的通货膨胀率}}{1+\text{另一国家的通货膨胀率}}$$

Put Option

The option to sell a specified quantity of one specified currency at a specified exchange rate on or before a specified future date.

看跌(货币)期权

看跌(货币)期权就是在指定的未来某个日期或之前，以指定汇率卖出指定数量的指定货币的选择权。

R

Risk Management

The policies and the measures taken by a company to manage its risk exposures in order to avoid or reduce risks.

风险管理

为了规避或者减少风险，公司制定相应的政策、采取适当的措施来对其风险敞口进行管理。

S

Smoothing(Interest Rate Risk Management)

Keeping a balance between fixed rate and floating rate borrowing. A rise in interest rate will make the floating rate borrowing more expensive but this will be compensated for by the less expensive fixed rate borrowing.

平滑(利率风险管理)

平滑(利率风险管理)就是指在固定利率债务与浮动利率债务之间保持平衡。当利率上升时，浮动利率的债务成本将提高，而这会由固定利率债务相对较低的成本来弥补。

【学习提示】

若企业有固定利率的债务，则当利率下降时有风险；若有浮动利率的债务，则在利率上升时有风险。因此，如果浮动利率的债务与固定利率的债务金额相当，则不管利率是上升还是下降，风险都可抵消。

Spot Rate

The exchange rate in currencies quoted now for immediate settlement(within two working days).

即期汇率

即期汇率就是现时报出的马上(一般在两个工作日内)结算的外汇交易的汇率。

【学习提示】

当前立即要结算的外币交易适用即期汇率。比如，到银行柜台兑换外币立即使用，就用即期汇率结算。

Structure of Interest Rates

The interest rates differ for different financial assets or the same financial assets in different markets or market segments.

利率结构

不同的金融资产或相同的金融资产在不同的市场或细分市场,其利率有差异。

T

Term Structure of Interest Rates

The way in which the yield on a bond varies with the length of the time to maturity. This can be depicted graphically by a yield curve.

利率期限结构

利率期限结构就是债券的收益率随着其到期时间的长短而变化的方式。利率期限结构可以用收益率曲线来形象地刻画。

Tick

The smallest movement in the contract price of the underlying futures. For currency futures, it is 0.000 1.

基点/最小变动价位

基点就是期货合约单位价格涨跌变动的最小值。例如,货币期货的最小变动价位为0.000 1。

Tick Size

The smallest price movement for a standard future contract. The calculation formula is minimum price movement×contact size. For example, if a currency future's contact size is ＄125 000, tick size＝0.000 1×＄125 000＝＄12.5.

点值

点值就是标准期货合约的最小价格变动值。计算公式为：点值＝价格最小变动基点×标准合约值。例如，一份标准期货合约值为125 000美元，则点值＝0.000 1×125 000＝12.5（美元）。

Transaction Risk

The uncertain movement in exchange rates between the agreement date and the settlement date will result in possible gain or loss on foreign currency payments or receipts.

外币交易风险

外币交易风险是指因合约日和结算日之间不确定的汇率变动而可能给有外币支出和收入的企业带来的收益或损失。

【学习提示】

外币交易风险会实实在在地影响企业实际的现金流流入或支出，是对现金流带来短期影响的风险。企业可以采取很多方法来规避外币交易风险。

Translation Risk

The uncertain movement in exchange rate between the transaction date and the financial reporting date will result in possible translation gain or loss when at reporting date the foreign currency assets and liabilities are translated into the home currency.

外币折算风险

外币折算风险是指由于交易日和报表日之间不确定的汇率变动,因此,在报表日把外币资产和负债折算成本币时,可能产生的汇兑收益或损失。

【学习提示】

外币折算只是会计上的账面处理,不对现金流造成实际影响。企业可以通过账面上一种外币资产和该种外币负债的对冲来规避外币折算风险。

Traded Option

A standard option that is traded in an option exchange.

交易所交易的期权

在交易所交易的标准期权。

【学习提示】

交易所交易的期权,定价透明,交易成本低,但只有有限的货币期权品种。

Y

Yield Curve

The curve that depicts the relationship between the gross redemption yield of the bonds and the length of time to maturity of the bonds. A normal yield curve slopes upward and a negative yield curve slopes downward.

收益率曲线

收益率曲线就是描述债券的到期期限长短与其到期收益率之间关系的曲线。正常的收益率曲线向上倾斜,而倒挂的收益率曲线向下倾斜。

Module Eight

Role of Senior Financial Adviser in Multinationals/跨国公司高级财务顾问的角色

本单元的学习目标：

(1)理解集团公司特别是跨国公司高级财务顾问的角色定位。

(2)掌握在制定公司财务战略以及四大财务决策时应综合考量的财务因素和非财务因素。

(3)能对企业的财务战略从财务和非财务方面进行评估。

(4)能在制定和评估公司财务战略时,充分考虑国际规则尤其是贸易规则的影响,特别是税收以及外汇管制对分红决策、转移定价决策以及公司组织结构和资本结构决策的影响,充分考虑子公司的管理者与总公司的管理者之间的代理问题,充分考虑国际金融市场的发展对公司财务的影响。

A

Arm's Length Standard

The most important concept on which transfer pricing of multinationals is based, it means that all intra-firm trades of multinationals should be priced as if they took place between unrelated parties in an arm's length transaction at a fairly competitive market.

公平交易标准

公平交易标准是跨国公司制定转移定价所遵循的最重要的概念。它是指跨国公司内部交易的转移价格应参照无关联公司之间在公平竞争的市场上公平交易的价格。

Availability Bias

People usually base their decisions mainly on information available and ignore unavailable information, so that judgement bias is resulted in. This can explain why the announced information will alter share prices shortly.

可得性偏差

人们经常主要根据自己可以得到的信息来进行决策而忽略那些还没得到的信息，从而形成了判断偏差。这可以帮助解释为什么公布的信息会很快地改变股价。

B

Business's Life Cycle

Different stages of a business's development, from commencement stage, to growth stage, to maturity stage and finally to down-turn stage.

企业生命周期

企业生命周期是指一家企业发展的各个阶段，从初创阶段，到增长阶段，再到成熟阶段，最后到衰退阶段。

C

Capitals

All resources and relationships that a business is using or will use to create value. In additional to financial capital, there are intellectual capital, social capital, human capital, manufactured capital and natural capital.

资本组合

资本组合就是企业现在或将要用来创造价值的所有资源和关系。除金融资本外，还有知识资本、社会资本、人力资本、制造资本以及自然资本。

Collateralized Debt Obligations (CDOs)

One form of asset-backed securitization (ABS). Debt instruments are issued backed up by a package of risky assets. The risks attached to these risky assets are then transferred to investors and the issuer obtains cash in advance.

债务担保证券

债务担保证券是资产支持证券化的一种形式。把风险资产打包作为担保而发行的债务工具。如此，这些资产的风险就转移给了投资者而发行商提前获得现金。

Comparable Uncontrolled Price (CUP) Method

The main method to establish an arm's length transfer price through looking for the price of a comparable product, either referring to a similar product being bought or sold by the multinational in a comparable transaction, or referring to a similar product being traded between two unrelated parties.

可比非受控价格法

可比非受控价格法是通过寻找一个可比产品的价格来确立公平转移价格的主要方法，可以参考这家跨国公司在可比交易中购买或出售类似产品的价格，也可以参考两家非关联公司买卖类似产品的价格。

Credit Crunch

A situation existing in the lending and borrowing market,

where banks are unwilling to lend money due to their lack of confidence in the economy and businesses are unable to obtain funds.

信贷紧缩

信贷紧缩是借贷市场上出现的一种情况——由于银行对经济缺乏信心从而不愿意提供任何信贷进而导致企业无法获得资金。

D

Dark Pools Trading Systems

Off-exchange trading platforms where large shareholdings are allowed to be disposed of without trading information being revealed in advance until after trades are completed.

黑池交易系统

黑池交易系统就是场外交易平台，在交易完成之前，允许在不提前披露交易信息的情况下处置大量股份。

Dividend Capacity

Funds available to pay out dividends to ordinary shareholders in any given year. Its calculation formula is: dividend capacity = profit after interest, tax and preference dividends − debt repayment, share repurchase, assets investment + depreciation, any capital raised through new share or debt issues.

分红能力/股利派发能力

分红能力就是在任何一年份可以用来给普通股股东派发股利

的可得资金。其计算公式为：分红能力＝扣除息税以及优先股股利后的利润－用来偿还债务、回购股票以及进行资产投资的资金＋折旧以及通过发行新股和新债而新筹集的资金。

【学习提示】

企业的分红能力主要来自权益自由现金流。

在计算集团公司的分红能力时，也要把子公司的分红能力考虑进去。而国外子公司给予总公司的分红可能有一些限制并且会缴纳额外的税，这都要考虑进去。

【知识点巩固与拓展】

Mayflower 公司今年的有关数据估计如下：息税前利润 100 000 美元，折旧等其他未支出现金的费用 12 000 美元，资本性支出 25 000 美元，额外的营运资本需求 10 000 美元。

公司所得税税率 30%。Mayflower 公司贷款总额 20 万美元，平均利率 6%。

计算 Mayflower 公司的分红能力。

Estimated information about Mayflower Ltd. in this year is as follows: PBIT \$100 000, depreciation and other non-cash expenses \$12 000, capital expenditure \$25 000, new working capital requirements \$10 000. Corporation tax rate is 30%. Mayflower has bank loans of \$200 000 with average interest rate 6%. Calculate dividend capacity.

Dividend capacity(分红能力)

$$=(\$100\,000-\$200\,000\times 6\%)\times 0.7+\$12\,000-\$25\,000-\$10\,000$$

$$=\$38\,600$$

E

Enhanced Scrip Dividend

The shareholders are given a choice on whether to take cash dividends or share dividends but the offering of shares dividends is often very generous that the shareholders are likely to choose share dividends rather than cash dividends.

增强型股票股利

股东可以选择是接受现金股利还是股票股利，但股票股利的发放通常是非常慷慨的，所以股东很可能选择股票股利而不是现金股利。

Entrapment

Management are trapped by their past decisions, and they are reluctant to admit they are wrong.

管理者陷阱

管理者陷在自己过去的错误决策所“挖的陷阱”里，不愿意承认自己的错误。

F

Financial Capital

Funds and other financial resources available, either obtained through financing activities or through operating activities.

金融资本

金融资本是企业通过融资活动或经营活动获得的资金和其他金融资源。

G

Goal Congruence

Striving for the achievement of consistent corporate goals by different levels of management, by management and employees of different departments over time.

目标一致

不同级别的管理者、不同部门的管理者和员工在不同的期间所追求的目标是一致的。

H

Herding

Decisions are made and actions are taken by following the decisions and actions by most people.

从众效应/羊群效应

从众效应是指人们通过遵循大部分人的决策和行为来做出自

己的决策并采取相应的行为。

Human Capital

Human resources available to innovate and create value for a business in the short and long term.

人力资本

人力资本是企业短期和长期内革新、创造价值所依赖的人力资源。

I

Integrated Reporting

An integrated report are produced to make visible six capitals of the business which reflects the reporting entity's ability to create and sustain value over the short, medium and long term. Six capitals include financial capital, manufactured capital, intellectual capital, social capital, human capital and natural capital.

综合报告

编制一份综合报告,以披露决定企业短期、中期以及长期创造价值并且持续创造价值能力的六大资本。六大资本包括金融资本、制造资本、知识资本、社会资本、人力资本以及自然资本。

Intellectual Capital

Intellectual property providing competitive advantage for a

business, such as patents, copyrights, trademarks and brand names.

知识资本

知识资本是为企业获得竞争优势的知识产权,比如专利权、版权、商标以及品牌。

J

Junior Tranche

The investment layer in securitization that bears very high risk and has a high potential yield and it ranks behind other tranches over claims on cash flows generated by the collateral.

劣后级

劣后级是资产证券化过程中的一个投资层级,承担非常高的风险但也有很高的潜在收益。在对担保品所产生的现金流分配中,它排在其他层级的后面。

M

Manufactured Capital

Manufactured tangible objects used in a business, such as buildings, equipment and infrastructure.

制造资本

制造资本是企业所使用的制造的有形物体，比如建筑物、设备以及基建设施。

N

Natural Capital

Natural resources provided by natural environment that are used in business activities, and the whole natural environment that a business's activities are based on, including water, land, minerals, forests, health of ecosystem.

自然资本

自然资本是用于企业各种活动中的、由自然环境所提供的自然资源，以及企业各种活动所基于的整个自然环境，包括水、土地、矿藏、森林以及整个生态系统的健康。

R

Risk Mitigation

The process through which a company reduces its risk exposure by taking measures such as hedging, insurance, or even avoiding risks completely.

降低风险

公司通过对冲、投保，甚至彻底规避风险等措施来降低风险的过程。

Risk Diversification

Reducing the impact of risks on earnings of a company through diversification of business areas.

分散风险

分散风险是指企业通过业务的多元化来降低风险对公司收益的影响。

S

Senior Tranche

The investment layer in securitization that bears low risk and has a low potential yield. It has priority in the claims on cash flows generated by the collateral over the junior tranches.

优先级

优先级是证券化的一个投资层级，低风险，低潜在收益。它对担保品所产生的现金流比劣后级有优先索求权。

Share Buyback（Repurchase）

Buying back shares outstanding by a company from its existing shareholders, either on open market or through private negotiation with shareholders.

股票回购

股票回购是指公司通过公开市场交易,或者通过跟股东私下协商,从现有股东手里买回其发行在外的股票。

Special Dividends

A cash return to shareholders that is far in excess of normal dividend payments.

特殊股利

特殊股利是给股东的现金回报,其金额远远超过正常的股利支付水平。

Social Capital

Social relationships with key stakeholders that are valuable to a business. For example, good relationships with customers will bring more sales orders for a business.

社会资本

社会资本是企业与主要利益相关方之间的社会关系,这对企业是非常有价值的。比如,与客户维持良好的关系将会给企业带来更多的销售订单。

T

Thin Capitalization

The capital structure of a company that there is a much greater proportion than usual of debt than equity.

资本弱化

一家公司的资本结构,其债务所占比例通常要高于权益占比。

Tranching

Dividing investors of CDOs into different investment layers so that one layer of investors takes more of the risk for higher potential return, and the other layer of investors takes less of the risk for a lower potential return. Different tranches rank differently as to the priority in claims to cash flows from the collateralized assets. The senior tranches have priorities over the junior ones.

投资分层

把担保债务凭证的投资者分成不同层级,某个层级的投资者承担更多的风险但有更高的潜在回报,而另一个层级的投资者承担更少的风险但有更低的潜在回报。不同的层级在对担保资产所产生的现金流索求时优先顺序不同。优先级比劣后级优先。

Module Nine

Advanced Investment Appraisal/高级投资评估

本单元的学习目标：

(1)掌握折现现金流法(DCF)中有关投资评估的方法，特别是项目久期(project duration)、在险价值(valuation at risk)，以及修正的内部收益率(MIRR)；掌握多期资本约束(multi-period capital rationing)时投资决策的方法。

(2)掌握布莱克-斯克尔斯(BSOP)模型，熟悉影响期权价值的各变量，了解这个模型的缺陷；能够识别、归类并评估投资项目的实物期权，特别是用BSOP模型去计算并评估实务期权的价值。

(3)熟悉资本结构有关理论，掌握财务风险和经营风险的变化对企业资本成本以及项目投资评估的影响；熟练运用调整净现值(APV)来进行项目投资评估。

(4)熟悉新兴的融资方法，根据企业具体的情况建议合适的融资渠道，或评价所选融资渠道的适宜性；掌握久期和修正久期等概念，了解其优缺点，并用其来评估利率变动对公司负债风险的影响；掌握收益率曲线以及风险溢价等概念，能够用其评价企业信用风险和信用评级变化对公司债务资本成本的影响。

(5)熟练运用基于资产、收益以及现金流的各种方法对企业的权益进行估值;掌握自由现金流和权益自由现金流的概念并用其对企业进行估值;解释如何用 BSOP 模型对企业的权益进行估值,以及如何用 BSOP 模型对债务违约风险以及债务价值进行估计。

(6)评估国际投资项目,特别要考虑汇率变化的风险;选择合适的国际融资渠道,尤其要考虑如何用国际债务融资来管理风险。

A

Adjusted Present Value (APV)

The net present value of a project undertaking by an all-equity company is adjusted to add the effects of financing the project with debts. The effects of financing the project with debts include but are not limited to tax relief of interest payments, issue cost of debts and any subsidies obtained on the loan. $APV = NPV$ (as if ungeared) $+ PV$ of tax relief and benefits of any loan subsidy-issue cost of new debt.

调整净现值

对全权益公司项目的净现值进行调整,要加上债务融资对项目的影响。债务融资对项目的影响包括但不局限于利息支付的节税效应、新债务的发行成本以及贷款所获得的补贴等。用公式表示:调整净现值=净现值(全权益、无杠杆情况下)+节税以及贷款补贴所获效益的现值—新债务的发行成本。

【学习提示】

利息支付所减的税、贷款补贴等债务融资效应用债务资本成本来折现。无杠杆 NPV 计算时用无杠杆公司的权益资本成本来折现。

【知识点巩固与拓展】

Futurebright 公司拟出资 2 000 万美元投资一个新的项目。新项目在接下来的 5 年内每年可以产生 520 万美元的现金流。

2 000 万美元的投资中有 1 200 万美元是以 6%的年利率借来的。这笔债务的发行成本为税后 100 000 美元。

公司目前的权益资本成本为 13%，企业所得税税率为 20%。目前以市值计量的负债权益比为 50∶50。

计算 APV，无杠杆公司的权益资本成本的计算用 M&M 公式。

第一步：计算无杠杆情况下的 NPV。

$13\%=Ke^{i}+0.8(Ke^{i}-6\%)\times 50/50$

$Ke^{i}=10\%$

$NPV=520\times 3.791-2\ 000=-28.68$ 万(美元)

第二步：计算利息支付所减税的现值。

每年减税$=1\ 200\times 6\%\times 0.2=14.4$ 万(美元)

年金现值系数(6%,5 年)$=4.212$

现值$=14.4\times 4.212=60.7$ 万(美元)

第三步：发行成本 100 000 美元。

第四步：计算 APV。

$APV=-286\ 800+607\ 000-100\ 000=220\ 200$(美元)

Futurebright plc. is planning to invest \$20 million now for a new project. The project will generate annual cash flows of \$5.2 million for the next 5 years.

\$12 million of the \$20 million investment will raised by borrowing at an interest rate of 6% per annum. The issue cost of the debt is estimated to be \$100 000(net to tax).

The company's existing cost of equity is 13% and corporation tax rate is 20%. Currently the ratio of debt to equity based on market value is 50∶50.

Calculate APV, with the ungeared cost of equity being calculated using M&M formula.

Step1: NPV as if ungeared.

$13\%=Ke^i+0.8(Ke^i-6\%)\times 50/50$

$Ke^i=10\%$

$NPV=\$5.2m\times 3.791-\$20m=\$-0.286\ 8m$

Step 2: present value of tax relief of interest payments.

Tax saved on annual interest paid $=\$12m\times 6\%\times 0.2=\$0.144m$

Discount factor (6% for 5 years) $=4.212$

$PV=\$0.144m\times 4.212=\$0.607m$

Step 3: issue cost \$100 000.

Step 4: APV.

$APV=-\$286\ 800+\$607\ 000-\$100\ 000=\$220\ 200$

B

Base Currency

An exchange rate is the price at which one unit of a currency can be in exchange for another currency. The currency that is quoted to one unit in an exchange rate quotation is base currency. And another currency is counter currency (the reference or term currency). For example, CNY 6.5435/USD, US dollar is the base currency, CNY is the counter currency.

基础货币

汇率通常使用另一种货币所表示的一个单位某种货币的价格。而在汇率报价中一个单位的某种货币即基础货币，而另一种货币为参照货币。比如，1 美元等于 6.543 5 元人民币，美元是基础货币，人民币是参照货币。

Benchmarking

A practice of establishing an internal standard or an external comparator, identifying areas of underperformance through comparison with this target or comparator and finding ways of improving.

对标

对标就是先确立内部标准或者外部参照者，再通过与标准或参照者的对比来发现不足之处并找到改进办法的过程。

Black-Scholes Option Pricing Model(BSOP)

A model of calculating the value of options by incorporating the various determinants of option value. The formula for valuing a call option at time 0 is: $C_0 = P_a N(d_1) - P_e N(d_2) e^{-rt}$ [P_a is PV of cash inflows of underlying investment, P_e is the exercise price of the option or the cost of underlying investment, r is the risk-fee rate of return, t is time to expiry in years, $d_1 = \frac{\ln(Pa/Pe) + (r + 0.5s^2)t}{s\sqrt{t}}$, $d_2 = d_1 - s\sqrt{t}$. $N(d_x)$ is the cumulative probability from the normal distribution table for the value of d_x]. The formula for valuing a put option is: $P = C - P_a + P_e e^{-rt}$ (C is the value of a call option, P is the value of a put option).

布莱克－斯科尔斯期权定价模型

把影响期权价值的各种因素都考虑进去、用来计算期权价值的一个模型。在时点 0，看涨期权价值的计算公式是 $C_0 = P_a N(d_1) - P_e N(d_2) e^{-rt}$ [P_a 是标的资产未来现金流的现值，即标的资产的现行价格，P_e 是标的资产的执行价格或标的资产的投资成本，r 是无风险利率，t 是距到期日的年数，$d_1 = \frac{\ln(Pa/Pe) + (r + 0.5s^2)t}{s\sqrt{t}}$，$d_2 = d_1 - s\sqrt{t}$，$N(d_x)$ 标准正态分布随机变量将小于或等于 d_x 的累计概率]，看跌期权价值的计算公式是 $P = C - P_a + P_e e^{-rt}$（$C$ 是看涨期权的价值，P 是看跌期权的价值）。

【学习提示】

也可用 BSOP 公式来估计实物期权的价值。

【知识点巩固与拓展】

Futurebright 公司正在考虑一个现值为 600 万美元的投资项目。该项目有机会在第四年投资 1 000 万美元扩张进一新的市场。标准差为 0.25，无风险利率为 4%，资本成本为 11%。

评估该扩张期权的价值。

该项目在第四年的现值为 1 000 万美元，那在时点 0 的现值，即 $Pa=1\,000$ 万$\times 0.659=659$ 万(美元)，$Pe=1\,000$ 万(美元)，$t=4$，$s=0.25$，$r=0.04$，$e^{-rt}=0.852$

$$d_1=\frac{\ln(Pa/Pe)+(r+0.5s^2)t}{s\sqrt{t}}$$

$$=[\ln(659/1\,000)+(0.04+0.5\times 0.25^2)\times 4]/0.25\times\sqrt{4}$$

$$=-0.26$$

$$d_2=d_1-s\sqrt{t}=-0.26-0.25\times\sqrt{4}=-0.76$$

$$N(d_1)=N(-0.26)=0.5-0.102\,6=0.397\,4$$

$$N(d_2)=N(-0.76)=0.5-0.276\,4=0.223\,6$$

$$C_0=P_aN(d_1)-P_eN(d_2)e^{-rt}$$

$$=659\times 0.397\,4-1\,000\times 0.223\,6\times 0.852$$

$$=71.379\,4 \text{ 万(美元)}$$

Futurebright plc. is now considering a project with an NPV of $6 million. The project will have an opportunity to expand into a new market at Year 4 with an investment cost of $10 million. The standard deviation is 0.25, risk-free rate is 4% and the cost of capital is 11%.

Evaluate the value of the option to expand.

The value of the project is \$10 million at Year 4, the present value at Year 0 is

$Pa = \$10m \times 0.659 = \$6.59m$

$Pe = 10m, t = 4, s = 0.25, r = 0.04. e^{-rt} = 0.852$

$$d_1 = \frac{\ln(Pa/Pe) + (r + 0.5s^2)t}{s\sqrt{t}}$$

$= [\ln(6.59/10) + (0.04 + 0.5 \times 0.25^2) \times 4] / 0.25 \times \sqrt{4}$

$= -0.26$

$d_2 = d_1 - s\sqrt{t} = -0.26 - 0.25 \times \sqrt{4} = -0.76$

$N(d_1) = N(-0.26) = 0.5 - 0.1026 = 0.3974$

$N(d_2) = N(-0.76) = 0.5 - 0.2764 = 0.2236$

$C_0 = P_a N(d_1) - P_e N(d_2) e^{-rt}$

$= \$6.59m \times 0.3974 - \$10m \times 0.2236 \times 0.852$

$= \$713\,794$

C

Capital Investment Monitoring

Introducing and implementing controls (for example, financial analysis) to reduce the probability of risk occurrence or to reduce the impact of risk exposures during the capital project investment decision-making process.

资本投资监督

资本投资监督是指在资本项目投资决策的过程中，通过引入并实施一系列的控制措施(比如财务分析)来减少风险发生的概率或减少风险对企业的影响。

Credit Spread(Credit Risk Premium)

The extra return above risk-free rate required by debt investors for bearing credit risk.

信用风险溢价

信用风险溢价是指因为承担了信用风险，债务投资者所要求的高于无风险利率的那部分额外的报酬。

D

Duration

Referring to Macaulay duration, the weighted average time taken to deliver the cash inflows of an investment, the weights being proportion of the present value of the cash inflows contributed in each period. The formula is: $D=(1\times PV_1+2\times PV_2+\cdots+n\times PV_n)/\sum_{i=1}^{n}PV_i$ (PV_i is the present value of cash inflows in period i discounted at current required yield by investors).

久期

参考麦考利久期，一项投资的现金流入所需时间的加权平均值，权数为每期现金流现值在投资所得现金流总现值中的占比。公式:$D=(1\times PV_1+2\times PV_2+\cdots+n\times PV_n)/\sum_{i=1}^{n}PV_i$($PV_i$ 为

第 i 期的现金流用目前市场所要求的收益率来折现的现值)。

E

Evaluating International Investments

Cash flows of international investments are often in foreign currency. In evaluating international investments, first convert cash flows in foreign currency to home currency using an appropriate exchange rate, and then discount cash flows in a suitable discount rate to get the net present value of the investment. Also, other factors affecting international investments must be considered, such as tax issues, exchange controls and political risks.

国际项目投资评估

国际投资项目的现金流通常是外币。在评估时,先用合适的汇率把外币现金流折算成本币现金流,然后用恰当的折现率把折算过来的本币现金流折现,计算出投资项目的净现值。并且要考虑其他影响国际投资的因素,比如税收、外汇管制以及政治风险等。

Exchange Controls

Controlling rules and measures imposed by a government to restrict the flow of foreign currency into and out of the country usually to protect reserves of foreign currency and to defend their home currency. For example, a government may restrict the payment of dividends to foreign shareholders.

外汇管制

外汇管制是指政府为限制外币进出而实施的管制法规和措施,通常是为了保护外汇储备以及维护本国货币。例如,政府可能限制向国外股东派发股利。

F

Financial Distress Costs

As debt financing increases, chances of failure to pay interests and repay capital due to lack of cash on hand increase, a company may fall into financial distress, and finally may even go bankrupt. The costs associated with this situation are financial distress costs. Financial distress costs can be classified into direct financial distress costs and indirect financial distress costs. Direct financial distress costs include the legal and administrative costs associated with financial distress. Indirect financial distress costs include agency cost of debt and loss caused by adverse effects of financial distress on business operating.

财务困境成本

随着企业的债务增加,企业由于手头资金短缺而不能还本付息的可能性增加,企业就可能陷入财务困境,甚至最后会破产。这种状况所导致的成本称为财务困境成本。财务困境成本可划分为直接财务困境成本和间接财务困境成本。直接财务困境成本包括与财务困境相关联的法律和行政管理成本。间接财务困境成本包括债务代理成本以及由于陷入财务困境对企业的经营产生负面影响而导致的损失。

Free Cash Flow(FCF)

Cash flows that can be freely available to debt and equity investors after considering new capital expenditure and working capital requirements. $FCE = PBIT - \text{tax} - \text{additional investments in assets} + \text{Non-cash expenses(eg. depreciation)} + \text{any new capital raised}$.

自由现金流

在考虑新的资本支出和营运资本需求后，可以自由分配给债务和权益投资者的现金流。自由现金流＝息税前利润－所得税－额外的资产投资＋无现金支出的费用（比如折旧）＋新筹集的资金。

【知识点巩固与拓展】

Futurebright 公司拟收购 Mayflower 公司所有的股权。假设每年的现金流相同，关于 Mayflower 公司未来每年的有关信息估计如下：

息税前利润 100 000 美元，折旧等其他未支出现金的费用 12 000 美元，资本性支出 25 000 美元，额外的营运资本需求 10 000 美元。公司所得税税率 30%。Mayflower 公司的贷款总额为 200 000 美元，平均利率 6%。Mayflower 公司与 Futurebright 公司属于同一行业，财务杠杆同为 20%（债务在总资本中占的比例）。Futurebright 公司的权益资本成本为 14%。请给 Mayflower 公司的股权估值。

自由现金流$=100\ 000\times 0.7+12\ 000-25\ 000-10\ 000$

$=47\ 000$(美元)

加权平均资本成本$=14\%\times 80\%+6\%\times 0.7\times 20\%=12\%$

公司价值$=47\ 000/12\%=391\ 667$(美元)

股权价值$=391\ 667-200\ 000=191\ 667$(美元)

Futurebright plc. is planning to make a bid for all the equity capital of Mayflower Ltd. The following yearly information about Mayflower in the future is estimated, assuming a constant cash flows each year. PBIT \$100 000, depreciation and other non-cash expenses \$12 000, capital expenditure \$25 000, new working capital requirements \$10 000. Corporation tax rate is 30%. Mayflower has bank loans of \$200 000 with average interest rate 6%.

Mayflower and Futurebright are in the same business sector and they both have a gearing level of 20% (debt/total capital employed).

Futurebright's cost of equity is 14%, Value the equity of Mayflower.

$FCF = \$100\ 000\times 0.7+\$12\ 000-\$25\ 000-\$10\ 000$

$= \$47\ 000$

$WACC=14\%\times 80\%+6\%\times 0.7\times 20\%=12\%$

Value of Mayflower$= \$47\ 000/12\%= \$391\ 667$

Value of equity$= \$391\ 667- \$200\ 000= \$191\ 667$

Free Cash Flow to Equity(FCFE)

Cash flows that can be freely distributable to shareholders after considering new assets investment, paying interest and repaying debt capital. $FCFE = PBIT$ − interest − tax − additional investments in assets − debt repayment + Non-cash expenses (eg. depreciation)+any new capital raised.

权益自由现金流

在考虑新资产的投资以及债务的还本付息需求以后，可以自由分配给股东的现金流。权益自由现金流=息税前利润−利息费用−所得税−额外的资产投资−还债资金+无现金支出的费用（比如折旧）+新筹集的资金。

【知识点巩固与拓展】

沿用上面自由现金流的例子。用权益自由现金流来给 Mayflower 公司的股权估值。

权益自由现金流=47 000−200 000×6%×0.7=38 600（美元）

权益资本成本 14%，则：

股权价值=38 600/14%=275 714（美元）

Continuing with the example for FCF, using FCFE to value the equity of Mayflower.

FCFE= \$47 000− \$200 000×6%×0.7= \$38 600

Cost of equity=14%

Value of equity= \$38 600/14%= \$275 714

Intrinsic Value

The value of an option if it was exercised now, that is the difference between the current price of the underlying asset and the exercise price of the option. Intrinsic value of a call option＝Max[(current price of the underlying asset－exercise price of the call option),0]; Intrinsic value of a put option＝Max[(exercise price of the put option－current price of the underlying asset),0].

(期权)内含价值

(期权)内含价值是指如果现在行使期权所具有的价值,即标的资产的当前价格与期权执行价格之间的差额。看涨期权的内含价值＝Max[(标的资产的当前价格－看涨期权的执行价格),0];看跌期权的内含价值＝ Max[(看跌期权的执行价格－标的资产的当前价格),0]。

M

M&M's Formula for K_e

$K_e = K_e^i + (1-T)(K_e^i - K_d)\frac{V_d}{V_e}$ (K_e is cost of equity of a geared company, K_e^i is the cost of equity of an ungeared company, K_d is before-tax cost of debt, V_e is the market value of equity, V_d is the market value of debt). This formula reflects the effect on cost of equity of debt financing, such as the tax relief of interest payments and the increase in financial risk etc.

M&M 计算杠杆公司权益资本成本的公式

$K_e = K_e^i + (1-T)(K_e^i - K_d)\frac{V_d}{V_e}$ (K_e 是杠杆公司的权益资本

成本，K_e^i 是无杠杆公司的权益资本成本，K_d 是税前债务资本成本，V_e 是权益的市值，V_d 是债务的市值)。这个公式反映了债务融资对权益资本成本的影响，比如利息支付的节税效应以及财务风险的增加等。

Macaulay Duration

The weighted average time taken to deliver the cash inflows of an investment, the weights being proportion of the present value of the cash inflows contributed in each period. The formula is: $D=(1\times PV_1+2\times PV_2+\cdots+n\times PV_n)/\sum_{i=1}^{n}PV_i$ (PV_i is the present value of cash inflows in period i discounted at current required yield by investors).

麦考利久期

一项投资的现金流入所需时间的加权平均值，权数为每期现金流现值在投资所得现金流总现值中的占比。公式：$D=(1\times PV_1+2\times PV_2+\cdots+n\times PV_n)/\sum_{i=1}^{n}PV_i$（$PV_i$ 为第 i 期的现金流用目前市场所要求的收益率来折现的现值）。

【知识点巩固与拓展】

A 公司发行了一债券，票面利率为 6%、面值为 100 美元，于三年后以高于面值 3% 的价格赎回。当前债券到期收益率为 5%。计算这种债券的久期。

年份	现金流($)	折现系数(5%)	现值($)	现值×年数
1	6	0.952	5.712	5.712
2	6	0.907	5.442	10.884
3	109	0.864	94.176	282.528
合计			105.33	299.124

久期=299.124÷105.33=2.84(年)

Company A issued a 6% bond with a nominal value of $100 redeemable at 3% premium in three years' time. The required yield is 5%. Calculate the duration of the bond.

Yr.	*CF*($)	*DF*(5%)	*PV*($)	*PV*×*Yr*
1	6	0.952	5.712	5.712
2	6	0.907	5.442	10.884
3	109	0.864	94.176	282.528
Total			105.33	299.124

Duration=299.124÷105.33=2.84(years)

Modified Duration

It is calculated as: Macaulay duration/(1+yield). It is a useful measure of the sensitivity of a bond price to changes in interest rates.

修正久期

计算公式:修正久期$=\dfrac{\text{麦考利久期}}{1+\text{所要求收益率}}$。它是衡量债券价格对利率变化敏感度的一个有用指标。

【知识点巩固与拓展】

沿用麦考利久期的例子。久期为 2.84 年，投资者要求的收益率为 5%。计算修正久期。

修正久期＝2.84/(1＋5%)＝2.70

投资者要求的收益率每增加 1%，债券价格就下跌 2.70%。

Continuing with the example of Macaulay duration. The duration of the bond is 2.84 years, the required yield is 5%. Calculate the modified duration.

Modified duration＝2.84/(1＋5%)＝2.70. That is if the required yield rises by 1%, the bond price will fall by 2.70%.

Modified IRR(MIRR)

The internal rate of return (IRR) that would result if it was assumed that the project cash flows are reinvested at the cost of capital of the company instead of the IRR. The formula to calculate MIRR is as follows: $MIRR=\left(\frac{PV_R}{PV_I}\right)^{1/n}\times(1+r_e)-1$ (PV_R is the present value of return phase, PV_I is the present value of the investment phase, r_e is the cost of capital). The assumption about the reinvestment rate is more realistic and there is only one MIRR.

修正内部收益率(MIRR)

假设项目所获得的现金流以公司的资本成本而不是内部收益率(IRR)再投资时产生的内部收益率。计算修正内部收益率的公式：$MIRR=\left(\frac{PV_R}{PV_I}\right)^{1/n}\times(1+r_e)-1$（$PV_R$ 是回报期间的现金流现值，PV_I 是投资期间的现金流现值，r_e 是资本成本）。修正内部收益率关于再投资回报率的假设更现实，而且只有一个修正内部收益率。

【知识点巩固与拓展】

一个 4 年期的项目，每年的现金流如下（单位：百万美元）：第 0 年 −200；第 1 年 120；第 2 年 180；第 3 年 −20；第 4 年 200。目前的资本成本 14%。计算 MIRR。

$PV_R = 120\times0.877+180\times0.769-20\times0.675+200\times0.592=348.56$ 百万（美元）

$PV_I=200$ 百万（美元）

$MIRR=(348.56/200)^{1/4}\times(1+14\%)-1=30.98\%$

A four-year project will generate the following cash flows (in \$m): Year 0 (200); Year 1 120; Year 2 180; Year 3 (20); Year 4 200. The current cost of capital is 14%. Calculate MIRR.

$PV_R=\$120m\times0.877+\$180m\times0.769-\$20m\times0.675+\$200m\times0.592=\$348.56m$

$PV_I=\$200m$

$MIRR=(348.56/200)^{1/4}\times(1+14\%)-1=30.98\%$

O

Option to Expand

If the project concerned is successful, other investment opportunities will be available to follow. These further investments brought about by the underlying project are options to expand, and will add value to the project concerned.

拓展期权

如果所评估的项目投资成功，随后就会带来其他投资机会。这些所投项目带来的额外的投资机会就是拓展期权，会给所评估的项目增值。

【知识点巩固与拓展】

拓展期权(option to expand)、递延期权(option to delay)、转移部署期权(option to redeploy)、退出期权(option to withdraw)都是实物期权(real options)。拓展期权和递延期权都需要企业将来出资，故两者是看涨期权(call option)。而转移部署期权和退出期权将来会为企业节省资金或使企业收到资金，故两者是看跌期权(put option)。

Option to Delay

If a company has a right to choose to invest now or to postpone to a later time, the company has an option to delay. This option to delay will add value to the project concerned.

递延期权/择机期权

如果一家公司有权选择是现在投资还是推后投资，该公司就获得了递延期权。递延期权将会增加所投项目的价值。

Option to Redeploy

If the project concerned fails, the company can switch the assets of the project to another project. The company has an option to redeploy, and this option to redeploy will add value to the project concerned.

转移部署期权

如果所投项目失败，公司则可以把该项目的资产转移部署到另一项目。公司就拥有转移部署期权，这种转移部署期权会增加所投项目的价值。

Option to Withdraw

If the project concerned fails, the company has the option to cease the project anytime during the project life and to sell the assets for some salvage value. This option is an option to withdraw, and it adds value of the project.

退出期权

如果所投项目不成功，公司就可以在项目投资周期内任何时间选择停止项目并把项目资产卖掉以获得一些残余价值。这就是退出期权，它将增加所投项目的价值。

P

Post-audit

Monitoring and reviewing the financial returns and risks of

the investment project after the commencement of the project and during the project life, and measures being taken to address any concerns to ensure the success of the investment.

事后审计(投资)

事后审计是指在项目开始后以及整个项目投资周期，监督并审核投资项目的财务回报和风险，以及为解决问题所采取的措施，以确保所投项目成功运行。

Project Duration

The average time over which a project originates cash inflows. Project duration = time period × % of the present value of cash inflows in each year. For example, the present values of cash inflows for a project are as follows: Year 1 \$400; Year 2 \$500; Year 3 \$500; Year 4 \$600. The project duration = 1×400/2 000 + 2×500/2 000 + 3×500/2 000 + 4×600/2 000 = 2.65 (years). The higher the project duration, the higher the risk and uncertainty of a project.

项目久期

项目久期是指一个项目产生现金流的平均时间。项目久期＝年份×该年现金流的现值占项目总现金流入现值的比例。例如，一个项目现金流入的现值如下：第一年 400 美元；第二年 500 美元；第三年 500 美元；第四年 600 美元。项目久期＝1×400/2 000＋2×500/2 000＋3×500/2 000＋4×600/2 000＝2.65(年)。久期越长，项目的风险和不确定性越大。

【知识点巩固与拓展】

一个 4 年期的项目，每年的现金流如下(单位：百万美元)：第 0 年 －200；第 1 年 120；第 2 年 180；第 3 年 －20；第 4 年 200。目前资本成本为 14％。请计算项目久期。

现金流入年份的现值计算如下(单位：百万美元)：

第 1 年 120×0.877＝105.24

第 2 年 180×0.769＝138.42

第 4 年 200×0.592＝118.40

合 计 362.06

项目久期＝1×105.24/362.06＋2×138.42/362.06＋4×118.4/362.06＝2.36(年)

A four-year project will generate the following cash flows (in $m): Year 0 (200); Year 1 120; Year 2 180; Year 3 (20); Year 4 200. The current cost of capital is 14%. Calculate the project duration.

Present value of cash inflows(in $m):

Year 1 120×0.877＝105.24

Year 2 180×0.769＝138.42

Year 4 200×0.592＝118.40

Total 362.06

Project duration＝1×105.24/362.06＋2×138.42/362.06＋4×118.4/362.06＝2.36(years)

R

Real Options

Actual right to make choices in relation to an investment project. This gives flexibility to investors and the flexibility significantly increases the value of the underlying project. The investing company may have the option to expand, the option to delay, the option to redeploy or the option to withdraw.

实物期权

实物期权是公司对所投项目拥有的选择权。这给予投资者一定的灵活性，而这种灵活性大大增加了所投项目的价值。投资公司可能有拓展期权、择机期权、转移部署期权或者退出期权。

Return Margin

The extent to which MIRR exceeds the cost of capital, that is: return margin $= MIRR -$ cost of capital. It reflects the extent to which a new project is creating value.

回报差率

回报差率就是指修正内部收益率高出资本成本的程度。计算公式为：回报差率＝修正内部收益率－资本成本。它反映了一个项目创造价值的能力。

【知识点巩固与拓展】

项目 A 的内部修正收益率为 14.9%，项目 B 的内部修正收益率为 16%。公司目前的资本成本为 14%。计算回报差率并据此评论两个项目的优劣。

项目 A 的回报差率＝14.9%－14%＝0.9%

项目 B 的回报差率＝16%－14%＝2%

根据回报差率，项目 B 胜出。

MIRR of Project A is 14.90%, MIRR of Project B is 16%, the current cost of capital of the company is 14%. Calculate the return margin of Project A and B respectively and comment on which project is better.

Return margin of A＝14.9%－14%＝0.9%

Return margin of B＝16%－14%＝2%

B is a better project, according to return margin.

Risk-adjusted Discount Factor

Discount factors of a risk-adjusted discount rate, that is if a project is of high risk, the discount rate should be adjusted higher accordingly to reflect the higher risk premium required by investors.

风险调整的折现系数

这是根据风险而调整过的折现率的折现系数。如果一个项目的风险比较高，那折现率也要相应地调高，以反映投资者所要求的更高的风险溢价。

S

Syndicated Loan

A group of banks work together as a syndicate to provide a loan to a borrower.

银团贷款

银团贷款是指几家银行组织起来形成一个银团，一起给借款方提供贷款。

T

Time Value

The value of an option =intrinsic value + time value. There are chances for the value of an option to increase and to exceed intrinsic value between now and the time to expiration. The difference between the market price of an option and its intrinsic value is the time value of the option. The more time an option has until expiry, the larger its time value.

（期权）时间价值

期权的总价值＝内含价值＋时间价值。从现在至到期日，期权的价值有机会超过内含价值。期权的市价与其内含价值之差就是时间价值。从现在至到期日，时间越长，时间价值越大。

V

Value at risk (VaR)

The worst outcome over a set period with only $x\%$ chance of being exceeded [at a $(100-x)\%$ confidence level]. For example, 95% value at risk means the worst NPV that a project produces at a 95% confidence level. 95% value at risk $=1.645\times$ standard deviation $\times\sqrt{\text{time period of the project}}$. 99% value at risk $=2.326\times$ standard deviation $\times\sqrt{\text{time period of the project}}$.

在险价值

在设定期限内的最坏结果，只有 $x\%$ 的可能性被超过[在 $(100-x)\%$ 的置信水平]。例如，95%的在险价值指在95%的置信水平下一个项目的最低 NPV。95%的在险价值 $=1.645\times$ 标准差 $\times\sqrt{\text{项目周期}}$。99%的在险价值 $=2.326\times$ 标准差 $\times\sqrt{\text{项目周期}}$。

【知识点巩固与拓展】

某项目的 NPV 为 600 万美元，标准差为 160 万美元。项目周期为 5 年。计算 95%置信水平的在险价值。

$VaR=1.645\times160\times\sqrt{5}=589$ 万(美元)，即该项目最差的 NPV 为 589 万美元，只有 5%的概率该项目的 NPV 会低于 589 万美元。

A project has a NPV of \$6 million and a standard deviation of \$1.6 million per annum. The project life is five years. Calculate the value at risk at a 95% confidence level.

$VaR = 1.645 \times \$1.6m \times \sqrt{5} = \$5.89m$, ie, the worst NPV of the project is \$5.89m, there is only 5% chance of being even worse.

Module Ten

Acquisitions and Mergers/收购与兼并

本单元的学习目标：全面（从战略、财务、法规等方面）评估兼并与收购方案及其融资方案，包括对兼并与收购方案估值。

C

Cash Offer

Acquiring a target company's shares by offering cash.

现金收购

现金收购是指通过向目标公司支付现金来购得其股权。

Commercial Due Diligence

Undertaking investigations in due diligence to assess the target company's commercial status, such as the competition, the appropriateness of the business plan, the distribution channel and the customer base etc.

商务尽职调查

商务尽职调查是指通过尽职调查来评估目标公司的商务状况，比如竞争状况、商业计划的合理性、分销渠道以及客户基础等。

Cost Synergy

Extra cost savings resulting from an acquisition, for example, better terms negotiated from suppliers, cost savings from sharing facilities between the acquirer and the acquiree.

成本协同

成本协同是指一项收购所带来的额外的成本节省，比如，跟供货商谈判获得更优惠的购买条款，购买方和被购买方由于在设施方面的共享而节省的成本。

Crown Jewels

Valuable assets of the target company which attract investors are disposed of to make the target company itself less attractive as a take-over target. It is one of the defensive tactics against a take-over.

"皇冠之珠"防御

目标公司因其优质资产而吸引投资者来收购，所以处置了这些优质资产，目标公司作为收购目标的吸引力就下降。这是反收购策略之一。

D

Defensive Strategies against a Takeover

Strategies a company adopts to counter against a hostile takeover, including both pre-bid and post-bid defences.

反收购的防御战略

这是一家公司为了应对恶意收购而采取的战略,包括在接到收购报价之前以及之后的各项防御策略。

Due Diligence Investigation

Investigating a target company in due diligence to assess its status in legal, financial, commercial or other aspects for the various purposes. An acquiring company will undertake a due diligence investigation of the target company before a take-over is finalized in order to make sure it is a good target.

尽职调查

出于各种不同目的对目标公司诸如法律、财务、商务和其他方面进行尽职调查。一家收购公司将在收购完成前对目标公司进行尽职调查以确保这是一个优质收购标的。

F

Financial Synergy

Extra financial benefits resulting from an acquisition. For example, a company with positive-NPV projects is acquired by a company with adequate cash, then extra NPV can be earned. Other financial benefits may include tax savings and risk diversification etc.

财务协同

财务协同是指收购所带来的财务方面的额外效益。例如，一家拥有正的净现值项目的公司被一家资金充裕的公司所收购，就可以投资这些项目并取得额外的净现值。其他方面的财务效益还有税负减少、风险分散等。

Financial Due Diligence

Investigations in due diligence are undertaken to assess the financial status of a target company, mainly to verify the financial information provided by the target company.

财务尽职调查

财务尽职调查是对目标公司进行尽职调查，以评估目标公司的财务状况，主要是验证目标公司所提供的财务信息。

G

Golden Parachutes

A large sum of payments are promised to board members or senior executives when they leave the company. It is one of the defences against a hostile take-over, as it increases the cost of take-over.

“金降落伞”防御

向董事会成员及公司高管承诺，在他们离职时，公司将向他们支付一大笔款项。这是防御恶意收购的一项策略，因为它增加了收购的成本。

Growth Strategies

Strategies adopted to achieve the growth objectives of a company. A company can expand its business through internal development, acquisitions & mergers and joint ventures.

增长战略

这是为达到增长目标，公司所采取的战略。一家公司可以通过内部开发、兼并与收购以及合营等方式来达到扩张业务的目的。

L

Legal Due Diligence

Investigating in due diligence the target company to check for any legal concerns. For example, investigate any pending litigation and compliance checks.

法律尽职调查

尽职调查目标公司,去查验任何关于法律方面的问题。比如,调查未决诉讼,以及合规检查等。

Litigation or Regulatory Defence

A defensive strategy employed by a target company against a hostile take-over by inviting an investigation by the regulatory authorities or by suing for a temporary order on a court to stop the bidder from purchasing any more of its shares.

诉讼或监管防御

这是一家目标公司为了反恶意收购而采取的防御措施,主要是向监管部门申请对收购行为予以调查,或向法院起诉收购方以取得法院临时命令,以阻止收购方购买公司更多股权的行为。

M

Maximum to Pay for an Acquisition (Post-acquisition P/E Valuation)

It is calculated as : value of the combined company − pre-acquisition value of the bidder. Value of combined company = earnings of the combined company × new P/E ratio.

收购方最高出价(购并后市盈率估值法)

计算公式如下:收购方最高出价=购并后合并公司的价值−出价方收购前的价值,购并后合并公司的价值=合并公司的收益×新的市盈率。

【知识点巩固与拓展】

Futurebright 公司正考虑购买 Mayflower 公司所有的股权。Futurebright 公司目前的市盈率为 25,收益为 12 亿美元。Mayflower 公司目前的市盈率为 15,收益为 6 亿美元。合并后因为协同效应而创造的额外收益为 2 亿美元。合并后公司新的市盈率为 30。计算 Futurebright 公司收购 Mayflower 公司所支付的价款最多为多少。

合并公司的收益=12 亿+6 亿+2 亿=20 亿(美元)

合并公司的价值=20 亿×30=600 亿(美元)

Futurebright 公司合并前价值=12 亿×25=300 亿(美元)

最高出价=600 亿−300 亿=300 亿(美元)

Futurebright plc. is considering to acquire the entire share capital of Mayflower Ltd. Futurebright currently has a P/E ratio of 25 and earnings of ＄1 200 million. Mayflower currently has a P/E ratio of 15 and earnings of ＄600 million.

It is estimated that there will be ＄200 million earnings increase due to synergies created by the takeover and P/E ratio of the new combined company is 30. Calculate the maximum to pay for the acquisition of Mayflower by Futurebright.

Earnings of the combined company = ＄1 200m + ＄600m + ＄200m = ＄2 000m

Value of the combined company = ＄2 000m × 30 = ＄60 000m

Pre-acquisition value of the bidder = ＄1 200m × 25 = ＄30 000m

Maximum to pay for the acquisition = ＄60 000m − ＄30 000m = ＄30 000m

Mandatory Bid Rule

One of the rules of the EU Take-over Directive. Once the bidder has accumulated a certain percentage of shares, the bidder is required to provide to the remaining shareholders a fair price in case that the bidder exploit its position at the expense of minority shareholders.

强制报价规则

这是欧盟《购并法令》中的一条规则。一旦收购方的股权累积到一定比例，就要求收购方给予其他股东一个公允报价，以防收购方为了自己的利益而牺牲了少数股东的利益。

Mixed Offer

Acquiring a target company's shares by a combination of cash offer and paper offer. The payment for the acquisition is partly in cash, partly in share exchange.

混合型收购

混合型收购是指通过支付现金和股权交换两种形式的结合来购得目标公司的股权。部分以现金支付,部分用股权交换。

O

Organic Growth

The growth a company achieves by expanding its business and increasing its sales through its own resources. Organic growth is in contrast to inorganic growth, such as growth through acquisitions and mergers.

有机增长

有机增长是指依靠自身资源来扩张业务、增加销售从而取得的公司增长。有机增长与无机增长形成对比,比如通过购并所实现的增长。

P

Paper Offer

Purchasing the target company's shares by issuing shares to

pay for the acquisition.

股权交换收购

股权交换收购是指通过发行新股给目标公司购得其股权。

Poison Pills

One of the defensive strategies against hostile take-overs. The target company takes measures to make its shares too expensive to be acquired. The target company may issue new shares to existing shareholders at a discount or issue convertibles which will be converted to ordinary shares should the acquisition take place.

"毒丸"防御

这是反恶意收购的一种防御策略。目标公司采取措施使收购其股权的成本增加。目标公司可以折价发行新股给现有股东，或者发行可转换证券，一旦收购发生，这些可转换证券就会马上转成普通股。

The Principle of Equal Treatment

One of the principles underlying the EU Take-over Directive. It requires the bidder to offer to the remaining minority shareholders the same terms that is offered to earlier shareholders to acquire the controlling interest.

平等待遇原则

这是欧盟《购并法令》中的一条原则。它要求并购方向剩余的少数股东许诺的条款应与其从先前股东手里取得控制权益所许诺的条款相同。

R

Reverse Takeover

A smaller quoted company takes over a larger unquote company by a share -for-share exchange. A reserve takeover enables the unquoted company to obtain a stock market listing.

反向收购

反向收购是指一家规模较小的上市公司,通过以股换股方式,收购了一家规模更大的非上市公司。反向收购使这家非上市公司的股票得以上市。

Revenue Synergy

Additional revenue obtained after the acquisition as a result of sharing of marketing resources and an enhanced market power.

收入协同

收入协同是指收购之后,因营销资源的共享和市场力量的壮大而获得的额外收入。

S

Squeeze-out Rights

In order to protect the interests of the bidder in an acquisition, once the bidder has acquired a specific percentage of the equity, the bidder is given the right to force minority shareholders to sell their shares. Squeeze-out rights enable the bidder to acquire 100% of the equity once the threshold percentage has been reached.

挤出权利

为了保护并购过程中收购方的利益，一旦收购方取得了一定比例的股权，收购方就有权强制少数股东出售其股权。挤出权利使收购方一旦持股比例达到规定的门槛，就可以购得100%的股权。

V

Value Added by the Acquisition (Post-acquisition P/E Valuation)

It is calculated as: value of the combined company − pre-acquisition value of the bidder and the target company. Value of combined company = earnings of the combined company × new P/E ratio.

购并增值(合并后市盈率估值法)

计算公式如下:购并增值=购并后合并公司的价值−购并前收购方与被收购方价值之和,购并后合并公司的价值=合并公司的收益×新的市盈率。

【知识点巩固与拓展】

Futurebright 公司正考虑购买 Mayflower 公司所有的股权。Futurebright 公司目前的市盈率为 25，收益为 12 亿美元。Mayflower 公司目前的市盈率为 15，收益为 6 亿美元。合并后因协同效应而创造的额外收益为 2 亿美元。合并后公司新的市盈率为 30。计算 Futurebright 公司收购 Mayflower 公司后所增加的价值。

合并公司的收益＝12 亿＋6 亿＋2 亿＝20 亿(美元)

合并公司的价值＝20 亿×30＝600 亿(美元)

Futurebright 公司合并前价值＝12 亿×25＝300 亿(美元)

Mayflower 公司合并前价值＝6 亿×15＝90 亿(美元)

购并增值＝600 亿－390 亿＝210 亿(美元)

Futurebright plc. is considering to acquire the entire share capital of Mayflower Ltd. Futurebright currently has a P/E ratio of 25 and earnings of ＄1 200 million. Mayflower currently has a P/E ratio of 15 and earnings of ＄600 million.

It is estimated that there will be ＄200 million earnings increase due to synergies created by the takeover and P/E ratio of the new combined company is 30. Calculate value added by the acquisition of Mayflower by Futurebright.

Earnings of the combined company

＝＄1 200m＋＄600m＋＄200m＝＄2 000m

Value of the combined company＝＄2 000m×30＝＄60 000m

Pre-acquisition value of Futurebright

＝＄1 200m×25＝＄30 000m

Pre-acquisition value of Mayflower＝＄600m×15＝＄9 000m

Total of pre-acquisition value

$= \$30\ 000m + \$9\ 000m = \$39\ 000m$

Value added $= \$60\ 000m - \$39\ 000m = \$21\ 000m$

Value Added by the Acquisition（Post-acquisition Cash Flow Valuation）

It is calculated as: value of the combined company − pre-acquisition value of the bidder and the target company. Value of combined company is valued using post-acquisition group cash flows discounted by post-acquisition group WACC.

购并增值（合并后现金流估值法）

计算公司如下：购并增值＝购并后合并公司的价值－购并前收购方与被收购方价值之和。购并后合并公司的价值是把购并后合并公司的自由现金流用购并后合并公司的加权平均资本成本折现所得到的现值。

【知识点巩固与拓展】

Futurebright 公司拟收购 Mayflower 公司所有股权。该公司打算支付 21 亿美元，所有款项都由利率 6.5%的债务融资。

目前，Futurebright 公司共有 2 亿股股票，股价为每股 150 美元，债务 20 亿美元（税前利率 6%），权益 β 为 0.90。

目前，Mayflower 公司共有 1 亿股股票，股价为每股 90 美元，债务 9 亿美元，权益 β 为 1.50。

无风险利率 5%，市场平均回报率 9%，企业所得税税率 30%。

假设购并前，所有现有债务的利率平均为税前6.5%。

购并后，Futurebright公司目前业务的自由现金流为35亿美元，Mayflower公司目前业务的自由现金流为9亿美元，协同效应增加的现金流为2亿美元。计算购并的增值以及Futurebright公司的最高出价。

Futurebright公司购并前的股权价值

=2亿×150=300亿(美元)

Mayflower公司购并前的股权价值=1亿×90=90亿(美元)

两家公司购并前的股权总价值

=300亿+90亿=390亿(美元)

把权益β去杠杆：

Futurebright公司的资产β

=300/(300+20×0.7)×0.90=0.86

Mayflower公司的资产β=90/(90+9×0.7)×1.50=1.40

购并后的资产β=0.86×(300/390)+1.40×(90/390)=0.98

合并公司的总债务=20亿+9亿+21亿=50亿(美元)

合并公司的权益β=0.98×(390+50×0.7)/390=1.07

合并后的权益资本成本=5%+1.07×(9%-5%)=9.28%

合并后 *WACC* =9.28%×390/(390+50)+6.5%×[50/(390+50)]×0.7

=8.74%

合并公司的自由现金流=35亿+9亿+2亿=46亿(美元)

合并公司的价值=46÷8.74%=526.32亿(美元)

合并公司的权益价值=526.32亿-50亿=476.32亿(美元)

购并增值=476.32亿-390亿=86.32亿(美元)

购并方最高出价=476.32亿-300亿=176.32亿(美元)

Futurebright plc. is considering to acquire the entire share capital of Mayflower Ltd. Futurebright plans to pay \$2 100 million and all funds are raised by new debts at 6.5%.

Currently, Futurebright has 200 million shares which are priced at \$150 per share and \$2 000 million of debts (paying interest at 6% pre-tax) and an equity beta of 0.90.

Currently, Mayflower has 100 million shares which are priced at \$90 per share and \$900 million of debts and an equity beta of 1.50.

The risk-free rate is 5%, market rate is 9%, corporation tax rate 30%. Assuming the interest rate of all existing debts will be 6.5% pre-tax on average after acquisition.

After acquisition, free cash flows of Futurebright's existing business are estimated to be \$3 500 million per year, free cash flows of Mayflower's existing business are estimated to be \$900 million. And there will be synergies of \$200 million post-tax per year.

Calculate value added by the acquisition of Mayflower by Futurebright and calculate the maximum to pay by Futurebright.

Pre-acquisition value of Futurebright

$=200\text{m}\times \$150=\$30\ 000\text{m}$

Pre-acquisition value of Mayflower

$=100\text{m}\times \$90=\$9\ 000\text{m}$

Total pre-acquisition value $=\$30\ 000+\$9\ 000=\$39\ 000\text{m}$

De-gearing equity beta: asset beta of Futurebright

$=30\ 000/(30\ 000+2\ 000\times 0.7)\times 0.90=0.86$

Asset beta of Mayflower

$=9\ 000/(9\ 000+900\times 0.7)\times 1.50=1.40$

Post-acquisition asset beta

$=0.86\times(30\ 000/39\ 000)+1.40\times(9\ 000/39\ 000)$

$=0.98$

Total debts of the combined company

= \$2 000 m+ \$900m+ \$2 100 m= \$5 000m

Equity beta of the combined company

$=0.98\times(39\ 000+5\ 000\times0.7)/39\ 000=1.07$

Post-acquisition $K_e=5\%+1.07\times(9\%-5\%)=9.28\%$

Post-acquistion *WACC*

$=9.28\%\times39\ 000/(39\ 000+5\ 000)+6.5\%\times[5\ 000/(39\ 000+5\ 000)]\times0.7=8.74\%$

FCF of the combined company

= \$3 500m+ \$900m+ \$200m= \$4 600m

Value of the combined company

= \$4 600m/8.74%= \$52 632m

Total value of equity after acquisition

= \$52 632m− \$5 000m= \$47 632m

Total value added

= \$47 632m− \$39 000m= \$8 632m

Maximum value to pay

= \$47 632m− \$30 000m= \$17 632m

W

White Knights

A defensive strategy adopted by a targe company against a

hostile take-over where the target company itself finds another friendly company to act as a counter-bidder and makes the cost of take-over too high to be accepted by the hostile bidder.

“白衣骑士”防御

这是反恶意收购的一种防御策略，即目标公司自己找另一家友好的公司去竞价收购，从而使恶意收购方因收购成本过高而退出收购。

Module Eleven

Corporate Reconstruction and Reorganization/公司重组

本单元的学习目标：

(1)评估财务重组(financial reconstruction)战略的适宜性，考虑财务重组对资本市场投资者的影响以及对公司价值的影响；

(2)根据公司的具体情况，提出企业重组的具体方案的建议，评估分拆公司方案的优缺点，指出管理层收购可能存在的财务问题。

B

Business Reorganization

Reorganizing the operations and the structure of a business in order to achieve a higher level of performance. Unbundling is a form of business reorganization.

企业重组

为了使企业业绩达到更高的水平，企业重组其业务及其组织结构。企业分拆是企业重组的一种形式。

Buy-in Management Buy-out(BIMBO)

Selling a part of or the whole of a business to a management team which is composed of both existing management(MBO) and outsider managers (MBI).

外部经理人参与的管理层收购

将企业的一部分或全部出售给由现有管理层(MBO)和外部经理人(MBI)共同组成的管理团队。

D

Divestment(Sell-off)

The practice of selling off part of a business to a third party in order to release funds and concentrate resources on core areas of strategic value. The part that is disposed off is usually of very low strategic value or even a loss-maker.

资产剥离(抛售)

为了释放资金，把资源集中到有战略价值的核心领域，而将企业的一部分出售给第三方的行为被称为资产剥离(抛售)。被处置的部分通常具有非常低的战略价值甚至是亏损业务。

Demerger(Spin-off)

The opposite of a merger. It involves splitting the whole company into two or more separate and independent bodies. And a new company is created for each new independent body and existing shareholders are given a stake in each of the new separate companies.

企业分拆

这是跟兼并相反的操作。把整个公司拆分为两个或两个以上分开的、独立的实体。并且每个独立的实体成立一家新公司，现有的股东获得每家拆分出去的新公司相应的股份。

E

Equity Ratchet

In order to protect itself against the dilution in value of its shareholding in a specific company, the private equity provider will set demanding financial targets when providing equity finance to the company. Once the company to be invested fails to hit targets, extra shares will be transferred to them at no additional cost.

棘轮条款

为了保护自己所持某公司股权的价值不被稀释，私募权益资金的提供方在向该公司注入权益资金时将设定苛刻的财务目标。一旦被投资公司没有达到这些财务目标，就应免费向私募股权的投资方提供一定数量的额外的股票。

F

Financial Reconstruction

Restructuring a company's finances, that is changing the capital structure of the firm.

财务重组

财务重组是对企业的财务进行重组，即改变其资本结构。

Financial Reconstruction Scheme

A scheme employed by a company to reorganize its capital structure. A company may reconstruct its finance when it owes too much debts and is in danger of going bankrupt due to a high interest payment and capital repayment burden. The creditors may be persuaded to accept equity shares or new debts, or the company may attract new investors to inject fresh capital, or just change its dividend policy to increase its equity base. Sometimes, a company may reconstruct its capital structure just as part of a strategy to create value for the owners of the company. The company may undertake a leveraged buy-out, or a share repurchase scheme, or attract new capitals injections.

财务重组计划

这是公司对其资本结构进行重整的计划。当一家公司因欠债太多、还本付息压力太大而陷入即将破产的危险境地时，公司可以进行财务重组。它可以说服债权人以债换股或以债还债，或者吸引新的投资者向企业注资，或者仅仅改变股利政策来增加权益基础。有时，公司重组资本结构只是将其作为为所有者创造价值战略的一部分。公司可以进行杠杆收购，或回购股票，或只是吸引新的注资。

L

Leveraged Buy-out (LBO)

A publicly listed company is acquired by a specially established private company who funds the acquisition by substantial borrowing. After the acquisition, the public company goes private and its shares stop to be traded on a stock exchange.

杠杆收购

杠杆收购是指一家公开上市的公司被一家专门设立的非上市公司收购，收购的资金是通过大量的借债来筹集的。在杠杆收购后，这家上市公司变成非上市公司，其股票从此停止在证券交易所买卖。

M

Management Buy-in

Selling the whole or part of a business to a team of outside managers, as opposed to the business's own managers.

外部管理者收购

把企业整体或一部分出售给外部管理团队，而不是企业自己的管理者。

Management Buy-out(MBO)

Selling the whole or part of a business to its own management team.

管理层收购

把企业整体或一部分出售给企业自己的管理团队。

Mezzanine Finance

Finance that has some characteristics of both debt and equity. It is a financing method that lies between equity and debt. Convertible debt and preference shares are forms of Mezzanine finance.

夹层融资

这是一种介于权益与负债之间的融资方法。它是既具有某些债务特征，又具有某些权益特征的融资方式。可转债和可转优先股都是夹层融资方式。

N

Negative Covenants

Conditions set in a loan agreement that are intended to restrict certain behaviours of a borrower and protect the interests of creditors. A negative covenant is a ‘cannot-do’ list. For example, a typical negative covenant may state that the borrower cannot dispose important assets without the consent of lenders.

贷款协议中的消极条款

这是在贷款协议中设定的用以限制借款方行为、保护债权人利益的条款。消极条款就是一个借款方“不能做什么”的清单。比如，一条典型的消极条款就是规定借款方未经债权人同意不得处置重要资产。

P

Positive Covenants

Conditions set in a loan agreement that a borrower must follow to take positive actions to protect creditors’ interests. For example, a typical positive covenant may state that the borrower must provide quarterly and annual financial reports to the lender.

贷款协议中的积极条款

这是在贷款协议中设定的借款方必须遵循的、用以保护债权人利益的正面的积极的条款。例如，一条典型的积极条款规定借款方必须向债权人提供季度和年度财务报告。

Private Equity

Equity finance provided to start-ups or other small and medium-sized unquoted companies through private negotiations, also including equity finance provided for an management buy-out (MBO).

私募股权投资

私募股权是指通过私下协商，投向初创企业以及其他未上市的中小企业的权益资本，也包括为管理层收购（MBO）而提供的权益资本。

U

Unbundling

Restructuring a business by reorganizing it into a number of separate parts. Typical types of unbundling include divestment, management buy-out (MBO) and demerger. Divestment and MBO raise cash for the business, and demerger brings no cash inflows into the business.

企业分拆重组

这是指通过把企业分拆成若干个独立的部分来对企业进行重组。典型的企业分拆重组形式有资产剥离、管理层收购以及企业拆分。资产剥离和管理层收购为企业筹集资金，而企业拆分不会给企业带来任何的资金流入。

Module Twelve

Working Capital Management/营运资本管理

本单元的学习目标：

(1)了解资金管理职能在公司的短期财务管理和长期财务管理以及为公司创造长期价值中发挥的作用；

(2)熟悉各种金融工具及金融衍生品，能根据企业具体的外汇风险和利率风险管理需要，选择并评估合适的风险管理方法和对冲工具。

A

American Option

The option that the buyer has the right to exercise at any workday before the expiry date.

美式期权

购买方有权在到期日前的任何工作日选择行使权力的期权，就是美式期权。

At the Money

An option is at the money when the exercise price is equal to the market price.

平值

期权平值是指当其执行价格等于市场价格时。

B

Basis

The difference between the spot price and the futures price of the underlying assets. Basis＝futures price－spot price.

基差

基差是指标的资产的即期价格与期货价格之差。基差＝期货价格－即期价格。

【知识点巩固与拓展】

当前英镑兑美元的即期汇率为 1 英镑等于 1.363 5 美元，3 个月的远期汇率为 1 英镑等于 1.353 8 美元。

基差＝1.353 8－1.363 5＝－0.009 7

The current spot rate is USD 1.363 5 per £, the current three-month forward rate is USD 1.353 8 per £.

The basis＝1.353 8－1.363 5＝－0.009 7

Basis Risk

A gradual reduction in the difference between the spot price and the futures price (the basis) over time will usually be assumed. But in reality, there is risk that the basis will not decrease as assumed, and there is a possibility that the basis will even increase.

基差风险

一般假设随着时间的推移即期价格与期货价格之差(基差)会逐步减少。但现实中,基差可能并不会如预期的那样减少,甚至还存在增加的可能性。

C

Centralized Treasury

The policies and important decisions about treasury management of the company are all made by a centralized treasury department based at head office. And the funds are managed centrally.

集中的资金管理

公司关于资金管理的政策以及重大决策都由总部的资金管理部制定。资金也集中管理。

Currency Futures

An agreement with a futures exchange to fix the exchange rate for a set standard amount of currency for a specified time period.

货币期货

货币期货是与期货交易所签订的合约，在指定的期间以固定的汇率来交易指定的标准数量的货币。

【学习提示】

用货币期货对冲外汇交易风险，如果有外币应付款，则在期货市场上买进外币；如果有外币应收款，则在期货市场上卖出外币。

【知识点巩固与拓展】

Futurebright 公司是一家英国上市公司，目前有一笔 5 月 30 日的 500 万美元的应付款。今天是 1 月 1 日，英镑兑美元的即期汇率为 1 英镑＝1.437 7 美元。6 月份英镑期货的价格为 1 英镑＝1.310 3 美元。5 月 30 日，即期汇率为 1 英镑＝1.298 9 美元。6 月份英镑期货的价格变为 1 英镑＝1.300 1 美元。计算用期货对冲，5 个月后的结果。\$/£期货，每单标准为 125 000 英镑。

第一步：确立对冲策略(现在)。

5 月 30 日的应付款为 500 万美元，应该买进 500 万美元，同时卖出英镑来对冲。即卖出 6 月份的\$/£期货。

5 000 000÷1.310 3＝3 815 920(英镑)

3 815 920÷125 000＝31(份)

第二步：实际交易结算结果(5 月 30 日)。

5 000 0000÷1. 298 9=3 849 411(英镑)

第三步：期货结算结果。

1 月 1 日	卖出期货	1. 310 3
5 月 30 日	买进期货	1. 300 1
汇率差		0. 010 2

期货市场利润=0. 010 2×125 000×31=39 525(英镑)

第四步：综合结果。

500 万美元应付款的英镑成本

=3 849 411−39 525

=3 809 866(英镑)

Futurebright plc. is a UK company. It has a $5m payable in 30 May. Today is 1 January. The spot rate is £1=USD 1. 437 7 and June sterling futures price is USD 1. 310 3 per £. By 30 May, the spot rate is USD 1. 298 9 per £. And June sterling futures price moves to USD 1. 300 1 per £. Calculate the outcome of the futures hedge in five months' time. $/£ futures contract size is £125 000.

Step 1: set up the hedge (now).

A $5m payable in 30 May needs to be hedged by buying 5m dollars while selling out sterling, that is selling June sterling futures.

5 000 000÷1. 310 3=£3 815 920

3 815 920÷125 000=31(contracts)

Step 2: outcome of the actual transaction (30 May).

5 000 000÷1. 298 9=£3 849 411

Step 3: outcome of the futures.

1 Jan. selling sterling futures	1. 310 3
30 May buying sterling futures	1. 300 1

Difference 0. 010 2

Profit on the future=0. 010 2×125 000×31=£39 525

Step 4: net outcome.

Sterling cost =3 849 411−39 525=£3 809 866

D

Decentralized Treasury

The policies and important decisions about treasury management of the company are all made at divisional/subsidiary level. And the funds are managed decentrally.

分散的资金管理

公司关于资金管理的政策以及重大决策都由分部或子公司自己来做。资金也是分散管理。

Delta

One of the Greeks (risk factors that affect the value of options). Delta =change in an option price/change in the price of the underlying assets. It measures how much an option's value changes as the underlying asset value changes. $N(-d_1)$ for a put option and $N(d_1)$ for a call option.

For example, delta of a call option is 0. 7. When the price of the underlying shares increases $1, the price of the option will increase $0. 7. Another example, delta of a put option is −0. 4. When the price of the underlying shares decreases $1, the price of the put option will increase ＄0.4.

For long call options (and short put options), delta has a value between 0 and 1, for a long put option (and short call options), delta has a value between 0 and －1. The closer the value of delta to 0, the more insensitive the price of the option to the price changes in underlying assets. When delta＝0, the option is out of the money. When delta＝－1 (put option) or ＋1(call option), the option is in the money.

Delta 值

希腊值(影响期权价值的风险因素)之一。Delta＝期权的价格变化÷标的资产的价格变化。它计量了期权价格随标的资产价格变化的程度。看跌期权的 Delta 是$N(-d_1)$，看涨期权的 Delta 是$N(d_1)$。

比如，某看涨股票期权的 Delta 为 0.7。当股票价格上涨 1 美元时，期权价格上涨 0.7 美元。再如，某看跌股票期权的 Delta 为－0.4，当股票价格下跌 1 美元时，期权价格上涨 0.4 美元。看涨期权的多头(或看跌期权的空头)，Delta 值处于 0 和 1 之间。看跌期权的多头(或看涨期权的空头)，Delta 值处于 0 和－1 之间。Delta 值越接近 0，意味着期权价格对标的资产价格的变动越不敏感。当 Delta＝0 时，期权是虚值。当 Delta＝－1(看跌期权)或 Delta＝＋1 时，期权是实值。

【学习提示】

ACCA 全球考，希腊值中只有 Delta 会涉及计算题。

Delta Hedge

It is used to determine the number of options required to hedge the risk of holding a certain quantity of underlying assets using the value of delta. For example, the required number of shares to sell under put options = number of shares ÷ delta. The number of option contracts=number of shares÷(delta× size of contract).

Delta 对冲

用 Delta 值确定需要多少期权合约去对冲所持有的一定量的标的资产。比如:看跌期权需要卖出的股票数=所持有的股数÷Delta;需要卖出的股票看跌期权合约数=所持有的股数÷(Delta×单期权合约的标准股数)。

【知识点巩固与拓展】

公司 A 拥有 Spright 公司 200 万美元的股票,假设看跌期权的 Delta 值为 0.42,则需要用看跌期权卖出多少股股票来对冲股票价格下跌带来的持股风险?假设股票期权都是以 100 股股票为单位交易的,那需要购买多少份期权?

看跌期权卖出的股数=2 000 000/0.42=4 761 905

看跌期权合约数=4 761 905/100=47 619

Company A owns $2 million shares in Spright plc., if the delta value of the put options is 0.42, what is the number of shares that need to be sold under a put option to hedge this holding risk? And assume that the option contracts are for the purchase or sell of units of 100 shares. What is the number of put options purchased?

The number of shares to sell under put options

=2 000 000/0.42=4 761 905

The number of put options purchased=4 761 905/100=47 619

Direct Rate/Quote (Exchange Rate)

The exchange rate which is quoted per unit of foreign currency. For example, for a UK company, the direct quote between sterling and US dollar is as follows: £0. 8794 per USD.

直接标价法(汇率)

直接标价法就是以外币作为标准货币的汇率表示方法。例如，对于一家英国的公司，英镑和美元之间汇率的直接标价如下：1 美元=0. 879 4 英镑。

E

Effective Futures Rate

The effective exchange rate of a foreign currency receipts or payments after being hedged with currency futures. Effective futures rate =closing spot－change in future rate =opening future's rate－closing basis.

期货对冲后的有效汇率

这是指一笔外币收入或支出在用货币期货对冲以后的有效汇率。有效汇率=结算时即期汇率－期货平仓和建仓时的汇率差=期货建仓时的汇率－平仓时基差。

【学习提示】

建议用期货建仓时的汇率减去平仓时的基差这种计算方法来计算有效汇率。

【知识点巩固与拓展】

Futurebright 公司是一家英国上市公司，目前有一笔 5 月 30 日的 500 万美元的应付款。今天是 1 月 1 日，英镑兑美元的即期汇率为 1 英镑＝1.437 7 美元。6 月份英镑期货的价格为 1 英镑＝1.310 3 美元。5 月 30 日，即期汇率为 1 英镑＝1.298 9 美元。6 月份英镑期货的价格变为 1 英镑＝1.300 1 美元。如果用 6 月份英镑期货来对冲交易风险，计算有效汇率以及 500 万美元的英镑成本。

方法 1：

期货平仓和建仓汇率差＝1.300 1－1.310 3＝－0.010 2

有效汇率＝结算时即期汇率－汇率差

　　　　＝1.298 9－(－0.010 2)＝1.309 1

英镑成本＝5 000 000/1.309 1＝3 819 418(英镑)

方法 2：

平仓时基差＝1.300 1－1.298 9＝0.001 2

有效汇率＝期货建仓时的汇率－平仓时基差

　　　　＝1.310 3－0.001 2＝1.309 1

英镑成本＝5 000 000/1.309 1＝£3 819 418

Futurebright plc. is a UK company. It has a ＄5m payable in 30 May. Today is 1 January. The spot rate is £1＝USD 1.437 7 and June sterling futures price is USD 1.310 3 per £. By 30 May, the spot rate is USD 1.298 9 per £. And June sterling futures price moves to USD 1.300 1 per £. Calculate the effective futures rate if using June sterling futures to hedge transaction risk and calculate the sterling cost of ＄5m.

Method 1:

Difference = closing futures price − opening futures price

= 1.300 1 − 1.310 3 = −0.010 2

Effective rate = closing spot rate − difference

= 1.298 9 − (−0.010 2) = 1.309 1

Sterling cost = 5 000 000/1.309 1 = £3 819 418

Method 2:

Closing basis = 1.300 1 − 1.298 9 = 0.001 2

Effective rate = 1.310 3 − 0.001 2 = 1.309 1

Sterling cost = 5 000 000/1.309 1 = £3 819 418

European Options

Options that the buyer has the right to exercise only at the expiry date.

欧式期权

期权的购买者只能在到期日才有权行使权利的期权就是欧式期权。

【学习提示】

注意欧式期权与美式期权的区别。欧式期权只有到期日才行权,而美式期权是到期日前的时间都可行权。ACCA考试一般采用欧式期权。

Exchange-traded Currency Options

An agreement with an exchange to obtain the right not the obligation to buy or sell the option contract currency at a strike exchange rate on (or before) a specified future date after paying a premium.

交易所交易的货币期权/场内货币期权

这是与交易所签订的期权合约，买方在支付了期权费后，获得在将来以敲定的汇率在某个指定的日期（或之前）购买或出售期权合约货币的权利而非义务。

【学习提示】

根据企业将来是要卖出还是买进期权合约货币来决定是买看跌期权还是看涨期权以对冲风险。如果是买进期权合约货币，则需要买进看涨货币期权（call option）；如果是卖出期权合约货币，则需要买进看跌货币期权（put option）。

【知识点巩固与拓展】

Futurebright 公司是一家英国上市公司，目前有一笔 5 月 30 日的 500 万美元的应付款。今天是 1 月 1 日，英镑兑美元的即期汇率为 1 英镑=1.437 7 美元。$/£ £31 250 期权（多少美分/£）的当前每份合约的期权费信息如下：

看涨期权			
敲定价格	6 月	9 月	12 月
1.423 0	3.24	3.60	3.89
1.446 8	2.16	2.41	2.85
1.470 0	1.45	1.97	2.27

看跌期权			
敲定价格	6 月	9 月	12 月
1.423 0	1.24	1.60	1.89
1.446 8	1.29	1.91	2.15
1.470 0	1.45	2.07	2.77

5 个月的远期汇率为 1.450 0 美元/英镑。

要求：假设最后行权，计算用期权对冲的英镑成本。

第一步：确定对冲策略。

5 月 30 日有美元的应付账款，需要买进美元，卖出英镑。英镑是期权合约货币，故买进 6 月份的 \$/£看跌期权合约。选取敲定价格 1.470 0。

需要的期权合约数＝5 000 000/1.470 0÷31 250＝109(份)

需要支付的期权费＝0.014 5×31 250×109＝49 391(美元)

期权费折成英镑＝49 391/1.437 7＝34 354(英镑)

第二步：期权市场行权。

行权支付的英镑＝109×31 250＝3 406 250

行权买进的美元＝3 406 250×1.470 0＝5 007 187.5

多出 7 187.5 美元，远期汇率为 1.450 0，折成英镑＝7 187.5/1.450 0＝4 957(英镑)

第三步：综合结果。

行权英镑成本 3 406 250 英镑＋期权费 34 354 英镑－多出 7 187.5 美元的远期市场英镑收入 4 957 英镑＝3 435 647 英镑

Futurebright plc. is a UK company. It has a \$5m payable in 30 May. Today is 1 January. The spot rate is £1＝USD 1.437 7.

The details for \$/£ £31 250 options(cents per £):

Calls			
Strike price	June	September	December
1.423 0	3.24	3.60	3.89
1.446 8	2.16	2.41	2.85
1.470 0	1.45	1.97	2.27

Puts			
Strike price	June	September	December
1.423 0	1.24	1.60	1.89
1.446 8	1.29	1.91	2.15
1.470 0	1.45	2.07	2.77

Five-month forward rate is \$1.450 0 /£.

Calculate the sterling cost if the option is exercised.

Step 1: set up the hedge.

There are 5 million dollars payable on 30 May. The company needs to purchase dollars and sell sterling. Sterling is the option contract currency, so buy June \$/£ put options. The strike price is 1.470 0. Number of option contracts = 5 000 000/1.470 0 ÷ 31 250 = 109 premium = 0.014 5 × 31 250 × 109 = \$49 391

Premium = 49 391/1.437 7 = £34 354

Step 2: options market outcome.

Exercise option 109 × 31 250 = £3 406 250

3 406 250 × 1.470 0 = \$5 007 187.5

Surplus \$7 187.5, five-month forward rate 1.450 0, 7 187.5/1.450 0 = £4 957.

Step 3: net outcome.

Exercise options 3 406 250＋premium 34 354－surplus 4 957 ＝£3 435 647

Exchange-traded Interest Rate Options

An agreement with an exchange to obtain the options on interest rate futures to pay or receive interest at a pre-agreed rate on a standard notional amount over a fixed standard period (usually three months) in the future.

交易所交易的利率期权/场内利率期权

这是与交易所签订的期权合约，标的资产是利率期货，公司获得将来按事先指定的利率支付或收到一标准的名义金额在指定的标准期间(通常为 3 个月)的利息的选择权。

F

FOREX Swap

A short-term swap that involves a spot currency transaction where a company buys or sells a foreign currency at spot rate, and an offsetting forward currency transaction where the company sells or buys the same amount of the foreign currency as spot transaction at forward rate. One spot transaction is combined with one forward transaction going the opposite direction. It is a useful hedging tool for exchange rate risk.

外汇掉期

这是一项短期互换交易，一方面是即期外汇交易，公司以即期汇率买进或卖出外币，另一方面是远期外汇交易，用以对冲即期外汇交易，公司以远期汇率卖出或买进与即期交易相同数量的同样外币。外汇掉期是一项即期交易与相反交易方向的一项远期交易相结合。它是一种有用的汇率风险对冲工具。

Forward Rate Agreements

A forward contract with a bank to receive or pay interest at a pre-determined forward rate on a notional amount over a fixed period of time in the future. A forward rate agreement effectively fixes the interest rate of a future borrowing or investment by counterbalancing the impact that interest rate movements have on the interest cost of an actual loan or on the interest revenue of an actual investment.

远期利率合约

这是与银行签订的远期合约，公司在未来支付或收取按事先确定的远期利率计算的名义金额的贷款或投资在一段固定期间的利息。远期利率合约有效地把将来某笔借款或投资的利率固定下来，远期合约正好抵消了利率变动对实际贷款的利息成本或实际投资的利息收入的影响。

G

Gamma

Gamma＝change in delta value÷change in value of the underlying assets. It measures the extent to which delta changes with the change in value of the underlying assets. When an option is at the money or close to expiry, the gamma has the highest value. The higher the gamma value, the more difficult to maintain a delta hedge.

Gamma 值

Gamma＝Delta 值的变化÷标的资产的价值变化。它衡量了 Delta 值随着标的资产价值变化而变化的幅度。当期权到期或接近到期时，Gamma 值最高。Gamma 值越高，维持 Delta 对冲越难。

The Greeks

Measures looking at how changes in the value of option are affected by such risk factors as the value of the underlying asset, the exercise price, the risk-free interest rate, the volatility of the underlying asset and the time to expiration.

希腊值

希腊值用于衡量诸如标的资产的价值、执行价格、无风险利率、标的资产价值的波动性以及期权到期时间长短等风险因素对期权价值的影响程度。

I

Indirect Rate/Quote

The exchange rate which is quoted per unit of home currency. For example, for a UK company, the exchange rate between sterling and US dollar is quoted as follows：USD 1.3284 per £.

间接标价法(汇率)

间接标价法是以本国货币作为标准货币的汇率表示方法。比如，对于一家英国公司，间接标价法表示的英镑兑美元的汇率为：1 英镑=1.328 4 美元。

Initial Margin

A deposit that is put into a client's margin account when the client initiates a trading position in the futures exchange.

初始保证金

这是期货交易所的客户在初始建立交易头寸时要存入保证金账户的一笔定金。

In the Money

The option is in the money when the exercise price is more favourable than the spot price.

实值

当期权的执行价格比即期价格优惠时，期权就是实值期权。

Interest Rate Collars

Buying an option and selling another option with the aim of raise revenue to reduce the cost of the option bought. For a borrower, an interest rate collar involves buying a put option to cap the cost of borrowing and selling a call option at a lower rate. For an investor, an interest rate collar involves buying a call option to establish a floor for the interest rate and selling a put option at a higher rate.

利率领子安排

买进一个期权并卖出另一个期权，目的是用卖出期权的收入去抵减买进期权的成本以增加收入。对于借款方，利率领子安排就是买进一项看跌期权，从而把借款的利率成本封顶，并以较低利率卖出一项看涨期权。对于投资方，利率领子安排就是买进一项看涨期权从而把投资利率兜底，并以较高利率卖出一项看跌期权。

【知识点巩固与拓展】

Futurebright 公司拟在 3 个月后借款 500 万美元并且借 6 个月。现在是 3 月 1 日。3 个月的利率期货期权(合约量 100 万美元，期权费%)的信息如下：

看涨期权		
敲定价格(美元)	3 月	6 月
96.00	0.116	0.201
96.25	0.025	0.078
96.50	0	0.086

看跌期权		
敲定价格(美元)	3 月	6 月
96.00	0.022	0.090
96.25	0.125	0.265
96.50	0.390	0.412

合约在相应月份月底到期，目前 LIBOR 为 3.6%。

假设实际贷款利率为 LIBOR+1%。6 月 1 日，LIBOR 为 5%，6 月利率期货价为 5.1%。

列示买进利率 4%的看跌期权、卖出利率 3.5%的看涨期权的领子安排的结果。

第一步：3 月 1 日确立对冲方案。

Futurebright 公司从 6 月份开始支付贷款利息，所以应买进 6 月份的利率看跌期权。

敲定价格=100-4=96(美元)

合约数=贷款金额/每单合约量×贷款期长/合约期长

=500/100×6/3

=10(份)

净期权费率=0.090%-0.086%=0.004%

第二步：6 月 1 日实际贷款，贷款利率=LIBOR+1%=5%+1%=6%。

第三步：结果。

3 月 1 日，看跌期权，支付利率 4%。

6 月 1 日，买进期货合约，收到利率 5.1%。

利差(利润)=1.1%。

综合结果：

0.004%+6%-1.1%=4.904%

500 万美元贷款的最终利息成本

=4.904%×5 000 000×6/12

=122 600(美元)

Futurebright plc. is planning to borrow \$5m for six months in three months' time. Now is 1 March. Options on three-month futures(\$1m contract size, premium cost in %) are as follows:

Calls		
Strike price($)	Mar.	June
96. 00	0. 116	0. 201
96. 25	0. 025	0. 078
96. 50	0	0. 086

Puts		
Strike price($)	Mar.	June
96. 00	0. 022	0. 090
96. 25	0. 125	0. 265
96. 50	0. 390	0. 412

Contracts expires at the end of each month.

LIBOR is 3. 6% now, and assuming that the loan is taken out at a fixed rate of LIBOR+1% . LIBOR on 1 June is 5%. June interest rate future price is 5. 1%.

Illustrate the outcome of a collar with a put at 4% and the call at 3. 5%.

Step 1: set up the hedge(1 March).

Futurebright will paying interest from June, so a June put option is needed.

Strike price= $ 100− $ 4= $ 96

Number of contracts=loan amount/contract size×loan period/length of contract=5m/1m×6/3=10 contracts

Net premium=0. 090%−0. 086%=0. 004%

Step 2: actual loan (1 June).

at LIBOR +1%=5%+1%=6%

Step 3: outcome.

Option market outcome:

1 Mar. put option to pay interest at 4%.

1 June contract to buy, receive interest at 5.1%.

Profit 1.1%

Net outcome:

0.004%+6%−1.1%=4.904%

Interest cost of \$5m loan=4.904%×\$5m×6/12=\$122 600

Interest Rate Futures

Standard contracts with a futures exchange to pay or receive interest at a pre-determined rate on a standard notional amount over a fixed standard period (usually three months) in the future. For an investor, a futures contract to buy is needed, because the buyer will receive interest. For a borrower, a futures contract to sell is needed because the seller will pay interest.

利率期货

这是与期货交易所签订的标准合约，在将来，按事先确定的利率支付或收取名义金额的贷款或投资在固定的标准期间（一般为3个月）的利息。对于投资方，买进利率期货，买方将收到利息；而借款方要卖出期货，卖方将支付利息。

【学习提示】

有资金需要投资的公司，需买进利率期货以收到利息；有借贷需求的公司，需卖出利率期货以支付利息。

【知识点巩固与拓展】

Futurebright 公司拟在 3 个月后借款 500 万美元，期限为 6 个月。现在是 3 月 1 日。3 个月金额为 100 万美元的利率期货报价为：

3 月　95.10

6 月　96.00

9 月　96.10

这些期货合约都在对应的月底到期。现在，LIBOR 为 3.6%。Futurebright 公司的借款利率为 LIBOR+1%。

假设贷款从贷款起始日以固定利率 LIBOR+1%计息。

如果 6 月 1 日 LIBOR 为 5%，请计算用利率期货对冲贷款利率风险的最后结果。

第一步：3 月 1 日，确立对冲策略。

卖出期货合约份数=对冲金额/一份合约金额×贷款期长/期货合约期长=500/100×6/3=10

贷款始于 6 月 1 日，故 Futurebright 公司需卖出 10 份 6 月份的利率期货，利率为 4%。

第二步：6 月 1 日实际贷款。

Futurebright 公司以 6%的利率借款 500 万美元。

第三步：6 月 1 日，期货结算结果。

现在——3 月 1 日。

6 月期货　4.0%

LIBOR　3.6%

基差　0.4%

6 月 1 日还剩一个月的基差=0.4%/4=0.1%

6 月 1 日，6 月利率期货的价格应为 5%+0.1%=5.1%

3 月 1 日，支付利息　4.0%(建仓)

6 月 1 日，收到利息 5.1%（平仓）

利差（利润） 1.1%

第四步：6 月 1 日，综合结果。

实际借款利率 6.0%

减去：期货利润 1.1%

净利率 4.9%

500 万美元贷款实际支付利息＝4.9%×5 000 000×6/12＝122 500（美元）

Futurebright plc. is planning to borrow ＄5m for six months in three months' time. Now is 1 March.

The prices quoted on standardized ＄1m three-month contracts are as follows：

March	95.10
June	96.00
September	96.10

Contracts expires at the end of each month.

LIBOR is 3.6% now and Futurebright can borrow at a rate of LIBOR plus 1%.

Assuming that the loan is taken out at a fixed rate of LIBOR +1% at the start of the loan. Calculate the outcome of the interest rate futures hedge if LIBOR is 5% on 1 June.

Step 1：1 March，set up the hedge.

Contracts to sell are required.

Number of contracts＝exposure/contract size×loan period/length of contract＝＄5m/＄1m×6/3＝10

The loan will start in 1 June，so Futurebright needs to sell 10 of June interest futures contract at 4%.

Step 2：1 June，take out the actual loan.

Futurebright will borrow ＄5m at 6%.

Step 3：1 June，the outcome of the futures.

Now—1 March	
June future	4.0%
LIBOR	3.6%
Basis	0.4%

1 June, only 1 month remaining, the basis is 0.4%/4 = 0.1%，the future price should be 5%+0.1%=5.1%.

1 Mar. pay interest at 4.0%(open)

1 June receive interest at 5.1%(close-out)

Difference(profit)=1.1%

Step 4:1 June，net outcome.

Actual borrowing rate	6.0%
Less:Profit on interest future	1.1%
Net borrowing rate	4.9%

So interest paid on ＄5m loan=4.9%×＄5 000 000×6/12=＄122 500.

Interest Rate Put Option

An option where the buyer has the right to sell (pay interest) at a pre-determined rate on a standard notional amount over a fixed period in the future.

利率看跌期权

这是一种卖出期权合约，其购买者有权在未来按照事先确定的利率支付名义金额的贷款在固定的标准期间的利息。

【学习提示】

利率看跌期权(interest rate put option)的买方获得了按确立的利率支付利息的选择权;利率看涨期权(interest rate call option)的买方获得了按确立的利率收到利息的选择权。

Interest Rate Call Option

An option where the buyer has the right to buy (receive interest) at a pre-determined rate on a standard notional amount over a fixed period in the future.

利率看涨期权

这是一种买进期权合约,其购买者有权在未来按照事先确定的利率收取名义金额的投资在固定的标准期间的利息。

【知识点巩固与拓展】

Futurebright 公司拟在 3 个月后借款 500 万美元,借 6 个月。现在是 3 月 1 日。3 个月的利率期货期权(合约量 100 万美元,期权费%)的信息如下:

看涨期权		
敲定价格(美元)	3 月	6 月
96.00	0.116	0.201
96.25	0.025	0.078
96.50	0	0.086

看跌期权		
敲定价格(美元)	3月	6月
96.00	0.022	0.090
96.25	0.125	0.265
96.50	0.390	0.412

合约在相应月份月底到期,目前LIBOR为3.6%。

假设实际贷款利率为LIBOR+1%。6月1日,LIBOR为5%,6月利率期货价为5.1%。请列示用利率为3.5%的利率期权对冲利率风险的结果。

第一步:3月1日,确立对冲方案。

Futurebright公司从6月份开始支付贷款利息,所以应买进6月份的利率看跌期权。

敲定价格=100-3.5=96.5(美元)

合约数=贷款金额/每单合约量×贷款期长/合约期长

=500/100×6/3=10(份)

期权费率为0.412%。

第二步:6月1日实际贷款。

贷款利率=LIBOR+1%=5%+1%=6%

第三步:结果。

3月1日,看跌期权,支付利率3.5%。

6月1日,买进期货合约,收到利率5.1%。

利差(利润)=1.6%

综合结果:

0.412%+6%-1.6%=4.812%

500万美元贷款的最终利息成本

=4.812%×5 000 000×6/12

=120 300(美元)

Futurebright plc. is planning to borrow \$5m for six months in three months' time. Now is 1 March. Options on three-month futures(\$1m contract size, premium cost in %) are as follows:

Calls		
Strike price(\$)	Mar.	June
96.00	0.116	0.201
96.25	0.025	0.078
96.50	0	0.086

Puts		
Strike price(\$)	Mar.	June
96.00	0.022	0.090
96.25	0.125	0.265
96.50	0.390	0.412

Contracts expire at the end of each month.

LIBOR is 3.6% now, and assuming that the loan is taken out at a fixed rate of LIBOR+1%. LIBOR on 1 June is 5%. June interest rate future price is 5.1%.

Illustrate an option hedge at 3.5%.

Step 1: set up the hedge(1 March).

Futurebright will pay interest from June, so a June put option is needed.

Strike price 100−3.5=96.5

Number of contracts=loan amount/contract size×loan period/length of contract=5m/1m×6/3=10 contracts

Premium: 0.412%.

Step 2: actual loan (1 June).

at LIBOR +1%=5%+1%=6%

Step3: outcome.

Option market outcome:

1 Mar. put option to pay interest at 3.5%.

1 June contract to buy, receive interest at 5.1%.

Profit 1.6%.

Net outcome:

0.412%+6%−1.6%=4.812%

Interest cost of \$5m loan

=4.812%×\$5 000 000×6/12

=\$120 300

Interest Rate Swap

An arrangement whereby two parties swap interest rate commitments with each other. A company with a fixed-rate loan can make a swap so that it ends up with paying interest at a floating rate. The counterparty of the swap with a floating-rate debt ends up with paying interest at a fixed rate. Interest rate swaps allow companies to take advantage of differences in interest rates in different markets for borrowing to manage interest costs.

利率互换

双方交换利率合约的一种安排。一家拥有固定利率贷款的公司通过利率互换，变成以浮动利率支付贷款利息。而互换的另一方原先拥有的是浮动利率的债务，通过利率互换，变成以固定利率支付这笔债务的利息。利率互换可允许公司充分利用不同借贷市场的利率差异来管理利息成本。

【知识点巩固与拓展】

Futurebright 公司与 A 公司的借款利率信息如下：

公司 利率	Futurebright	Company A
固定利率	6%	5%
浮动利率	LIBOR+1%	LIBOR+0.6%

在互换安排中，银行向双方各收费 0.2%。

请列示如何通过互换使两家公司均受益。

第一步：计算互换的潜在利得。

Futurebright 公司的利率为 LIBOR+1%的浮动利率贷款换成固定利率贷款。A 公司的利率为 5%的固定利率贷款则换成浮动利率贷款。

利得=(6%−5%)+(0.6%−1%)=0.6%

减去收费后利得=0.6%−0.2%×2=0.2%

双方各分 0.1%。

第二步：互换，互动利率为 LIBOR，互换利得 50∶50 分配。

如不互换所付利率	6%	LIBOR+0.6%
	Futurebright	A 公司
实际贷款	LIBOR+1%	5%
+互换收费	0.2%	0.2%
+互换：浮动	(LIBOR)	LIBOR
+互换：固定	4.7%	(4.7%)
互换后所支付净利率	5.9%	LIBOR+0.5%
利得分配	0.1%	0.1%

The borrowing rate for Futurebright plc. and Company A are as follows:

Rates	Futurebright	Company A
Fixed	6%	5%
Variable	LIBOR+1%	LIBOR+0.6%

A bank would charge 0.2% fees to both parties in a swap arrangement.

Illustrate how an interest rate swap would benefit both companies.

Step 1: potential gain from swap.

Futurebright's variable loan at LIBOR+1% can be swapped to a fixed-rate loan. And Company A fixed-rate loan at 5% can be swapped to variable-rate loan.

Gain =(6%−5%)+(0.6%−1%)=0.6%

Gain after fees=0.6%−0.2%×2=0.2%

Each party 0.1%.

Step 2: swap, variable rate at LIBOR, splitting gain 50 : 50.

Position if no swap	6%	LIBOR+0.6%
	Futurebright	Company A
Actual loan	LIBOR+1%	5%
+Fees	0.2%	0.2%
+swap: variable	(LIBOR)	LIBOR
+swap: fixed	4.7%	(4.7%)
Net Position after swap	5.9%	LIBOR+0.5%
gain split	0.1%	0.1%

L

Long-position

A trader buys in a financial instrument, a commodity or a currency with the expectation that the asset bought will rise in value.

多头

交易者买进某种金融工具、某种商品或者某种货币，以期买进的资产将来能够升值。

M

Maintenance Margin

The minimum balance in an investor's margin account. If losses are made to reduce the margin account below the maintenance margin, the investor will be required to restore the margin account to its maintenance margin level.

维持保证金

这是投资者保证金账户的最低限额。如果损失使保证金账户金额低于维持保证金，投资者就会被要求追加保证金以使保证金账户余额恢复到维持保证金水平。

Marking to Market

The process of calculating the gain or losses on futures contracts at the end of each trading day and the gain or losses being received or paid from the margin account on a daily basis.

逐日盯市

在每个交易日结束时计算期货合约的利得和损失，并且每日收到利得或从保证金账户支付损失。这个过程就叫逐日盯市。

O

Options on Futures

The underlying assets of interest rate options are interest rate futures.

期货期权

利率期权的标的资产是利率期货。

Out of the Money

The option is out of the money when the exercise price is less favourable than the spot price.

虚值

当期权的执行价格不如即期价格优惠时，期权就是虚值期权。

Over-the-counter Options (OTC Options)

Option contracts that entered into directly with a bank.

场外期权

场外期权就是与银行直接签订的期权合约。

P

Put Option

An option to sell underlying assets with the expectation of the value in underlying asset will fall.

看跌期权

预期标的资产的价值将下降而卖出标的资产的期权就是看跌期权。

R

Rho

It measures the extent to which the change in option price is in response to interest rate changes. An option's rho is the amount of change in value of the option for 1% change in the risk-free rate of interest. Rho is positive for call options and negative for put options. Long-term options have larger rho than short-term options.

Rho 值

Rho 值计量利率变化所引起的期权价格的变化幅度。一个期权的 Rho 就是无风险利率每变化 1%，期权价值的变化幅度。看涨期权的 Rho 是正的，看跌期权的 Rho 是负的。长期期权比短期期权的 Rho 要大。

S

Short Position

A trader sells a financial instrument, a commodity or a currency with the expectation that the price of the asset will fall.

空头

交易商卖出某种金融工具、某种商品或者某种货币，以期这项资产价格下降。

Spread（Exchange Rate Quotations）

The difference between the bid price and the ask price of a foreign currency quoted by a bank.

买卖价格之差（汇率报价）

这是银行报出的外币的买进价与卖出价之间的差额。

Swaption

An option on swaps, giving the holder the right but not the

obligation to enter into a swap with the seller.

互换期权

这是以互换作为标的资产的期权，期权的持有者获得了与期权的卖方签订互换合约的权利而非义务。

Synthetic Foreign Exchange Agreements(SAFEs)

A kind of non-deliverable forward currency contracts. The two counter parties settle the profit or loss (calculated as the difference between SAFE rate and the prevailing spot rate upon settlement) on a notional amount of a currency (the SAFE's face value).

远期外汇综合协议(SAFEs)

这是一种不用实际交割货币的货币远期合约。合约双方只对名义金额的某种货币(SAFE 面值)的汇率差(SAFE 汇率与结算日的即期汇率之差)进行结算。

T

Theta

The change in option's price (specifically time premium) over time. Theta measures how much value is lost over time through retaining the option. Theta is usually negative. And often expressed as an amount lost per day.

Theta 值

Theta 值就是期权的价值(确切地说是时间价值)随时间的流逝而变化的金额。它计量了因保留期权而损失的时间价值。Theta 值一般为负。经常的表示方式是每天损失多少。

Treasury Management

Handling all financial matters of a company. Treasury management involves in liquidity management, funding management, risk management and corporate finance, and also helps in setting corporate financial objectives and strategy.

资金管理

处理公司所有财务事项。它涉及流动性管理、筹资管理、风险管理以及公司财务,也会帮助企业制定财务目标和财务战略。

V

Variation Margin

When an investor's balance in the margin account is below maintenance margin, a margin call will be sent to the investor, and on next trading day, the investor needs to recover the balance of the margin account to the maintenance margin level by paying an extra margin. This extra margin is called variation margin.

追加保证金

当某投资者的保证金账户余额低于维持保证金时,投资者会收到保证金催付通知，然后在下一个交易日，投资者就需要额外支付一笔保证金把保证金账户余额恢复到维持保证金水平。额外支付的这笔保证金被称为追加保证金。

Vega

Vega=change in option price/change in volatility of the underlying assets. Vega is the change in value of an option resulting from a 1% change in the implied volatility of the underlying assets. It reflects the sensitivity of the option price to the change in its implied volatility. Long-term options have larger vegas than short-term options.

Vega 值

Vega=期权价格变化÷标的资产波动率变化。Vega 是标的资产波动率每变化 1%，期权价格的变化金额。它反映了期权价格相对标的资产波动率变化的敏感程度。长期期权比短期期权的 Vega 值大。